THE FILMS OF NICHOLAS RAY

THE POET OF NIGHTFALL

New Edition

Geoff Andrew

bfi Publishing

This new edition first published 2004 by the
British Film Institute,
21 Stephen Street,
London W1T 1LN

The British Film Institute is the UK national agency with responsibility for encouraging the arts of film
and television and preserving them in the national interest.

First published in 1991 by Charles Letts & Co. Ltd

Cover design by Ketchup, Lambeth, UK
Cover illustrations: (front) James Mason, Christopher Olsen and Barbara Rush in *Bigger than Life*, 1956;
(back) Jim Backus and James Dean in *Rebel Without a Cause*, 1955.

Designed and set by Ketchup, Lambeth, UK
Printed in the UK by Cromwell Press, Trowbridge, Wiltshire

British Library Cataloguing-in-Publication Data
A catalogue record for this book is available from the British Library

ISBN 0–84457–000–2 (hbk)
ISBN 0–84457–001–0 (pbk)

Contents

Acknowledgments

For their help, encouragement and/or understanding, in the first edition of this book I thanked: my parents, Cortina Butler, Brian Case, Tom Charity, Bernard Eisenschitz, Tom Farrell, Simon Field, Philip French, Wally Hammond, the late John Houseman, Peter Howden, Jim Jarmusch, Julia Judge, James Leahy, David Meeker, Susan Ray, Tony Rayns, Chris Rodley, Jonathan Rosenbaum, Markku Salmi, Martin Scorsese, Alison Starling, David Thompson, Adrian Turner, Peter von Bagh, Sheila Whitaker, Amanda Wood and Tom Milne, who read and offered valuable advice on the manuscript. Just as I still adhere to what I wrote then, so my gratitude to the above remains undiminished.

But this is a new edition, and I must add some more names to those deserving of mention. Thanks, then, to James Quandt of Cinemathèque Ontari, for giving me the idea of letting my thoughts about Ray's work see the light of day once more; to Andrew Lockett, head of BFI Publishing, for enabling me to do that, and for being a sympathetic editor; to Sophie Contento, for help with stills; to my friend and colleague Tom Charity, for reading and providing insightful comments on the new material; to Victor Erice and Jos Oliver, another two Ray aficionados; to my colleagues in the National Film Theatre programming team, especially Julie Pearce, Waltraud Loges and Jim Hamilton (aka Mr Johnny Guitar), for agreeing to mount another Ray retrospective; and not least to my mother Olive and my wife Ane for their continuing support and patience as I embarked on yet more work.

To these last two loved ones, and to the memories of my father-in-law Sebastian and my own father Len, this book is dedicated.

Preface: Postscript to the First Edition (1991)

It is, perhaps, ironic that Britain's first published book on the films of Nicholas Ray should have been written more than a decade after his death, and by someone who first encountered the director's considerable talent at the very time his career in commercial film-making was coming to an end. One of the earliest movies I can clearly remember appreciating as an adults' rather than a children's film, is *55 Days at Peking*, which I saw at the age of nine or ten, during its initial British run, at a none too lavishly appointed cinema in my then home town of Northampton.

Of course, I was too young then to know what a director was or did, let alone to recognise or notice Nicholas Ray's name on the credits. But I can recall, even now, being deeply affected by the sheer scale and beauty of both the images and the story; I was saddened by Ava Gardner's needless, lonely but oddly calm death; amazed by the exotic pomp of the Chinese Imperial Court; excited by the huge, expertly staged scenes of battle; and choked – probably to tears – by the moment when Charlton Heston held out his hand to the little orphaned Chinese girl to take her on his proud horse away from the cruel carnage, to America and 'home'. Obviously, what I saw in that film had nothing whatsoever to do with my own safe, happy childhood in a far from exciting Midlands town – at least, not in its story and visual spectacle. But on an emotional level, it touched my heart, while at the same time it gave me an inkling of the harsh complexity of the world of grown-ups, a complexity whose existence I had never even guessed at from the movies I had seen hitherto.

Not that the movie changed my life, of course, though it did make me want to see other films that offered a more adult account of the world than had been available to me in the endless series of cartoons, adventure serials and innocuously cheerful 'family entertainment' that had constituted most of my movie education up to that time. Ray's identity remained unknown to me until my early twenties, when a cinema I was then managing – the Electric, in London's Portobello Road – put on a season of his work. Due to the frustrating vagaries of distribution, the retrospective was necessarily incomplete, but I was able to renew my acquaintance with *55 Days at Peking* (its capacity to impress and move me had not diminished at all with the passage of the years!) and, in addition, I found myself confronted by still more astonishing examples of the director's ability to explore and express mature human emotions through purely cinematic means.

Like many other young people, I had already become an admirer of *Rebel Without a Cause*; but *They Live by Night, In a Lonely Place, On Dangerous Ground, The Lusty Men*, and particularly *Bigger than Life* were nothing short of revelations. I wanted to know, now, why this man's films affected me so deeply, and I began searching out other examples of his peculiarly troubled sensibility at each available opportunity, with the result that finally, in 1986, I suggested to Sheila Whitaker, then programme director of London's National Film Theatre, that she let me mount as complete a retrospective of Ray's work as possible. Happily, she agreed, and with the exception of Ray's television work and shorts, I and many others were given the chance to see all his films again, on the big screen, within the space of a month. Since then, I have continued to watch Ray's films over and over again, and the enjoyment I derive from them has never waned; indeed, the more I see them, the more I realise how great was his artistry.

It was during that NFT season that I first properly saw how much *other* people enjoyed his work. I then decided it might be a good idea to put the many hours I had spent watching the films to more widely profitable use. It seemed shameful and ridiculous that such a fine film-maker had never had a thorough study of his work written in English, and the only way I could see that situation being rectified was to write one myself. Fortunately, I found in time a publisher who felt that such a book might be not only valuable but financially viable, and I was enabled at last to fulfil a long-term ambition, and in so doing, to offer, as it were, belated thanks to Nicholas Ray for all the pleasure his films have given me over the years. Indeed, writing the book supplied an additional excuse to watch the films again, not to mention an extra reward in that, in searching out video recordings of the movies I did not already possess, I was able to see, for the first time, Ray's very rarely seen television film *High Green Wall*, about which almost nothing, as far as I have been able to ascertain, had been written. (Which is why, besides its astoundingly sophisticated and cinematic style of expression, I have devoted so much space to a half-hour film.)

My purpose was to try to provide as clear and objective an assessment of Ray's achievements as possible, by offering a close, detailed textual description and analysis of each film, and by giving logically argued reasons for what I consider to be each film's strengths and weaknesses. Inevitably, in this I have failed to some extent, since there are no firm rules on what constitutes good film-making, and since we all carry so much emotional and intellectual baggage with us when we approach a film, a novel, a painting or whatever that any reaction is bound, in the end, to be hopelessly subjective. But perhaps this does not matter so very much in the end; for if in writing this book I have been able to convey just a little of what makes these films so perennially fascinating and enjoyable for me, there is a possibility that readers will turn to them again, and so discover highly rewarding facets of Ray's creativity for themselves. If I have succeeded in this respect, writing the book will have been worthwhile, because in Ray's work there are more than enough treasures for everybody.

Introduction

If the cinema no longer existed, Nicholas Ray alone gives the impression of being capable of reinventing it, and what is more, of wanting to.

Jean-Luc Godard, *Cahiers du cinéma*, February 1957

It was all in the script, a disillusioned writer will tell you. But it was never all in the script. If it were, why make the movie?

Nicholas Ray, *Sight and Sound*, August 1956

You're tearing me apart.

Jim Stark, played by James Dean, in *Rebel Without a Cause*

Why was Nicholas Ray so admired by, and such an inspiration to, the French critics of the 1950s who later became the directors of the *nouvelle vague*? The answer lies, perhaps, both in Ray's own oft-quoted observation about the limited contribution made to a film by its script – which highlights his decidedly non-literary approach to his chosen profession – and in the extreme sense of personal pain and *angst* evoked in a famous line from his best-known film.

For Ray was something of a maverick in Hollywood, a man whose deeply felt disillusionment, both with American life in general and with the American movie establishment in particular, manifested itself not only in his perennially troubled relationship with the Hollywood studios, but in the dramatic content and thrust of his work. His films were, for the most part, profoundly personal contributions to what was, and still is, something of a factory conveyor belt, specialising in the production of homogenised, undemanding mass entertainment; they expressed his awareness of inner torment, of solitude and despair, conflict and confusion, and did so through entirely cinematic means.

For Godard, Truffaut, Rohmer, Rivette and others, Ray was the ultimate *auteur*, an admirable example of the film artist whose patent intelligence, intensity of feeling and sheer love of cinema ensured that his creative signature might be easily and vividly discerned amongst all the dramatic bric-a-brac that constituted the American commercial cinema. A Ray film, for these eager, iconoclastic *enfants terribles*, represented a triumph of the individual over the safe, bland conformity of the system; indeed, the director's often unhappy dealings with studio moguls, and the lack of critical enthusiasm that greeted much of his work in his own country, probably served to enhance his reputation as a beleaguered rebel. He seemed, no doubt, the successor to such neglected figures as von Stroheim, Keaton and Welles – talents of massive ambition, originality and genius, crushed by a cautious, money-minded, philistine system.

In this respect at least, Godard and friends were to be proved right: Ray's pessimistic vision of life, his general dissatisfaction with the methods and ideals of the Hollywood mainstream, *were* finally his professional undoing. In December 1962, fifteen years after making his debut as director and with twenty movies to his name, he walked away from *55 Days at Peking* (the second of two epics he made for the producer Samuel Bronston, which had, ironically, given him the two biggest budgets of his career) and retired from the world of commercial film-making.

There were, of course, further projects, but few came to fruition, and by the time of his death in 1979 Ray had made only two more features, neither of which could possibly be considered part of the commercial mainstream. *We Can't Go Home Again* was an experimental independent movie made in collaboration with his students while he was teaching film at New York State University; *Lightning Over Water* was a partly fictional, partly documentary account of his own last weeks, spent battling against the ravages of cancer, co-directed by the German director (and long-time Ray *aficionado*) Wim Wenders.

Another European: it was perhaps sadly appropriate that Ray, an admirer of European 'art' cinema who frequently characterised his own predicament with a line ('I'm a stranger here myself') spoken by Sterling Hayden in his *Johnny Guitar*, should end his life working in close collaboration with a young foreigner, who was both a leading figure in another New Wave and a film-maker whose special interest was the exploration and depiction of melancholy, *angst* and alienation. America never properly recognised or rewarded Ray's enormous gifts as a film-maker, and even now very few of his films (with the exception of *Rebel Without a Cause*, whose importance is widely attributed to James Dean rather than Ray) are shown as often as they deserve.

This study of Ray's work, therefore, is undertaken partly in reaction against the critical neglect he has suffered at the hands of Anglo-Saxon writers on film. At the time of writing (1991), only one book about his work has appeared in English (and that is a jargon-filled and obscurely argued thesis which, for no good reason, focuses nearly all its attention on *Rebel Without a Cause*); there are at least three monographs, however, not to mention Bernard Eisenschitz's recent exhaustive biography, by French critics.

Why this should be the case is unclear, but a significant factor may possibly be a tendency of many English and American critics to approach film from a distinctly literary standpoint, thus rendering themselves at least partly insensitive to Ray's essentially cinematic means of expression. Perhaps, too, the fact that a large proportion of his output may be seen as somehow flawed – certainly, he himself tended in interviews to be severely self-critical – might account for the dearth of serious attention paid to his career; polished perfection is widely held as an ideal to which any proper artist should aspire. Ray's films rarely fulfil such expectations: some were studio chores for which he himself felt little affection (it is ironic that these were his most conventionally craftsmanlike, pro-

Judge not … Justice of the Peace Hawkins (Ian Wolfe) sells Bowie (Farley Granger) and Keechie (Cathy O'Donell) a cheap wedding in *They Live by Night*.

fessional films); others fell victim to producer interference; even his most satisfying works feature moments of baroque excess.

But immaculately polished works of art are not *necessarily* better than those whose imperfections exert their own peculiar power and interest; indeed, as Michael Wilmington has written in an article on Ray's RKO films in *The Velvet Light Trap*, 'the failures of a talented man are often more fascinating than the successes of a mediocrity; in an unguarded way they can tell us things which a "masterpiece" may not'. Restrained, classical perfection is not everything: *On Dangerous Ground*, for example, may be perceived as flawed by an uneven and broken-backed narrative structure; yet it is that very same formal awkwardness that gives Ray's portrait of a violent man riven by conflicting, contradictory impulses its raw emotional force. Like a few other directors (Welles, Fuller, Powell) whose artistic personalities were so powerful that they could barely be contained by the constrictions of tastefulness and genre, Ray seems sometimes hardly to have concerned himself with notions of balance, restraint and other 'respectable', more conventional modes of expression.

At the same time, however, he was not especially innovative, in terms either of technique or of form; for the most part, he worked in popular, traditional genres like the Western, the thriller, the war film and the melodrama. And it is precisely this tension, between his private sensibility and the constraints of a largely formularised mainstream cinema, that makes his work so interesting and so enduringly modern.

Not that Ray was not very much a product of his times; just as he himself appears to have been profoundly affected by the New Deal liberalism that swept America in the 1930s, so his work is a reflection of the post-war disillusionment felt by certain artists and intellectuals confronted by the bland optimism and inhibited conformism of the Eisenhower era. (It is perhaps not surprising, then, that he abandoned commercial film-making altogether in the 1960s, a decade when disillusionment with the American Way reached what may be seen as its zenith.) But the confusion, despair and sense of not belonging that mark much of his work are as relevant today as they were when he made the films, and Wenders is not the only director in whose movies Ray's influence may be discerned. Dennis Hopper, too, can be seen as following in the footsteps of the man who gave him his first acting role in a Hollywood film (in *Rebel Without a Cause*), while Jim Jarmusch – a student of Ray's before becoming his assistant on *Lightning Over Water* – now enjoys a successful career as a film-maker who works at a tangent to the commercial mainstream and who is concerned, at least partly, with the experiences of strangers in a strange land.

Ray's continuing importance, moreover, stems not only from his influence on other film-makers; that millions of young people still attest to the power of *Rebel Without a Cause* to sway the emotions is merely the most conspicuous example of the way in which Ray transcended his times with a vision of life that affects us all. Pain, anxiety, uncertainty, violence and loneliness are abiding elements of the human condition, and few directors, especially in Hollywood, have confronted them as directly, as uncompromisingly as Ray. Even in his most conventional movies, his pessimistically troubled sensibility is an active force in the characterisation, both of individuals and of society at large. Not only do many of his films end unhappily, but even a film as relatively impersonal and traditionally heroic as *Flying Leathernecks* is a dark study of doubt and fear, indelibly marked by an awareness of the bleak complexities of existence in the twentieth century.

At this point, before proceeding to examine Ray's thematic concerns, his stylistic methods and the films themselves in more detail, it is necessary to consider the question of authorship, a perennial problem in discussions of cinema, which is after all both industry and art, and a collaborative art form at that. In Ray's case, the issue is further complicated by the fact that, especially during the latter half of his career, at a time when he had managed to win at least some small measure of independence for himself, he was very often plagued by illness, which resulted in his being absent either from the set or from the editing room.

This, coupled with the interference from producers that beset his career from the very early years, has provoked some critics to dismiss his contribution to certain finished films as relatively negligible. Nevertheless, while one must, of course, bear in mind that Ray cannot be held altogether responsible for every scene, shot and line of dialogue in every film credited to his name, I should hope that this study will show that there *is*, throughout his career, an overall consistency – both thematic and stylistic – which suggests that his creative influence was a dominant factor in establishing the dynamics, tone and meaning of each particular movie. (While there is, too, the question of what actually happened whenever someone else took over the editing or direction, it is probably fair to assume in the majority of cases that his replacement either followed detailed instructions from Ray, or was working from a shooting script that Ray himself had helped to prepare.)

It is the purpose, here, not only to evaluate his work, but to establish what his artistic signature was and to suggest when it was likely to have been allowed free expression. Nor will those films that fall outside the parameters of what may be considered an 'archetypal' Ray film be regarded as necessarily inferior in quality; every artist has the right to change his views or style, and to create atypical works, and these are often of as much interest and value as others which are seen to fall more readily within a critical schema formulated by a writer long after the works themselves were produced.

There is also the problem of assigning authorship to the individual in a medium which involves, inevitably, as many collaborators as film. And indeed, this study is not intended as a simplistic exercise in auteurism. There are, of course, various critical methodologies that may be employed in discussing a film – historical, sociological, semiological, psychoanalytical and genre analysis, to name but a few – but in assessing the meaning and value of one man's body of work, a modified form of auteurism seems, quite simply, to be both the most lucid and the most useful. Nor does one deny the crucial importance of contributions made by producers, writers, cameramen, actors, editors and others if one focuses on the achievements of a director; he, after all, is normally the organising figure who determines how the various contributions of others might best be used to express his vision of the story at hand. (Even if he is personally without ideas or imagination, it is his function at least to accept or reject the suggestions of others.)

Moreover, since we are here considering the achievements of Nicholas Ray, he, more than any other figure, is the common denominator to the films in question, and our aim is to build a portrait of his artistic personality by tracing the kind of connections that may be made between those films. It is *his* work, rather than that of the writer Philip Yordan, the cameraman Joe MacDonald or the actor Robert Ryan, that is our subject here, and his life and films suggest that his personality was such that, for him, the job of film-making was *not* a question merely of accepting or rejecting the contributions of others, but of striving to give a film as much personal input as possible. It is for this reason that Ray surely warrants a study of his work based loosely upon the principles of the *politique des auteurs*, the critical tool with which Godard, Truffaut and their peers, in polemical mood, first attempted to rescue him from being unjustly consigned to the faceless anonymity of the Hollywood hack.

Rationalisation apart, however, the main impulse for writing this book is deeply personal. While the critical neglect that Ray has so far suffered at the hands of English-language writers on film suggests a need for this volume – which is intended not as a definitive study, but as a starting point for further such work – I could never have embarked on this project if repeated viewings of Ray's films had not already given me enormous pleasure. And it is in the hope that my attempts to illuminate his work will help others to derive a similar enjoyment that this tribute to one of the greatest directors in the history of cinema is offered.

Biographical Summary

For complete biographical details, see Bernard Eisenschitz, trans. Tom Milne, *Nicholas Ray: An American Journey* (Faber and Faber, London, 1993).

1911: On 7 August, Raymond Nicholas Kienzle born in Galesville, Wisconsin, youngest of four children in a middle-class family. His mother, of Norwegian stock, has strong artistic leanings; his disciplinarian father, the son of German immigrants, is a secret drinker.

1919: Family moves to La Crosse, Wisconsin. In high school, Ray is a member of the dramatic society.

1926–7: Ray writes and produces for local radio – including a version of Shaw's *Candida* – and wins a scholarship to University of Chicago, where he studies drama and architecture for one year.

1929–31: Attends University of Wisconsin in La Crosse.

1932–4: Moves to New York, changes his name to Nicholas or Nick Ray, and becomes involved with radical theatre groups, joining the Theatre of Action (formerly Workers Laboratory Theatre), associating (marginally) with the Group Theatre, and eventually joining the government's Federal Theatre Project. Also, during this period, spends time at Frank Lloyd Wright's Taliesin Fellowship in Green Springs, Wisconsin, and travels a little in Mexico. At some point is a member of the Communist Party. Meets Elia Kazan, John Houseman and others through his work in theatre.

1935: Appears on stage in *The Young Go First*, directed by Kazan; his first performance in mainstream theatre.

1936: Marries Jean Evans. Acts in *The Crime*, with Kazan. For The Living Newspaper's theatrical presentations of news events, stage-manages *Injunction Granted* for director Joseph Losey (also from La Crosse). Directs a theatre workshop at Birkwood Labor College in Katonah, NY.

1937–9: Son Anthony born. Works for theatrical branch of the Resettlement Administration (later Farm Security Administration). Travels widely in US, researching folk music (notably with Lomax brothers) for Library of Congress archives, organising theatre groups and meeting musicians such as Pete Seeger, Woody Guthrie, Huddie 'Leadbelly' Ledbetter, 'Blind Lemon' Jefferson and Billie Holiday.

1940: Returns to New York. Separated from Evans. Interest in folk music and culture leads to work with Alan Lomax on CBS radio's *Back Where I Come From*, a mixture of music and stories about US life.

1941–5: Ray declared unfit for military service, and divorced. Works as assistant to Houseman, then head of the Office of War Information's Voice of America, on propaganda programmes;

put in charge of folk music, and directs news programmes in various languages. Ray's name included on a list of suspected Communists but inquiry dropped after four days.

1944–6: First visit to Hollywood, where assistant to Kazan on *A Tree Grows in Brooklyn* and to Houseman on *Tuesday in November*, a propaganda short made for the OWI Overseas Branch. With Losey, stages for Dore Schary a Roosevelt memorial spectacular at the Hollywood Bowl, and the 1946 Oscar awards ceremony. In New York, works with Houseman on television version of *Sorry Wrong Number* (as director), and on Broadway production of musicals *Lute Song* (as Houseman's assistant) and *Beggar's Holiday* (as Houseman's associate), the latter Broadway's first racially integrated show, with music by Duke Ellington. Begins work on script of *Thieves Like Us*, later to become *They Live by Night*.

1947: Dore Schary, now RKO production chief, allows Ray to direct *They Live by Night*, first of six films made for the studio, to which he will remain contracted until 1952.

1948: Directs *A Woman's Secret* (and marries its star, Gloria Grahame) and, for Humphrey Bogart's Santana Pictures, *Knock on Any Door*. Works briefly and without enthusiasm on pre-production of *I Married a Communist* for RKO chief Howard Hughes, who, Ray claimed, 'protected' him from House Un-American Activities Committee blacklist. Son Timothy born.

1949: Directs *Born to Be Bad*, and, for Santana, *In a Lonely Place*. Marriage to Grahame breaks up.

1950: Directs *On Dangerous Ground* with Houseman producing. Works uncredited for Hughes for the next year or so, reshooting scenes for various films including *The Racket* and *Macao*. Divorced from Grahame.

1951: Directs *Flying Leathernecks*. Vainly plans to make film on gypsies, researched by Jean Evans, entitled *No Return* and eventually to become *Hot Blood*. Meets future wife Betty Utey for the first time, on set of *Androcles and the Lion*.

1952: Directs *The Lusty Men*. Leaves RKO to work independently for various studios, hoping – in vain – to set up his own production company.

1953: Directs *Johnny Guitar*.

1954: Directs *Run for Cover* and, for television, *High Green Wall*. Meets James Dean while working on story of *The Blind Run*, later to become *Rebel Without a Cause*.

1955: Directs *Rebel Without a Cause* and *Hot Blood*. Plans various films with Dean, who dies in car crash on 30 September while Ray promoting *Rebel* in Europe.

1956: Directs *Bigger than Life* and *The True Story of Jesse James*. Announces foundation of own production company to make *Passport*, but to no avail.

1957: Tired of Hollywood, directs *Bitter Victory* in France and Libya. Problems with producers result in illness, and drive him back to US to direct *Wind Across the Everglades*.

Ray in discussion with James Dean on the set of *Rebel Without a Cause*.

1958: Heavy drinking exacerbates conflict with Budd Schulberg over making of *Wind Across the Everglades*. Directs *Party Girl* and marries dancer/choreographer Betty Utey.

1959: Daughter Julie born. Problems in making of international co-production *The Savage Innocents*. Moves to Rome, entertains plans to set up a film school in Switzerland.

1960: Directs *King of Kings*; again problematic. Moves to Madrid.

1961: President of Berlin Film Festival jury. Unrealised projects include films on Cyrus the Great of Persia and the children's crusade, *Circus World, The Road to the Snail* and *The Tribe that Lost Its Head*. Daughter Nikka born.

1962: Directing *55 Days at Peking*, collapses from exhaustion and is hospitalised. Kept away from set by producer Samuel Bronston (Andrew Marton and Guy Green complete the film); effectively the end of Ray's career as a commercial film-maker.

1963: Exile in Europe: opens restaurant Nikka's in Madrid. Continues to work on numerous projects, none of which come to fruition.

1964: Moves to Paris. Works on the editing of the foreign-language version of *Popioly* by Polish director Andrzej Wajda.

1965: Plans to film Dylan Thomas's *The Doctor and the Devils* fall through. Moves to the Baltic island of Sylt.

1968: Begins shooting (but never completes) *Wha-a-at?* on Sylt, in London and in Paris, where he becomes involved in general socio-political unrest, including protests against proposed removal of Henri Langlois from the post of head of the Cinémathèque Française.

1969: Returns to US, where meets Susan Schwartz. Shoots footage for a never-completed film on the Chicago Conspiracy Trial. Loses sight in right eye after embolism. Collaborates with the Film Group on the pre-production of a film about the Black Panthers, which later became *The Murder of Fred Hampton*.

1971: Teaches film at Harpur College, University of New York. As part of course, begins making, with his students, *The Gun Under My Pillow*, which later becomes *We Can't Go Home Again*.

1973: After first version of *We Can't Go Home Again* receives its premiere at the Cannes Film Festival, visits Amsterdam to shoot, overnight, *The Janitor*.

1974: Moves into a loft in New York's SoHo, with Susan Schwartz. President of San Sebastian Film Festival jury.

1976: Successfully undergoes treatment for alcoholism. Project *Murphy – City Blues* abandoned.

1977: Appears in Wim Wenders' *The American Friend*, and teaches acting classes for University of New York School of Arts and Lee Strasberg Institute, where he makes short films *Macho Gazpacho* and *Marco*. Diagnosed as suffering from cancer.

1978: Undergoes several operations. Appears in Milos Forman's *Hair*.

1979: Serves as informal advisor to former student and assistant teacher Jim Jarmusch on making of *Permanent Vacation*. Collaborates with Wenders on *Lightning Over Water*. Dies 16 June.

Themes and Style

With some justification, Nicholas Ray might be described as the first home-grown film-poet of American disillusionment, an accolade that goes some way towards explaining his importance for European directors (and, indeed, American independent film-makers working outside the Hollywood mainstream) during the 1960s and the early 1970s. It is true that certain other directors – most notably, perhaps, Fritz Lang, Billy Wilder, Douglas Sirk, Alfred Hitchcock and Otto Preminger – also made films offering what can be seen as a cynical, alternative vision of the American Dream, thus refuting the bland homilies implicit in the vast majority of Hollywood productions. But one must bear in mind that these men were all outsiders, from Europe, casting a detached and critical eye over the mores of their adopted country. Moreover, their cynicism tended to be an all-embracing world view rather than a commentary made in particular response to American society itself. They also differed from Ray in the very fact that their attitude *was* cynical, aloof and remote.

Ray, conversely, was a native American whose work, indelibly marked by personal experience, constitutes a despairing anthology of the problems faced by his compatriots during the twentieth century, a pessimistic yet oddly romantic account of the violence, alienation and confusion that he seems to have felt were the inevitable concomitants of rampant individualism trapped within a culture devoted to conformism and materialism. For the most part, Ray's films are bereft of cynicism; with the exception of the few he made as studio chores, he repeatedly identified with his protagonists, and encouraged his audience to join him in that sympathetic identification. His misguided, lonely victims of a callous and complacent society are followed in close-up; it is the world around them that is presented as corrupt, malign and in need of moral re-education.

To anyone who has read Bernard Eisenschitz's biography of Ray, it will already be clear that Ray's experiences, interests and the particular circumstances of his career before becoming a film-maker were at least partly reflected in several recurring thematic elements in his films: the pressures and deceptions of family life; the equivocal function of drink (or drugs) as social lubricant and evil, and as private panacea; the way architecture and environment affect or reflect personality; the conflict between the needs of the individual and the demands of society; the role of outsiders and minority groups in a conformist world.

Ray may also be seen as one of a number of film-makers – Joseph Losey, Jules Dassin, Elia Kazan, John Berry, Abraham Polonsky, Robert Rossen amongst others – whose involvement with the Communist Party and/or various radical theatre groups during the New Deal 1930s led to the making of 'social conscience' movies that approached the many problems of contemporary America from a vaguely liberal or even downright left-ist perspective. In this respect, his work may be understood partly as emanating from, and contributing to, a rather nebulous movement of intellectuals and liberal sympathis-ers, just as, of course, it is possible to examine his individual films purely in the context of how they relate to other examples of the genre to which they belong.

But Ray was a fiercely independent artist with a troubled, highly idiosyncratic sensi-bility, and both the socio-political and the generic elements in his films are inflected, to a greater or lesser degree throughout his career, by his private sympathies, antagonisms, doubts and ambivalences. In this sense, 'a Ray film' exists simultaneously as a cultural document, an exercise in genre and a personal artistic statement; while I shall be look-ing, in passing, at both the cultural and generic parameters – the wider socio-political and industrial context – of his work, it is the specific stylistic qualities and thematic con-cerns which recur in his films that I shall be examining in my attempt to create a rounded, intelligible portrait of Ray the film-maker. And since form and content are inevitably intertwined in a film, either reflecting or working at odds with each other, so, in this analysis, they will be examined concurrently, rather than separated according to some artificial critical methodology.

The close inter-relationship between form and content, style and theme, in Ray's work is immediately evident if one considers his approach to what may be defined as the arche-typal Ray hero or, more precisely, protagonist. Not only did he repeatedly focus on char-acters for whom he felt great emotional and moral sympathy, but that very act of identification was expressed using essentially cinematic means. While there are no instances in his work of the voice-over so beloved of thriller directors during the late 1940s and early 1950s – the cinematic equivalent of the novel's first-person narrative – Ray, instinctively it seems, achieved this sympathetic identification simply by staying close to his central characters. A typical Ray hero, however flawed, is on screen, the focus of attention, throughout the film. The camera never leaves him for reasons of plot devel-opment or to provide a wider social perspective; there are no distractions. While exter-nal factors do clearly affect the protagonist, we are rarely allowed to view the world around him as a separate entity that exists independently of him; in Ray's films, society exists insofar as it colours the lives of his central characters.

This tendency towards a kind of delirious solipsism, expressed both through the struc-ture of the script and through visual composition, highlights two recurring thematic elements in Ray's work: the sense of isolation felt by the hero, and his ambivalent, trou-bled relationship with society at large. Frequently, a film will make explicit verbal refer-ence to the isolation from and wretched connection with the external world experienced by Ray's ill-starred loners. Indeed, the opening pre-credits sequence of his very first film, *They Live by Night*, might stand as the perfect introduction to his work as a whole: in extreme close-up, ironically accompanied by the lyrical strains of the song 'I Know Where I'm Going', we are shown two young lovers tenderly caressing one another, while subti-tles explain that, 'This boy … and this girl … were never properly introduced to the world we live in.' The film then proclaims its status as a thriller by means of a dynamic over-head travelling shot, taken from a helicopter, of a car driven at full speed by desperate fugitive convicts through a bleak landscape; but Ray's deepest concerns have already been made plain by that initial statement of sympathies.

Solitude, vulnerability and a sense of being unprepared for the task of coping with the cruel ways of the world are, time after time, the handicaps suffered by his doomed but beautiful losers, whose awareness of their predicament often extends to a stark and abrupt verbal articulateness, frequently laced with dark irony. In *Johnny Guitar*, Sterling Hayden's eponymous gunslinger insists that, 'I'm a stranger here myself' (a phrase at one point considered by Ray as a possible title for *They Live by Night*); in *Bitter Victory*, Richard Burton's Captain Leith acknowledges the absurdity of his role in a futile wartime raid by pointing out, with an air of lucid resignation, that he kills the living and saves the dead; and in *On Dangerous Ground*, the gulf that Robert Ryan's Detective Jim Wilson feels exists between himself and the urban environment in which he works is evoked in a brutally honest exchange with his partner, 'Pop' Daly:

> WILSON: Garbage, that's all we handle. Garbage! How do you live with it?
> DALY: I *don't* live with it. I live with other people.

The loneliness and vulnerability that afflict many of Ray's characters find their poetic, symbolic counterpart in his visual and narrative use of night. The dark hours, for Ray, serve a dual function: on the one hand, night may be a time of great anxiety, danger and solitude; on the other, it may serve as a cocoon-like refuge from the harsh realities of the outside world. Seldom is it presented as a time for sleeping; rather, it brings the onset of love or death, and, either way, it is evoked with a melancholy lyricism that prompted François Truffaut, when writing of *Johnny Guitar*, to describe Ray as 'the poet of nightfall'.

Another recurrent motif that mirrors the dangerous, menacing solitude experienced by most of his protagonists is that of the hunt, a narrative structure characteristic not only of his crime-thrillers and Westerns, but also, to a greater or lesser degree, of *Rebel Without a Cause, Wind Across the Everglades, The Savage Innocents* and even *King of Kings*. Inevitably, Ray's romantic individualism leads him to focus less on the predator than on the prey, while night provides temporary refuge. Equally interesting is the way in which nature, as opposed to the city, is often seen as offering the possibility of relative safety, salvation or redemption; a number of the films – *They Live by Night, On Dangerous Ground, Rebel Without a Cause* and *Wind Across the Everglades* – feature verbal and visual references to animals.

The protagonists in Ray's films are frequently those who, in other Hollywood movies of the time, either would have been deemed evil, criminal or simply unpleasant (and, therefore, unworthy of serious, rounded characterisation), or would have been relegated to the margins of the drama while more monolithically good or bad characters held centre-stage. The means by which he obtains and holds our understanding and sympathy for these outcasts, outlaws, losers and loners is to reveal, and indeed emphasise, facets of a human personality that, though realistic, are seldom shown in the mainstream commercial cinema.

Characterisation for Ray seems to have centred, to an unusual degree, on notions of

Was God wrong? From on high, Ed Avery (James Mason) takes it upon himself to teach Lou (Barbara Rush) and Wally (Walter Matthau) a lesson in moral responsibility, in *Bigger than Life*.

polarisation and reversal of audience expectations: delving beneath and beyond the veneer of conventional film stereotyping, in search of a real complexity of human motivation, he exposes violence in the quiet and sophisticated, gentle sensitivity in the murderer, weakness and vulnerability in the apparently self-sufficient. *In a Lonely Place* focuses on Bogart's intelligent and romantic screenwriter Dixon Steele, who becomes almost psychopathically brutal when his temper is aroused; in *Bigger than Life*, James Mason's suburban schoolteacher Ed Avery, homely and conscientious, is catalysed by medically prescribed drugs into believing himself dull and into giving way to a hitherto latent, darker side of his character that turns him into a tyrannical, megalomaniac patriarch, with homicidal tendencies towards his own family. Conversely, in *They Live by Night* Farley Granger's juvenile killer Bowie is at heart a warm, considerate and nervous innocent, while in *The Lusty Men* Robert Mitchum's Jeff McCloud, a seemingly tough and totally independent rodeo-rider who lives only for the here and now, conceals beneath his proud façade a quiet, aching nostalgia for his home and past, and an unexpectedly tender respect for the woman he has grown to love.

Ray uses these formal strategies of reversal and *apparent* contradiction not for the sake of novelty or to play with genre conventions; rather, they fulfil a dual purpose. On the one hand, his characters are plausible as realistic, complex human beings, rather than two-dimensional film caricatures; their inconsistency is simply part of the acute psychological detail with which they are invested by Ray's unsentimental but compassionate gaze. On the other hand, and equally relevant to his purpose, the notion of characters beset by inner contradictions is fundamental to his thematic concerns; his 'heroes', flawed to a man, are torn apart by the destructively conflicting impulses they sense within them. Ray's work, after all, is primarily about pain and tension.

Tension – a sense of things being somehow so out of balance, so unstable, so fragile, that the whole edifice of a personality, a relationship or a society will fall apart – is virtually a *sine qua non* of Ray's work, informing (as we shall see later) not only his narrative and visual style and his tangential relationship to the Hollywood mainstream but the subject matter of all his films. For this most troubled of film-makers, tension was invariably a question of bitter, painful conflict, frequently ending in death. The protagonist at least, if not the minor characters, is prey to fierce, often irreconcilable and contradictory impulses within his psychological make-up, expressed in many instances as a battle between, on the one hand, an innate tendency towards violence and, on the other, a need to repress those instincts in order to live peacefully with others. Conflict is also a crucial factor in dealing with the world; it regularly arises in three basic forms: between two (types of) individuals (male/female, young/old, master/servant, and so on); between an individual and the family or society he lives with; or between one group (or culture) and another.

Indeed, Ray's work is full of contradictory opposites, which create still further, more abstract forms of tension: between the desire for love and a need for independence, between innocence and experience, integrity and survival, hope and reality. The tension in Ray's films is often manifested through structures rooted in antithesis and balance: the characters, in particular, are frequently depicted as being somehow complementary opposites of each other. In *Party Girl*, crippled Tommy Farrell enters into a fragile relationship with dancer Vicky Gaye; in *King of Kings* Christ's pacifism meets its opposite in the revolutionary terrorism of Barabbas. Similarly, narrative itself may feature two diametrically opposed situations or locations, as in *On Dangerous Ground*, which suddenly shifts from the menacing darkness of the city to the snowy landscapes of the seemingly safer country.

Despite occasional happy endings (some of which seem to have been forced upon Ray, and few of which are unqualified by doubt, ambiguity and irony), these struggles, both internal and external, frequently result in destruction, of life, love or ideals. For Ray, life and the world are spaces in which his characters strive to hold on to their very self, with their integrity intact; innocence is a short-lived blessing, an almost dreamlike state; happiness, too, is merely temporary. Love and friendship, which offer the highest chance of contentment, for the most part provide only a brief respite from the isolation of existence, and frequently carry in their wake their own special, dangerous drawbacks of suspicion, misunderstanding, betrayal and embittered disappointment. Hell, in Ray's films, is not simply other people (who, after all, can at least *appear* to alleviate, if only temporarily, the sense of alienation and solitude felt by his protagonists); rather, it is the external *and* the internal world. Hell is also one's self.

In film after film, Ray's heroes bear within them the seeds of their own destruction; Dixon Steele (*In a Lonely Place*), Nick Romano (*Knock on Any Door*), Jeff McCloud

(*The Lusty Men*), Jesse James (*The True Story of Jesse James*) and James Leith (*Bitter Victory*) are merely the most obvious examples. There is a dark, paradoxical irony in the way that their attempts to avoid compromise, to fight social injustice or, quite simply, to escape an overwhelming sense of solitude and futility, bring about the demise either of themselves or of a relationship which they have dreamed of as offering the potential for a better life. Bowie (*They Live by Night*), Romano, McCloud, Jesse and Leith all die; Steele loses the women he loves, Jim Stark (in *Rebel Without a Cause*) loses his only male friend, and Ed Avery (in *Bigger than Life*) almost kills his beloved son and wrecks his marriage.

But it is not only a character's inner qualities, the critical flaws in his tortured soul, that wreck the dream of a happier, more fulfilling existence. Ray, while showing us the larger world through the peculiarly tormented perceptions of his protagonists, was sufficiently aware, socially and politically, to realise that we do not live in a vacuum, that we are deeply affected by external factors. His protagonists fall victim not only to their own spiritual demons, but to the society around them, with its pressures to conform and knuckle under; with the emphasis it places on the importance of respectability, success and material comfort; with its neglect and intolerance of the poor, the weak and those who are simply *different*. To feel that one is isolated from the world is painful, but for the stranger, the outsider, the one who believes, wrongly or rightly, that he just does not fit in with the rest of society, living *in* the world is equally miserable. For Ray's misfits, dreams of belonging are generally fruitless, and loneliness is an inevitable, agonising condition of being alive.

The American Dream – of individual success and happiness, of the family that stays and plays together, of personal freedom – is repeatedly examined and found wanting by Ray's aching romantic pessimism. His sensitivity to the pressures exerted by society at large extends far beyond the impassioned if rather simplistically articulated indictment of poverty, inequality and complacency put into Bogart's mouth at the end of *Knock on Any Door*; until his last few films, made when he was working in Europe, he repeatedly located his victim-heroes in recognisably and specifically American settings.

This was partly, of course, a concomitant of his working in Hollywood, using traditional Hollywood genres. But Ray took those genres and settings and made them his own, often working against the grain in the same way that he did in the field of characterisation. *They Live by Night* is less a conventional *film noir* or gangster movie than a romantic elegy to beleaguered innocence and doomed love. *The True Story of Jesse James* is as much about the rebellious nature of alienated, brutalised youth as *Rebel Without a Cause*. Nobody who has seen *Johnny Guitar* would ever describe it as a conventional Western, while *Wind Across the Everglades* is such a bizarre hybrid as to defy generic categorisation. Even *Flying Leathernecks*, Ray's most anonymous and conventional film, feeds on personal conflict and anxiety rather than on traditional gung-ho wartime heroics.

Indeed, *Johnny Guitar*, in which the central gun-shooting rivals are women, is perhaps indicative of the way Ray preferred to *combine* what were traditionally seen as 'male' and 'female' Hollywood genres: to the 'masculine' thriller, war movie and Western, he brought tenderness and introspection, while in his 'feminine' romances and melodramas, outbursts of violence are unusually conspicuous. Time and again, genre clichés are both transformed and transcended, even as conventional iconography and motifs are requisitioned to demonstrate the unfeeling methods by which those who do not quite 'fit' are rejected, intimated and neglected by America and its institutions. The marriage parlour in *They Live by Night*; the urban hell of *On Dangerous Ground*; the rodeo arenas and bars of *The Lusty Men*; the homes, schools, police stations and hospitals of *Rebel Without a Cause* and *Bigger than Life*: in most Hollywood films, such locations would be familiar, respectable settings ripe for confirming the values of the American Dream, but in the cruel, cool world envisioned by Ray, they are translated into arenas of suffering and conflict, humiliation and disappointment.

And just as he investigated areas of life usually neglected by Hollywood (the rodeo-circuit nomads, the gypsies of *Hot Blood*, the Florida bird-poachers of *Wind Across the Everglades*), so he virtually invented new sub-genres of his own. *Wind Across the Everglades* and the European-funded *The Savage Innocents* (both, to some extent, presaged by the TV film *High Green Wall*) are perhaps the most bizarre, fusing fiction and semi-documentary, ethnology, ecology and Western-style thriller-devices. But others are also remarkable in this respect: *In a Lonely Place*, an intriguingly disenchanted view of Hollywood itself, merges *film noir* suspense and iconography into 'women's-weepie' romance with an originality surpassing even that of Max Ophuls's *The Reckless Moment* and *Caught*; *Rebel Without a Cause* popularised a new genre of its own – the teenage *angst*-and-revolt movie – almost single-handedly. For Ray genre was merely a convenient tool, which could be dispensed with or distorted according to the demands of his subject: America was his canvas, upon which he painted subtle strokes of bold, angry yet tender colour and movement to express his private feelings of isolation and despair. For him, the grasping insensitivity of his homeland, with its conformism and complacency, its capitalism and crime, was forever threatening to consume the confused outsider.

This view was, of course, partly a reflection of America during two crucial periods in Ray's life – the Depression, when he was first making his way in theatre and radio, and the years of the House Un-American Activities Committee witch-hunts, when he was attempting to establish himself as a film-maker. Other directors of his generation were also profoundly affected by the turbulence of the times, but none of them spent their entire careers speaking so obsessively and so eloquently of disenchantment. Ray's response to the world around him was virtually unique in Hollywood, in two respects: his films, made in a highly commercial, industrialised and profit-motivated environment, were nevertheless for the most part deeply personal expressions of his own despair; secondly, that despair was surely more than a merely incidental response to contemporary historical events. Though he was, without a doubt, a child of his times, one cannot but suspect that Ray's peculiar combination of romanticism and pessimism was born of a very private sensibility and would have been expressed, in one way or another, even had he lived during another age.

None the less, if one considers the settings for most of his films (the West, Hollywood, suburbia and the dark, crime-ridden cityscapes of *film noir*), it is clear that a specifically American experience was central to his purpose, and while his loner-heroes may outwardly appear to be part of American normality – cowboys, cops, screenwriters, teachers – they are as isolated from society at large as was the outlaw Jesse James (who, as Ray portrays him, was a simple farm-boy, embittered and confused by the Civil War and its aftermath, and driven into banditry by his desire to protect his own kinsfolk from persecution and cruelty). Typical, for Ray, is the predicament of Detective Jim Wilson in *On Dangerous Ground*, who is so brutalised by his job and his surroundings that he himself, though idealistic and efficient, turns increasingly to violence. Without a family to distract him from the depressing nature of his work, which he performs with a fanatical passion, he is simply unable to 'connect' with others; it is only when he is exiled upstate, to a snowy, rural environment that serves as the exact opposite to his night-time shifts in the city, that he can examine and come to terms, tentatively, with his own inner conflicts.

Significantly, Wilson's redemption is made possible not only by the death of a killer for whom he has come to feel some semblance of sympathy and understanding, but by his being confronted by two opposing but far from mutually exclusive forms of family love: the vengeful bloodlust of a murdered girl's father, and the protective warmth of the culprit's blind sister. (Ray's central characters frequently suffer from a physical wound or disability that mirrors psychological or spiritual torment: an example of his tendency to reveal inner emotions through external details. This symbolic dualism, however, is far from schematic or simplistic: while the fact that Tommy Farrell, the crooked lawyer in *Party Girl*, has a crippled leg reflects his moral weakness, Mary Malden's blindness in *On Dangerous Ground* is partly ironic in that she not only 'sees', that is, understands people more clearly than Wilson, but is far less cut off from the world than he is.)

Because Ray's protagonists see themselves as outsiders, as somehow different or abnormal (it is no accident that a number of them are adolescents, racked by confusion about what it means to be 'a man'), they are often driven to transgress the moral norms held dear by the conformist world in which they are required to live. Often, this transgression is presented in terms of an act of violence; it may also, however, be expressed through a general contempt for life as it is lived by the majority of Americans. In *Bigger than Life*, teacher Ed Avery shocks a parents' meeting by pouring contempt both on his pupils and on traditional methods of education; in *Rebel Without a Cause*, teenagers who see little value in emulating the lives of their parents gamble with death when they gather for the 'chickee run'. The reward for such acts of transgression, of pushing beyond the limits of what is deemed socially acceptable behaviour, is frequently death, either for the perpetrator or for another character who may be presented as a kind of *alter ego*.

Occasionally, that death is self-inflicted; often, however, it takes the form of a punishment inflicted by a cruel, hysterical and violently repressive society whose desire to exact an eye-for-an-eye retribution is so fervent that it commits what perhaps seemed to Ray an even more reprehensible act of murder: the lynching. (It is surely no accident that the dangerous and vengeful mob mentality depicted in films as diverse as *On Dangerous Ground, Johnny Guitar* and *Run for Cover* is evocative of the heated, paranoid emotions aroused by Senator Joe McCarthy and his cohorts during the anti-Communist witch-hunts.) Such hangings – the crucifixion of Christ in *King of Kings* may be seen as a further example – are entirely in keeping with Ray's vision of the relationship between

'All you can buy up these stairs is a bullet in the head': Vienna (Joan Crawford) protects her privacy from an invading mob in *Johnny Guitar*.

the individual and the world at large, stressing not only the vulnerability and solitude of a victim who is confronted with an undifferentiated, unfeeling mass, but also the fundamental injustice of a society where an innocent is often hurriedly and mistakenly presumed guilty by those who are themselves far from blameless.

In that lynching is a form of retribution that is commonly directed against a scapegoat and that ignores the fundamental concept of justice whereby the accused has the democratic right to defend himself in a fair trial, it bears some resemblance not only to the iniquities of the McCarthy hearings, but also to the primitive ritual of sacrifice. And indeed, the motif of sacrifice (intentional or otherwise) is a recurring element in Ray's films, lending an almost mythic clarity and power to his tales of human waste and redemption. In *They Live by Night*, a final letter suggests that Bowie has gone half-knowingly to his death in order that his wife and child might live their lives untainted by crime and punishment and prejudice; in *The Lusty Men*, Jeff McCloud's death drives his partner to forsake the dangerous glamour of the rodeo for a happier life with the woman both men love; and in *Rebel Without a Cause*, it is only when Jim Stark's friend Plato dies that Jim's parents finally realise how close they have come to losing their own son.

But the loss of human life, for Ray, always entails tragedy, and sacrifice is equally often shown as futile; *Bigger than Life* recoils in horror from Ed Avery's attempts to murder his own son (inspired by God's having commanded Abraham to kill Isaac), while in *Bitter*

Victory James Leith's death serves only to reinforce the self-loathing of Leith's rival and would-be killer through an awareness of his own moral bankruptcy. It matters little, in Ray's films, whether the sacrificial victim is the protagonist or a comparatively minor character functioning as his *alter ego*; for while acknowledging the pain of human existence, Ray also insists on its sanctity and worth. And it is because of this fundamental humanism that his characters are viewed with such compassion, and that a number of his films rail against capital punishment.

There are, however, slower, more insidious ways by which an individual's happiness and self-esteem may be eroded; for Ray, the family, that sacred cow of American movies, was a potential haven of repression, resentment and misunderstanding. Often, the protagonist's family will either have already broken up, or be on the brink of doing so; unreasonable demands may be made of one member by another for the sake of conformity and respectability; tensions are particularly rife between father and son, the latter feeling that the former has compromised the ideals of his youth. Ray's attitude, one feels, was not so much one of wanting to do away with the family, but simply one of wanting to improve it; while the *real* families shown or mentioned in *They Live by Night, Rebel Without a Cause, Hot Blood* and *Bigger than Life* are marked by a mood of inequality, recrimination and claustrophobia, in a number of other films *surrogate* familial relationships are established, revealing not only the characters' need to feel that they *belong*, but

The architecture of a scene: hauled into the police precinct, Jim (James Dean) makes initial contact with Plato (Sal Mineo) while Judy (Natalie Wood) looks on, in *Rebel Without a Cause*.

also the mutual equality and understanding that must be achieved in order for a relationship to provide stability and security. The friendship between Jim, Judy and Plato in *Rebel Without a Cause* becomes a substitute for the family love each is deprived of at home; in *Knock on Any Door* and *Run for Cover*, confused, embittered adolescents take up with older, more experienced men whom they regard as surrogate fathers; in *They Live by Night, The Lusty Men, Hot Blood, Wind Across the Everglades* and *Party Girl*, whole gangs and groups of outsiders cluster together, creating a form of extended family that offers protection against the outside world, mimicking the father–son relationships of domestic life. Often, these surrogate families, like their real counterparts, are destined to break up, for the most part violently, but for a while at least, like love between a man and a woman, they offer respite from the solitude of existence.

It is perhaps in evoking the tensions of domestic life that Ray's extraordinarily precise visual sense is most immediately noticeable. Not for nothing did he repeatedly acknowledge the influence of the architect Frank Lloyd Wright upon his work and ideas. No other American director has made such expressive use of space to suggest and delineate the inner lives of his characters. Though his depiction of the great outdoors in his Westerns, war films and epics was equally inspired and elegant, it is in his quasi-symbolic use of buildings that Ray most obviously excels. In film after film, a house becomes far more than just a home: a protective haven from the outside world, it also speaks of the tension between characters, of seemingly contradictory needs for independence and togetherness. Often (the saloon in *Johnny Guitar*, the family homes in *Rebel Without a Cause* and *Bigger than Life*), downstairs represents sociability, upstairs privacy and individual freedom. Staircases – diagonals that contrast with the more stable horizontals of the rooms – are therefore meeting points between private and public, dreams and reality, and more often than not the location of indecision, crisis and conflict. (Interestingly, Ray even contrives to work a stepladder into the narrative of the jungle-set TV film *High Green Wall*, at the very moment when McMaster introduces Henty to his library of Dickens novels, thus setting in motion the master–servant relationship that results in Henty's complete surrender of his own identity.)

Similarly, the *position* of a building mirrors its meaning for the protagonist; many of Ray's loner-heroes retreat to remote houses, in which they take refuge from the cruel realities of the world, while in the film *In a Lonely Place*, the way the apartments of Dixon Steele and Laurel Gray are simultaneously connected and separated by a courtyard reflects the way their fragile, hesitant relationship is at once defined by attraction and repulsion, communication and withdrawal. Landscape, too, is put to supremely expressive use by Ray: the desert of *Bitter Victory* incarnates the arid nature of Leith's futile cynicism, while the Florida swamps in *Wind Across the Everglades* reflect the murky, animalistic and quasi-primeval morality of Cottonmouth's murderous band of poachers.

This tendency towards a poetic, almost symbolic abstraction is present not only in Ray's use of setting, but in his compositions. Line, as might be expected of one so influenced by Wright, is of crucial importance, with horizontals evocative of rest and stability, diagonals of confusion, chaos, crisis and violence. (Certainly, it is arguable that no director, with the possible exception of Altman, has used the unwieldy format of the

CinemaScope frame so expressively or beautifully as did Ray.) Camera movement, too, serves meaning, with rapid travelling shots often accompanying violent action, and static shots – sometimes in close-up – depicting intimacy and introspection.

Moreover, Ray was one of the great colour film-makers, deploying a palette of pastel tones and primary colours to create mood and meaning. In *Party Girl* (which one enthusiastic French critic compared to the paintings of Cézanne), red is associated with violence and death, browns and greys with tranquillity and safety, while in *Bigger than Life*, Ed Avery's first visible bout of illness is accompanied by a shot of rows of yellow cabs, their sickly hues filling the screen, and Avery's initial, nightmarish visits to the hospital feature feverish compositions suffused with bloody reds. (Indeed, it may have been Ray's almost abstract interest in décor and colour, coupled with his experiences working in radio and as an archivist gathering folk music, that attracted him to the idea of making a musical. Although he never fulfilled this ambition, *Hot Blood* and *Party Girl* include musical dance sequences, and many later works feature actions so stylised that one is almost tempted to describe them as choreographed rather than directed.)

Nevertheless, however expressive Ray's *use* of colour and décor, the colours and décor themselves are always fundamentally *real*, rather than fantastic; they never challenge our faith in the plausibility of what we are seeing, but are fully integrated into the story. At the same time, this tendency towards abstraction and symbolism often lends Ray's work a dimension of classical myth, or tragedy. The director himself spoke of the overhead helicopter shots at the beginning of *They Live by Night* as representing the long arm of fate, while the flawed nature of his protagonists can be compared to the (admittedly more heroic) flaws that bring about the downfall of the noble figures of Greek or Shakespearean drama; certainly, Ed Avery's megalomania in *Bigger than Life* is a classic instance of *hubris*. More specifically, colour, costume and characterisation are frequently combined to endow an otherwise realistically depicted figure with a virtually symbolic significance: the grim, pallid, mask-like face and persistently black attire of Mattie in *They Live by Night* not only evoke her predicament as a kind of widow, but also suggest that she may be seen as Death itself; while the hysterical, unstoppable movements of the funeral-party-turned-lynch-mob in *Johnny Guitar* are reminiscent of the Furies of Greek myth. Such resonances are implicit, rather than explicit, but their effect is to emphasise the timelessness and universality of Ray's pessimistic vision of an unjust world.

It was not only the visual resources of his medium that Ray deployed to create and enrich meaning; sound and music, too, were tools that he would frequently use to Expressionist effect. (In this respect, as for Welles before him, the years he spent working in radio were doubtless of considerable value.) Even in his first film, the sound of passing trains (unseen, and with no narrative function) is utilised to suggest danger, culminating in the thundering roar that foreshadows and accompanies the death of Bowie: trains underline, too, moments of tension and violence in *Party Girl*, just as animal cries echo Henty's despair in *High Green Wall*. Moreover, events are prefigured or commented on by Ray's use of music and songs: again in *They Live by Night*, the strains of 'I Know Where I'm Going' contribute a sad and ironic counterpoint to the entrapment and haphazard flight of Bowie and Keechie, while the song 'Your Red Wagon' offers a sardonic gloss on society's callous, negligent attitude towards the pair's helpless predicament. Music also plays a crucial, *dramatic* role in *A Woman's Secret, Johnny Guitar, Hot Blood, The True Story of Jesse James* (which Ray originally planned as a kind of cinematic ballad), *Wind Across the Everglades, Party Girl, The Savage Innocents* and *55 Days at Peking*; sound was simply one further element in his total, all-embracing conception of *mise en scène*.

While Ray's methods were thus essentially cinematic rather than literary – with colour, composition, camera movement, décor and sound contributing as much to characterisation, meaning, and narrative and thematic development as did dialogue – his earlier work in the theatre with luminaries such as Kazan and Losey ensured that he was also an unusually sensitive and adventurous director of actors. Whenever possible, he took a great deal of care over casting his films, occasionally selecting comparatively unknown performers and often opting to work with actors more than once, with the result that the careers of a handful of figures – John Derek, Jay C Flippen, Gloria Grahame, Sumner Williams, Ian Wolfe and, most notably, Robert Ryan – are often remembered as having been inextricably associated with his own.

Moreover, Ray was well acquainted with the Method, and while few of his actors were from the Actor's Studio, many performances in his films have a Method-like intensity; it is well-known, too, that he liked to work in close collaboration with his actors, even favouring a certain amount of improvisation when the script failed to meet his satisfaction. (Despite this tendency, Ray was equally adept at eliciting strong performances from actors who came from totally different disciplines and backgrounds; Dean, of course, was associated with the Method, but Bogart, Mitchum, Ryan, Cagney and Heston were famous as Hollywood tough-guy heroes; Arthur Kennedy, Richard Burton and others were from the 'serious' legitimate theatre; Ida Lupino, Susan Hayward, Joan Fontaine, and Joan Crawford were best known for their roles in 'women's weepies'; Howard Da Silva was from the Group Theatre; Joseph Cotten was famous for his work in Orson Welles's Mercury Theatre; John Wayne, Ward Bond and Maureen O'Hara were from John Ford's repertory company; Burl Ives was better known as a folk singer; still others were more or less discovered by Ray himself.)

Most interesting, however, is the way Ray often cast his actors partly against type, and worked against the grain of their familiar screen personae. Just as he frequently explored unexpected qualities in an otherwise comparatively conventional character, so he would counteract an actor's most popular or recognisable attributes, or logically extend those attributes to achieve a fresh and revealing characterisation. Thus, in *The Lusty Men*, Robert Mitchum's taciturnity, usually offered as evidence of his being a strong, silent type, becomes an index of Jeff McCloud's unease with people, of his introverted shyness, of his private, painful sense of nostalgia, loss and loneliness: in *Johnny Guitar*, Joan Crawford's almost masculine hardness of appearance was not merely acknowledged but accentuated, to emphasise Vienna's determination to be accepted as an equal in a man's world; and in *On Dangerous Ground*, Robert Ryan's familiar tough-nut persona cracks beneath Ray's penetrating, compassionate gaze, to reveal a pathologically insecure, confused and lonely man. Even in the widely underrated epic *55 Days at Peking*, Ray, allowing for moments of startling intimacy, undermines and, in effect, humanises Charlton

Heston's heroic persona by having his hardened soldier stumble clumsily in his efforts to tell a young Chinese girl that her father is dead; it is clearly the most demanding task he has ever faced, since both courage *and* sensitivity are required.

Because Ray probed beneath veneers in this way, continually striving to reveal the real man or woman behind the mask that is presented to the world, many actors excelled themselves under his supervision, creating fresh, rounded, *understated* characterisations which are, nevertheless, often overwhelmingly powerful in their raw emotional honesty and their fraught, fragile humanity. Ray was justifiably proud of his work with James Dean, for whom he felt great affinity, and with Bogart ('For the first time he didn't have a prop; he didn't have a gun in his hands') whose performance in *In a Lonely Place* surpassed even his appearances for Howard Hawks. But others, too, did their best work for Ray: Mitchum, Ryan and James Mason were especially well served by his interest in vulnerability and sensitivity; Gloria Grahame, Richard Burton, John Derek, Charlton Heston, Ava Gardner, Farley Granger, Christopher Plummer, Natalie Wood, Susan Hayward, Burl Ives, Sal Mineo and many others also plumbed depths and nuances of character barely touched on by other film-makers.

Such performances, vivid, credible and affecting to this day, are simply one more example of Ray's determination to explore, using every tool at his command, film's capacity for depicting the pain, anxiety, confusion and sadness of human existence. And it is one of his very greatest achievements that he did so while making movies that were first and foremost popular entertainment; though the subject matter of his films was, more often than not, such that they might have been depressing, the sheer artistry on view, coupled with his profound compassion for his characters (who in turn show great grace and courage in attempting to face up to both their own inner conflicts and the injustices of the world about them), transforms the films into strangely uplifting experiences.

They Live by Night (1948)

SYNOPSIS: Three convicts – hardened criminals T-Dub and Chicamaw, and the 23-year-old
Bowie – have escaped from a penitentiary. They take refuge at the home shared by
Chicamaw's brother Mobley and Mobley's daughter Keechie. The three men immediately
plan a bank robbery (Bowie in order to obtain money to employ a lawyer who might clear
him of a murder conviction). They rent a house with the help of T-Dub's sister-in-law
Mattie, whose husband – T-Dub's brother – is himself in prison. The robbery is successfully
carried out, but after a car crash, Chicamaw shoots a policeman, and leaves the injured
Bowie in the care of Keechie. Bowie's gun, complete with fingerprints, is found at the scene
of the crime, and his dreams of proving his innocence are dashed; he takes to the road with
Keechie, whose reward-hungry father immediately betrays the fugitive couple. After they are
married by Hawkins, proprietor of a seedy wedding-parlour, they check into a remote motel.
Here, their happiness is eventually disturbed by a visit from Chicamaw, who persuades the
reluctant Bowie to join him and T-Dub in one more bank robbery. Their efforts end in
disaster: T-Dub is killed, and during their escape, Bowie and the irascible Chicamaw quarrel
and separate. Bowie returns to Keechie, who is angry with him for having deserted her for
his old cellmate; he learns that Chicamaw has been killed while breaking into a liquor store,
and that Keechie is expecting his child. They are recognised by a plumber, leave the motel
and try to find refuge in a town where Bowie is again recognised, this time in a nightclub.
Desperate, they make for the motel bought by T-Dub for Mattie, whose resentment of the
pair leads her to betray Bowie to the police in return for her husband's release from prison.
Meanwhile, Bowie, believing that he and Keechie will only be safe if they go to Mexico,
visits Hawkins, who refuses to help them. Returning to the motel, he decides that Keechie's
safety is dependent on his leaving her; but as he walks to their cabin to deliver a farewell
note – she is asleep – he is gunned down by the police. On his body Keechie finds the note,
an expression of his enduring love for her and their child-to-be.

Ray's first film was produced by his colleague John Houseman at the request of RKO's
liberal and adventurous executive Dore Schary – it remains one of the most impressive
directing debuts ever made in the history of the cinema. Although his only experience of
working in the medium had been as an assistant to Kazan on *A Tree Grows in Brooklyn*,
he appears, in hindsight, to have come to film-making with his artistic personality already
surprisingly mature: both stylistically and thematically, the film prefigures the best of his
later work, while his highly expressive use of the medium is remarkably assured and complete. Meaning is conveyed through a comprehensive grasp of cinema's various signifying
properties – script, acting, imagery, movement, light and sound – and one never feels that

Ray is stressing style simply for style's sake: form, throughout, is at the service of content.

They Live by Night is generally regarded as belonging to a group of movies, made during the 1940s and 1950s, that were later categorised as *film noir*: bleak, pessimistic thrillers or melodramas in which an atmosphere of paranoia and alienation, corruption and mystery is conveyed through dark, shadowy images frequently reminiscent of the Expressionist visuals of early German cinema. The film has been further categorised into a sub-genre consisting of a number of movies dealing with fugitive lovers on the run, of which the most notable other examples are Fritz Lang's *You Only Live Once* (1937), Anthony Mann's *Desperate* (1947), Joseph H. Lewis's *Gun Crazy* (1949), Arthur Penn's *Bonnie and Clyde* (1967), Robert Altman's *Thieves Like Us* (1973) – adapted from the same novel by Edward Anderson as the Ray film – and Terrence Malick's *Badlands* (1974).

Nevertheless, while there may be considerable interest in approaching *They Live by Night* from a generic perspective (it is instructive, for example, to examine how elements of irony, even of pastiche, crept into many later examples of the fugitive-couples subgenre), the film is probably more interesting in the way that it differs from most *film noir* and exists, perhaps primarily, as an example of Ray's obsessive and sympathetic fascination with outsiders confronted with and destroyed by an uncaring, corrupt society. For a predominant feature of *film noir* is its tone of world-weary cynicism, whereas Ray's passionate identification with his innocent protagonists is far from cynical; there is, indeed, an overwhelming *tenderness* in his film that is entirely at odds with the cool emphasis on macho violence and misogynist suspicion that characterises the mood of so many crime films of the 1940s and 1950s. As was suggested in the preceding chapter, Ray often merged 'masculine' and 'feminine' genres to create fresh, intriguing hybrids, and while it would be folly to claim that *They Live by Night* was a complete original – its generic components are far too pronounced for that – it is none the less true that the film is as much love story as thriller.

Generic considerations apart, a brief comparison with Altman's 'remake' immediately throws light, by contrast, on Ray's own special interests and intentions. In plot and characters, the films are remarkably similar; Altman's dialogue is, in fact, frequently identical to Ray's. In tone, however, they differ considerably. While *Thieves Like Us* is arguably the most tender and touching of the iconoclastic Altman's experiments with genre (others include *McCabe and Mrs Miller*, *The Long Goodbye* and *Nashville*), any affection he feels for his doomed lovers is ironically undercut, not only by a semi-humorous approach which insists on the absurd delusions and poverty of the characters' lives and dreams as compared to the myths purveyed by the radio and press, but also by the fact that his Bowie, like the novel's but unlike Ray's, *is* guilty of killing (admittedly in self-defence), and feels no remorse after Chicamaw's shooting of the policeman.

Altman's methods, as opposed to Ray's, may be seen as anti-romantic and anti-mythic (his Mattie is no Death-figure, but simply a pragmatic, careworn mother tired of bringing up her family alone while her husband festers in prison), and as concerned less with the central characters themselves than with the society around them. Bowie's visit to the state penitentiary in order to free Chicamaw (one of the few sequences for which there is no counterpart in Ray) stresses the greed and comfort of the prison governor's life despite the Depression, and draws attention to social inequality; lynchings of blacks are mentioned on the radio and an evangelical broadcast about the New Deal warns, ironically, of the need to keep America safe for democracy; when Bowie and Keechie make love in her father's run-down storeroom, its walls papered with old magazine covers and newsprint, a highly romantic transmission of *Romeo and Juliet* plays on the radio, lending a cruel irony to their doomed relationship. Perhaps even more significant is the difference between the two films' visual styles: where Ray lyrically stages most scenes at night, Altman mostly opts for dull grey daylight, emphasising the grim despair of the times; and where Ray reveals his sympathy for his protagonists with a predominance of close-ups, Altman uses long shots to create an objective distance between his characters and himself, and to suggest a more widespread, national malaise.

Ray's opening shot is, in fact, a statement of intentions and sympathies: a soft-lit, extreme close-up of Bowie and Keechie (at night) caressing each other chastely and tenderly, underlined by subtitles explaining that 'This boy ... and this girl ... were never properly introduced to the world we live in', accompanied by the tune 'I Know Where I'm Going'. The effect of this unusual, almost Brechtian pre-credits shot is at once poetic in its beauty and direct in its expressiveness: verbally, of youthful outsiders neglected by and in conflict with society; visually, of romantic intimacy and secrecy; aurally, of inexorable destiny. Already, in his very first shot for the cinema, Ray shows both his ability to create a rich complexity of meanings through a simple, precise image, and his strong sense of sympathy for the outcast. Form and emotional content are inextricably interrelated even before the credits sequence – an extraordinarily dynamic helicopter-shot of a speeding car driven in harsh daylight across a desolate landscape by T-Dub, Chicamaw and Bowie – which further reinforces the deterministic feeling as the characters career headlong to meet their fates, watched over by a lofty, all-seeing eye.

While the pre-credits close-up suggested both a love story and a social-conscience drama, the helicopter-shot introduces the iconography of the crime-thriller, thus indicating the hybrid nature of Ray's debut. Before a word has been spoken, Ray has plunged us into a world defined by stark polarities – night and day, secrecy and conspicuousness, rest and flight – between which Bowie, the narrative centre of the film, will be forever caught. Almost at once, when the car has screeched to a halt with a burst tyre, we are made aware that this boy, never properly introduced to the world, is not entirely comfortable in the company of experienced criminals like T-Dub and Chicamaw. T-Dub points a gun at the driver of the car they have hijacked; Chicamaw pushes the gun aside and brutally beats the man. Less interested in the physical display of violence than in its cause and effect, Ray cuts away from the beating to Bowie's shocked, fearful face; though part of this unholy alliance, he is not like his two colleagues. Indeed, when they continue their escape by running across the fields, he injures his foot and is left alone by T-Dub and Chicamaw, who go ahead to Mobley's house, promising to collect him later.

In the next scene, the first that takes place at night (the prologue was 'outside' the drama), Ray introduces a number of motifs that will reappear throughout the film. As Bowie awaits his friends in the dark, he is positioned behind a latticework arrangement of wooden supports for a billboard; the visual effect, very like a cage, suggests his entrap-

ment. At the same time, he is joined by a stray dog, the first of several references to animals that underline Bowie and Keechie's natural innocence and helplessness. The sound
of a train passing nearby is heard, fatalistically prefiguring the roar of a train that immediately precedes Bowie's death at the end of the film. And when at last Keechie arrives to
collect him, the entrapment motif is repeated, with the pair shot from behind a grille in
the back of the truck. The soft, hesitant rhythms of their first feint-and-parry dialogue –
a blend of duet and duel that foreshadows many such wary encounters between hero and
heroine in Ray's work – poetically evoke the suspicion and fear felt by the characters:

> BOWIE: You having trouble?
> KEECHIE: Could be.
> BOWIE: Who are you? You live around here?
> KEECHIE: Could be.
> BOWIE: You haven't had a couple of visitors lately, have you?
> KEECHIE: That wouldn't be a sore foot making you limp, would it?
> BOWIE: Could be.
> KEECHIE: I got some other stuff to pick up. Get in or we'll both get pneumonia.

Already, before the plot proper is under way, Ray is using dialogue, off-screen sound,
composition, movement and lighting to enrich both narrative and characterisation.
When the pair join T-Dub, Chicamaw, Mobley and Mattie at Mobley's house, the various relationships between characters continue to be economically and deftly drawn, as
much by glances and composition as by dialogue: Bowie, repeatedly towered over by T-
Dub and Chicamaw (in several shots he is framed between T-Dub's arms), is clearly
intimidated and influenced by the older men; Chicamaw's volatile instability is revealed
by the camera's panning back and forth with him when he paces the room in anger at
his being called 'One-Eye' Mobley in the newspapers; Mobley's moral weakness and
Mattie's strength are introduced by the way she looms over him upon their arrival at the
house; and when Chicamaw asks Bowie if he killed someone, he pauses before answering Yes, throwing a glance at Keechie, to whom he looks for approval, sensing her as a
fellow innocent.

The idea that it is the world at large which is corrupt is introduced when Mobley asks
for payment in return for hiding his brother and friends, and when T-Dub explains to
Bowie, who voices his disgust at the price of a second-hand car they need for their next
robbery, that the vendors are 'thieves just like us'. Even more central to Ray's thesis is
the fact that Bowie and Keechie are innocent lovers, their chances in life crippled (it is
no accident that he starts out with a limp) by a lack of family warmth and love. In their
first real conversation together, in the garage at night with Bowie repeatedly shot at a
lower level than the woman who will be his potential salvation, it emerges that Keechie
is not fond of her venal, drunken father (whom her mother deserted for a man running
a medicine show), and Bowie admits that his mother abandoned him in order to live
with his father's killer. Both are victims of circumstances beyond their control – it transpires that Bowie was arrested for murder simply because, unlike the carnival gang of
thieves he had been watching in action, he did not run away from the scene of the crime

– and the improbability of Bowie's escape from the trap that engulfs him is underlined by the paradoxical nature of his plans: to clear his name, through a lawyer, he must resort to crime to gain money. Indeed, Mattie (lent an almost mythic aura of Death by her morbid premonitions, her pallid, unsmiling face and her black, widow-like clothes) says of Bowie to Keechie, 'He's jail-bait. Maybe you'll be lucky. Maybe they won't send him back to prison. Maybe he'll get killed first.'

But Keechie is made of sterner stuff than to give up; like all Ray's protagonists, she and Bowie dream of a better life and feel impelled to rail against their destiny, but time is already running out. When the three men move on to prepare their robbery of a bank in Zelton, Ray brings time, rather than violence, to the fore: a clock stands outside the bank; Bowie visits a watchmaker (in order to accompany the man to the bank for change) and buys a watch for Keechie; before the robbery itself, a row between Mattie and Chicamaw ends with the woman smashing a mirror and Bowie shouting, 'That's seven years bad luck!' The watch is, in fact, of crucial symbolic importance for Ray. As Bowie sits in the car in Zelton, waiting for his colleagues to emerge from the bank (the robbery is never shown – Ray shot almost the entire sequence from inside the car), he is recognised by the watchmaker and in panic resorts to his first and only act of violence in the film. Even more important is the scene when, wounded after a car crash and tended by Keechie, he gives her the watch. Framed, as if imprisoned, by the brass bars of the bedstead on which he lies, he speaks of the money he now possesses, thus alienating Keechie's affections; only when he asks 'Who's yer fella, Keechie?', and remembers the

Innocents caught in a trap: Keechie (Cathy O'Donnell) tends to the wounded Bowie (Farley Granger).

watch (that is, his love for Keechie rather than his ill-won fortune), does the camera angle change so that he is 'freed' from his criminal life. But the gift's significance is ambivalent; without a clock to set it by, they live by a time that only *approximates* to that of the rest of the world; they are literally out of time, out of step with society. If the watch symbolises their love (they later note the time of their wedding, and Keechie herself buys Bowie a watch for Christmas), it also signifies the transience of their happiness together: when Bowie, against Keechie's wishes, chooses to join T-Dub and Chicamaw for one last robbery, the pair quarrel violently, almost to the point of parting, and her reply to his request for the time is, 'What difference does it make?'

The problems faced by Bowie and Keechie in trying to live like ordinary people, however much they may be 'thieves like us', are emphasised throughout. This is achieved not only by the night motif – darkness offers secrecy, warmth and rest, while daylight makes them conspicuous and vulnerable – but also by scenes like the one in which Chicamaw tells Bowie, 'One thing you gotta learn, kid, you gotta look and act like other people,' even as the camera, focused on his face, picks out the grotesque abnormality of his blind eye. Bowie and Keechie are, in fact, caught between two worlds: 'ordinary' law-abiding society and an incestuously close-knit criminal underworld. As a pair, their safety is repeatedly threatened by various groups of three: that of Chicamaw, T-Dub and Bowie challenges Bowie's loyalties to Keechie; Chicamaw/Mobley/Keechie, and T-Dub/Mattie/ Mattie's imprisoned husband are family knots that both inspire betrayal; even at the wedding, the witnesses whom Hawkins employs are his sister and brother-in-law.

As in Ray's later work, a triangular relationship is presented as closely knit, though liable to inner instability; when Chicamaw 'persuades' Bowie to join him and T-Dub in one more robbery, meanwhile complaining bitterly about public awareness of their exploits, he argues, 'It takes three to pull a trick, and you're number three, even if the papers do say you're number one.' The same motif is also present in Ray's imagery, which frequently frames three characters together, as well as in the script: Keechie claims that 'bad luck runs in threes'. And perhaps the couple's only hope of salvation lies in becoming a 'three' of their own, separate from the other family trios, and parents to an unborn child who Bowie says will 'just have to take his chances the same as us'. In the event, the child will not have it easy; like Bowie himself, and like so many Ray characters, he will have to learn to survive without the warm support of a strong father.

Just as we see almost no explicit violence in the film – the robberies are not shown; Chicamaw's shooting of the policeman is represented by a close-up of Bowie's startled face; the violence of Chicamaw's demands that Bowie rejoin the gang is symbolised by his clumsy, unthinking breaking of glass Christmas-tree baubles – so the film steers away from crime-thriller conventions in that the police who hunt for Bowie and Keechie are hardly depicted at all. Instead, 'normal' law-abiding society is characterised by a gallery of none too friendly or honest individuals: a nightclub owner who violently disarms Bowie, whom he has recognised, before throwing him out of town (rather than turning him in); an all too garrulous, inquisitive tourist-cabin proprietor who demands cash in advance as protection against 'fly-by-nights'; a woman on a bus too tired to stop her baby crying.

Central to Ray's depiction of the 'respectable' world is Hawkins, whose 'class B' mar-

Double standards: Bowie is run out of town by a nightclub proprietor (Curt Conway).

riage ceremonies – shown throughout from the point of view of Bowie and Keechie – emphasise the venal nature of society. From the first shot of his neon sign, flashing through the windscreen of the bus on which the lovers have made their night-time escape, Ray shows the cheap, profit-motivated sentimentality of Hawkins's debased tribute to human love. An organ, playing the wedding march, is heard by the fugitive couple as they sit in a crowded diner; having decided to marry, they stand between two Cupid gateposts, before proceeding hesitantly up the path to the door, followed by Ray's sympathetic camera. Inside, Hawkins's conversation centres on money; his performance of the ceremony is quick and perfunctory. But Ray is too sophisticated to invalidate an argument with caricature, and when Hawkins explains himself later, responding to Bowie's demand that he organise a passage to Mexico for the couple, he is genuinely sad that he has to disappoint the boy: 'Welchers, that's all we are … Son, I'd sure like that money; I'm old, and money's a real comfort to an old man. I believe in helping people get what they want as long as they can pay for it. I marry people 'cos there's a little hope they'll be happy. But I can't take this money of yours. No sir. In a way I'm a thief just the same as you are, but I won't sell you hope when there ain't any.'

Even Mattie, who finally betrays the young lovers, has her reasons – she wants to see her husband again – and when she goes to the police, who tell her that she is saving a lot of people a lot of grief, she replies, 'I don't think that's gonna help me sleep nights.' For Ray, society may be corrupt and self-serving, but it is not malicious; what makes Bowie and Keechie different *is* their innocence, which is all-embracing. Told by Bowie that girls normally have 'fellas', Keechie says, 'I don't know what other girls have'; just married, both confess to not knowing much about kissing; and when they drive across the Mississippi, Bowie says, 'Some day, I'd like to see some of this country we're travellin' through', to which she replies, 'By daylight, you mean? That'd be nice.' The sad point of this exchange is that they never will see the country together, the irony being that nature would seem the ideal habitat for this pair repeatedly likened, by themselves and others, to weasels, dogs, sheep and kittens.

There is no room for innocents in a world beset by poverty, violence and selfishness, no room at the inn; as Bowie and the pregnant Keechie are forced to flee their country-cabin retreat, 'clean away from everything except the sky and trees', it is Christmas, and a carol ('Noël, Noël, born is the King of Israel') plays on the radio. It is very soon after this that the couple decide to take a chance on joining the real world, albeit temporarily; after walking in the park (where Bowie expresses his delighted surprise at the absurd ways other people take their pleasure: golf, riding and so on), they visit a nightclub, and too shy to dance, have their predicament made plain by a singer's smiling rendition of the song 'Your Red Wagon' (which was, incidentally, the original working title for the film):

> Your business is your red wagon,
> What's in it is all your own,
> So don't load it up with troubles,
> 'Cos you're dragging it all alone.

With both the possibility of hiring a lawyer and a chance of escaping to Mexico denied him, the only path left to Bowie when he leaves Hawkins is one of self-sacrifice; he must go away, and leave Keechie safely alone to live with the child. Returning to Mattie's, he writes a farewell letter, promising to send for her, and walks across the darkened motel courtyard to the cabin where, through a window, he can see Keechie sleeping. Suddenly, a bright light (from a torch, but reminiscent of the harsh revealing glare of daylight) is shone upon him and he is shot down, dead. Keechie runs out into the light, finds the letter, and reads it with her back to us, before turning her head to mouthe in close-up, as the screen slowly fades to black, the words 'I love you'. Far from being a conventionally moralistic reprisal typical of a Hollywood whose censors insisted that crimes never go unpunished, Bowie's death is rather an expression of Ray's bitter-sweet, pessimistic concern for the fate of loners in a callous world. Plunged involuntarily into the light, Bowie is no longer allowed to live, but Keechie, sustained by his undying love, returns to the night which has kept their brief, fragile happiness safe and unsullied by the outside world, and which now, finally, ensures Bowie lasting peace and freedom.

Making *They Live by Night* was an untypically straightforward and happy experience for Ray; he was indeed fortunate in that his producer was the unusually sympathetic and very erudite Houseman, who had already supported Ray in his radio work – Houseman would go on to number amongst his film-productions some extremely fine movies directed by Max Ophuls, Vincente Minnelli, Fritz Lang, Joseph L. Mankiewicz and the young John Frankenheimer. While *They Live by Night* never achieved the success it deserved upon its initial release – sadly delayed for a couple of years, due to Howard

Hughes's purchase of RKO – it was at least received warmly by a handful of critics (notably the British), and has come to be widely regarded as one of Ray's most polished and satisfying works. Certainly, in its actors' performances, in its photography and in its script, the film lives up to Godard's description of it as having a B-movie budget and A-movie ambitions. But where the film impresses most is in its rich, subtle and complex vision of contemporary America (it may be seen partly as a study in moral relativism, which refutes the notion of ethical absolutes being applied to a society in turmoil); in its deft balancing of myth, realism and personal poetry; and in its sophisticated marshalling of film's various codes of expression to create a detailed web of allusions and symbolic motifs. Clearly, Ray's experience in radio influenced his inventive use of sound, while his work with Kazan probably helped his direction of the actors (all of whom provide carefully nuanced and vivid performances). But it is above all his precise, imaginative integration of style and theme which shows that, even in his first film, he was already fully in command of his medium.

A Woman's Secret (1949)

SYNOPSIS: When singer Susan Caldwell returns to the Park Avenue apartment she shares with Marian Washbourn, she announces her intention to abandon her career. The women argue and Susan retires to her room. Marian follows; a gunshot is heard by the maid, who enters Susan's room to discover Marian kneeling over the wounded singer. After Marian tells the police that she shot her flatmate, she is jailed but her musicologist friend Luke Jordan, sure of her innocence, demands that wealthy attorney Brook Matthews – Susan's fiancé – defend her. Marian repeats her tale, explaining that she resented the desire of her protégée Susan to lead her own life, and that she was given the gun by a strange soldier. Luke tells Inspector Fowler why he remains unconvinced of her guilt: Marian, a singer on the brink of stardom, had suddenly lost her voice and acted as mentor to the seemingly innocent Susan, whom they had first met as an out-of-work ingénue. But the young woman, ungrateful to Marian, had been a liability: during a trip to Paris she had left Marian suddenly to go to Algiers, while later, she had made up to part-time entertainment impresario Matthews, whose mother thought her a fortune-hunter. Intrigued by this story, Fowler's wife, fancying herself an amateur detective, investigates the scene of the crime and finds a key belonging to Susan. The key is traced to Lee Crenshaw, who awaits Susan's recovery at the hospital, and who confesses to having given the gun to Susan. It transpires that she had married Crenshaw, and that, having subsequently fallen for Matthews and received a telegram announcing her husband's imminent arrival, she had panicked and decided to kill herself; when Marian had found the gun in her room, there had been a struggle during which Susan had accidentally shot herself. In the hospital, Susan successfully begs Matthews for forgiveness; meanwhile, Marian, freed and reassured that Luke was never in love with Susan, virtually proposes marriage to him.

Having completed *They Live by Night*, Ray was invited by Dore Schary to undertake another project. This was to direct a film of Vicki Baum's novel *Mortgage on Life*; a script had been written by Herman J. Mankiewicz. Initially, Ray refused, but when a little later Schary asked a second time, he agreed. His lack of enthusiasm for the project is, however, immediately transparent; if *A Woman's Secret* is not exactly *bad*, it is without doubt Ray's most anonymous work, and he himself felt no affection for it.

Mankiewicz's script is indeed poor, even if its structure – centred on a series of flashbacks, two of which contradict one another – is vaguely reminiscent of his most famous screenplay, for Orson Welles's *Citizen Kane* (1941). Most damagingly, the plot features a number of implausible contrivances and obscurities (why, for example, does Marian choose to suffer in prison for her ungrateful protégée?), which the flashbacks fail to conceal, while the characters are nothing more than thinly drawn stereotypes: high-living sophisticates with hardly a moral qualm between them. Nor is the dialogue convincing; clearly, with lines like Fowler's observation that, 'A meal ticket don't have to be looked on as a meal ticket to be a meal ticket', Mankiewicz thought he was being witty, or profound, or both, but the effect on screen is clumsy and pretentious. For once, in fact, Ray chose to contribute little or nothing to the script, and filmed it almost unaltered; one can only deduce not that he found it too good to change, but that it left him completely uninterested.

It is certainly hard to imagine what Ray could possibly have found in the script to engage his interest or imagination. By his own admission he disliked flashbacks. And 'whodunit' mysteries never seem to have held any attraction for him. The characters (mostly rich, successful and urbane) are not loners, losers or outcasts, and despite the gunshot of the opening sequence, there is very little opportunity to explore the nature of violence and rebellion. Any nastiness is largely confined to the sarcastic and cynical dialogue, which mostly serves to alienate the audience from the gallery of smug, shallow and dimly motivated characters.

One may perhaps regret that Ray did not bring his experience of radio to bear on a story that at least begins with a scene in a radio studio. Presumably, the world envisioned by the film was so remote both from reality and from Ray's more populist interest in the medium that he simply felt no desire to take up any such ideas with Mankiewicz, who was the film's writer *and* producer; certainly, it is unlikely that a man with a detailed, specialist knowledge of traditional American folk music would have had any great affection

Moment of untruth: Fowler (Jay C. Flippen) questions Marian (Maureen O'Hara) at the scene of the crime.

for the songs inserted for Susan and Marian. Nor is anything made of the fact that Luke is a musicologist, other than that he is seemingly omniscient and the perfect accompanist for Marian (for which read: her ideal, supportive lover). If *A Woman's Secret* is to be examined in terms of its relationship to Ray's work as a whole, then we are left with the task of searching for minute, personal contributions to what is craftsmanlike but conventional studio fare. And few they are, though those that exist are not altogether without interest.

Perhaps the most noticeable aspect of the film is that the action takes place almost entirely indoors. (Establishing shots are included to place us in Paris and Algiers, but these are, on the one hand, stock footage and, on the other, patently a studio set, drawing attention to the film's comparatively low budget.) For the most part Ray frames and positions his actors in much the same way that any other director would – in order that they may be clearly seen and heard. He does, however, locate the opening argument, immediately before the shooting, on a staircase, for Ray a recurrent symbol of crisis and conflict; Susan stands above Marian, reflecting the way she has usurped her mentor's position in the musical world and come to exert an almost sadistic power over her. Then, after the incident with the gun, it is Marian who is positioned on the stairs, gazing down at Fowler; the fact that he is below her mirrors his ignorance and her knowledge of what has really happened. Staircases also figure at other key moments (notably when Marian and Luke first encounter Susan, who faints on her way out of an audition, thus winning their pity), while Luke's arrogance and anger at Susan's arrest is given physical expression when he kicks the furniture at the police station!

Apart from Ray's occasionally expressive use of décor, the chief interest of the film lies with the character of Susan, nominally the villain of the piece but clearly, for Ray, the most vivid and fascinating figure in a tapestry that includes a range of personalities from the blandly picturesque (the likeable Fowler and his eccentric wife) to the repellent (the abrasively suave, strong Luke, the risibly self-sacrificial Marian, the spineless Matthews). Obviously, this may have had a great deal to do with the talented Gloria Grahame, the 22-year-old actress Ray would marry (albeit disastrously and briefly); but all the same he may well also have been taken by the essential contradictions central to the role: a naïve, seemingly innocent young girl, who looks and sings like an angel, but who lies, cheats and exploits everyone around her. In retrospect, Susan may seem like a blueprint for the character of Christabel in Ray's second (and superior) 'women's film', *Born to Be Bad*; in *A Woman's Secret*, however, she is cast adrift in a two-dimensional world populated by tired movie stereotypes.

With his second film, Ray proved, once and for all, that he could direct actors, handle a modicum of suspense and narrate a story, however uninspired it might be. But there were no risks to be taken, no challenges to face; he simply revealed that he could do hack-work as professionally as any other contract director. As a result, the film, lacking the raw, jarring moments that permeate much of his best work, is also sadly without inspiration.

Knock on Any Door (1949)

SYNOPSIS: When 'Pretty Boy' Nick Romano is arrested and charged with killing a policeman, he insists that he has been framed and asks lawyer Andrew Morton, who also grew up on Skid Row, to defend him. In his opening speech at the trial, Morton recounts Nick's history, in order to demonstrate the morally debilitating effects of an adolescence spent in poverty among petty criminals. Morton himself partly accepts the responsibility for Nick's anti-social behaviour: some years ago, he had been too busy to defend the boy's father who, imprisoned for a killing carried out in self-defence, had died in jail. The impoverished Romano family had then been forced to move into a slum neighbourhood, and Nick had fallen in with bad company and embarked on a life of crime. A spell in a reform school had only embittered him, but a meeting with Emma – herself an orphan, burdened with a drunken aunt – combined with Morton's support had driven Nick to try to mend his ways. He had married Emma and found work, but then, provoked into a rage by his boss's prejudiced hostility, he had been fired, and had returned to his old life. Emma, pregnant and feeling betrayed, had committed suicide, and all hopes of Nick's salvation were dashed. In court, Morton successfully undermines the testimonies of the witnesses for the prosecution, but District Attorney Kerman picks holes in Nick's alibi and, by reminding him of his wife's death, browbeats him into confessing to the murder of the policeman. Morton, though angry that Nick lied to him, begs for clemency, arguing that society has brutalised Nick into anger and desperation; the judge, while moved by Morton's impassioned pleas, feels duty-bound to abide by the law. Nick is sentenced to death and led to the electric chair.

After the less than satisfying experience of making *A Woman's Secret*, Ray was fortunate when Humphrey Bogart – who had only recently set up his own production company, Santana – invited him to direct the film of Willard Motley's best-selling book *Knock on Any Door*. Inevitably, for reasons of censorship, the subject matter – an account of crime and poverty in 1930s Chicago, which included a candid treatment of sex and police brutality – had to be toned down for the cinema; moreover, coming to a project whose script had already been written, Ray was obliged to employ a flashback structure, a narrative format that he always disliked. That said, the material itself was close to his heart; he had been well acquainted with Chicago in the 1930s, and it allowed him not only to deal, as in *They Live by Night*, with the confusion and solitude of youth, but also to explore, from a liberal perspective, the moral worth of capital punishment.

Indeed, *Knock on Any Door* is both archetypal 'Ray film' *and* archetypal social-conscience drama; its flaws are, mostly, those which would appear to be more or less inherent in a genre that tends towards didactic overstatement. Unlike, say, *Rebel Without a Cause*, the film suffers from being too stridently explicit in its social pleading. The events recalled

On the streets of Chicago: Nick Romano (John Derek) learns to live fast ...

by Morton to 'explain' Nick Romano's decent into crime fall too neatly into place; his running commentary on his client's life and his final indictment of society are dramatically over-emphatic, underlining things we see quite clearly for ourselves. (Had Ray not been saddled with a flashback structure, this tendency towards didacticism might have been significantly reduced.) Nevertheless, the film remains an intelligent, deeply felt diatribe against social injustice and the death penalty. Crucially, and unlike so many heroes of the genre, Nick *is* guilty of the crime of which he has been accused; the dice are not artificially loaded in his favour, and the film is not a refutation of individual guilt, but an attack on a moral system which all too readily assumes it has the right to punish wrongdoers with cruelty and the vengeful taking of human life.

In some respects, *Knock on Any Door* conforms to a standard social-conscience drama format: Romano is the poor, misunderstood and impressionable teenager from the wrong side of the tracks. With his journey from wronged innocence to the electric chair, we are led to a simplistic conclusion: we, society, are guilty. But the wealth of detail used by Ray to embellish this thesis finally makes the film both powerful *and* very personal. Nick Romano – the name is from the novel, and not, as some suggest, a sign that we should see him as a surrogate for the director – is in many ways a more bitter version of Bowie in *They Live by Night* (John Derek's soft, dark, 'pretty boy' face and slim build are even a little reminiscent of Farley Granger): fragile, fatherless, anxious to prove himself 'a man', he seeks his salvation in both a lawyer and a young woman, and attempts to replace his real family, not only with the loafers, panhandlers and thieves he finds in the pool-halls and bars of Skid Row, but also with Morton and Emma. And if Nick differs from Bowie in that he appears to be innocent but is actually guilty of killing the policeman, he shares with Bowie his *fundamental*, existential innocence. His crimes are less premeditated than instinctual, a childlike response born of the frustration and rage that he feels at the injustice of life, as is evident when he manically empties his gun into the policeman's corpse in the film's opening scene. Romano *reacts*, rather than acts; each misdemeanour is preceded by what he considers an act of provocation or betrayal (his father's death in prison, a friend's death in the reform school, Morton's boss's cynical and uncharitable assumption that he can never go straight, an employer sacking him without justification).

Not that Ray absolves Romano of all responsibility for his actions: Emma, a paradigm of purity, never knew her father either and also lives in squalid poverty, while Morton repeatedly points out that he, who like Nick served time in reform school, managed to drag himself away from Skid Row. But the lawyer's success is seen *by Romano* almost as a rebuke, or as a betrayal of his roots: when Morton returns to Skid Row to check the boy's alibi, the lawyer is accused by an elderly drunk of 'slumming', and though he never entirely forgets his origins, his pride at having escaped them occasionally tempts him to let Romano fend for himself. Romano, in fact, could easily become a Morton, given the right breaks; but as the lawyer tells the jury, there are 'pinpoints of time' which govern any destiny.

For Ray, however, it is less these 'pinpoints of time' (that is, specific events) which mould Romano's character, than environment. The film's social-realist veneer may prompt comparisons with the documentary-influenced Hollywood thrillers of the late 1940s (*Brute Force*, *The Naked City*, *Call Northside 777*, and so on), but Ray's symbolic use of décor and composition transcends genre, and is characteristic of his own very special precision in the creation of mood and meaning. The facial close-ups, the cluttered rooms, crowded streets and dark, smoky pool-halls in which Romano grows up evoke a sense of claustrophobia that mirrors the boy's frustration. His movements are stifled and cramped by the lack of space around him, and only when he takes Emma to a park at night (in a sequence as lyrical as the scenes between Bowie and Keechie in *They Live by Night*), and during his brief excursion to the countryside with Morton, does he seem properly relaxed. When he and Emma confess their mutual love in the park, he remembers having been an altar-boy, quoting, 'And I go unto the altar of God, to God who giveth joy to my youth', with tragic, unwitting irony; the boy's innocence and happiness have been crushed by the urban environment, and there is little chance of escape or redemption.

That Romano is oppressed by the world he lives in is made plain throughout by Ray's highly expressive visual style – his use of stairways, for example. In the opening shot, a shadowy figure (who, it later transpires, is Romano) is seen behind the credits climbing up a dark stairway and emerging into the bustling streets where he will eventually kill the cop; as he is hunted by the police, the chase progresses up and down further staircases and fire escapes whose diagonals evoke panic, disorder and danger (a later chase,

following the robbery of an elevated-railway ticket office, similarly occurs on a steep staircase). At another point in the film, flames are used to convey a strong visual message.
When Romano and Emma are taken by Morton and his social-worker wife to a sumptuous restaurant, a waiter stands flambéing steaks behind Romano as he tells of his
dreams of better times (a job, a suit, a home of his own; like most Ray outsiders, he longs
for a normal life, and is attracted to Emma because she is different from most girls, who
'don't look like they belong to families'); the scene ends on Romano's promise that he
will try harder to go straight, and as he makes his vow the flames from the steaks suddenly flare up behind him, not only echoing his fiery temper but suggesting, perhaps,
that his dreams will go up in smoke.

Romano's hot-headed and self-destructive sense of urgency, embodied in his sadly
prophetic motto, 'Live fast, die young, and have a good-looking corpse', is calmed only
by Emma and Morton (who, as surrogate father and teacher, is repeatedly positioned
higher in the frame than Romano). Both fight against rather than endorse or provoke
his macho pride, the former by showing him love, the latter by beating him at his own
game (at one point Morton 'mugs' Romano in a dark alley to retrieve some stolen
money). Both, too, are aware of his sense of solitude. When Morton first meets Romano,
who begs him to help get his sick father released from prison, the lawyer says, 'Take it
easy, kid, I know how you feel', to which Romano replies, 'Nobody knows how *anybody*
feels.' Emma, meanwhile, believes he can go straight if he is not lonely, and understands
him because she, too, is alone; he is all she has. Indeed, the couple are linked together
in death as in life. When Romano, despairing at the corruption both of the world and of
himself, decides to abandon her and their unborn child (he has already told her repeatedly that he is no good for her) and to commit another robbery, he takes his gun from
its hiding place in their kitchen boiler, while she moves to the oven she will later use to
gas herself. And when he is finally broken down by Kerman, it is not out of remorse for
having killed the cop, but because, as the District Attorney points out, he caused his
wife's death; he feels guilty only of having betrayed, deserted and killed Emma, and goes
to the electric chair in a strangely tranquil mood, there, perhaps, to rejoin her in death.

Like Bowie, Romano's chances in life have been wrecked both by the underworld that
has corrupted him, and by the callousness of 'respectable' society. When Morton first
decides to defend the boy, his bosses warn him that, if he takes the case, he will ruin his
prospects of becoming a partner; when Romano serves time at a reformatory, the disciplinarian regime kills his best friend (and then lies about his death), turning Romano
into a hardened and embittered criminal. Repeatedly typecast in court as a 'hoodlum
killer', long before a verdict has been reached, he becomes the victim of Kerman's
irrational, personalised jealousy; the District Attorney makes snide references to the
defendant's 'pretty boy' looks and fingers a scar on his own face as he asks, irrelevantly,
if Romano is successful with girls. The law, in fact, has little to do with justice, and the
trial becomes a theatrical show (even the judge, who is patently down to earth, humane
and fair – we see that he sweats a lot – calls it 'a slugging match'). Appearances are everything: the DA's office has, it transpires, been providing lodging and respectable clothes
for prosecution witnesses in return for their testimonies; Morton advises Romano, as he

Love's labours lost: Nick watches his wife's funeral from afar.

takes the stand, that he should always look straight at the jury for maximum effect. Kerman, conversely, asks that Romano look at *him* and stares at aggressively close range into his eyes, downcast at last in shameful memory of Emma's death.

Romano's guilt having been established, Ray makes his point about the responsibility of society and the state through verbal *and* visual means. As spoken by Bogart, Morton's speech, eloquent and rhetorical in its denunciation of poverty, prejudice, neglect and inequality, is indeed moving, with the actor angrily spitting out his lines and bringing into play the full moral weight of his heroic screen persona. At the same time, Ray, who until this final plea for mercy has filled the courtroom with a plethora of colourful characters, suddenly adopts a far more abstract visual style to implicate us, the audience, and the unfeeling mechanism known as the state, in Romano's crimes. The sequence begins with the camera focused on a wooden seal of justice on the wall high above the judge, before panning down to the man himself, instrument of the state's power. As Morton brings his speech to an end, he alone is seen, speaking directly to the camera, which looks down on him from the position occupied by the judge; the appeal is made to us, and we too stand accused of having neglected Romano and all those like him: 'If he dies, we killed him.' Finally, Romano joins Morton, still looking up at the camera, and, as we hear the judge's off-screen voice admit that he is 'deeply moved' by Morton's speech but that he is obliged by the law to sentence Romano to death 'in the manner prescribed by the state', the camera moves still higher, so that our/its point of view is no longer that of the judge, but of the state insignia shown at the opening of the scene. Ray's final point is clearly but subtly expressed: the blame for Romano's death must not be placed on any single judge but on a state system which allows institutionalised killing to continue. And since it is we who elect our government, we ourselves must admit our share in the responsibility, not only for the crimes but also for the death of Nick Romano.

Flaws there are in *Knock on Any Door* (the didactic script and the rather maudlin characterisation of the unblemished, near-angelic Emma), but the film is for the most part a fascinating example of Ray's passionate identification with the underdog and of his ability to transcend predictable generic material by means of stylish, vividly detailed direction. Despite the occasionally schematic contrivance of its courtroom dialogues (which are, for all that, admirably paced and performed), it remains a key work in the director's early film career, reflecting back on the more lyrical and mythic *They Live by Night*, and looking forward to later movies like *Rebel Without a Cause* and *Run for Cover*. Ray himself was not entirely happy with it – he later confessed, 'I wish Buñuel had made *Los Olvidados* before I made *Knock on Any Door*, because I would have made a hell of a lot better film' – but his producers must have been pleased, for they took up their contractual option to have him make a second film for Santana. Unfortunately, Howard Hughes wanted Ray back at RKO to work on his infamous *I Married a Communist*, and Ray and Bogart would have to wait a while before teaming up again, to make *In a Lonely Place*.

Born to Be Bad (1950)

SYNOPSIS: Donna Fortes, who is engaged to be married to rich industrialist Curtis Carey, agrees to take as a lodger Christabel Caine, the seemingly innocent niece of Donna's boss, publisher John Caine. The girl is an immediate success with Curtis's and Donna's friends; the painter Gobby asks Christabel to sit for a portrait, while novelist Nick Bradley falls in love with her. Though Christabel is attracted to Nick and begins dating him, she is at the same time entranced by Curtis's wealth and sets about sowing doubts in his mind about Donna's reasons for wanting to marry him. Donna, dismayed by her fiancé's lack of faith in her, and angry at Christabel's scheming ways, leaves San Francisco for London: Christabel quickly takes advantage of Donna's absence and cleverly lures Curtis into a proposal of marriage. Nick, filled with contempt for her deviousness, goes on a tour to promote his latest book; when he returns some months later, however, Christabel, whose now obsessive interest in women's committees and charity groups barely conceals her lack of sexual passion for her husband, promises to leave Curtis for Nick, whom she presently visits under the false pretext of going to see a sick aunt. When Nick discovers that she has no intention of losing Curtis's fortune, he terminates their affair and Christabel returns home, only to learn from Curtis and her uncle that her aunt has died, and that they know about her rendezvous with Nick. Curtis insists that Christabel leave him and is later reconciled with Donna; meanwhile, Christabel, who was the victim of a car accident as she drove away from Curtis's house, is first cited as correspondent in a divorce case involving her doctor, and then embarks on an affair with her lawyer. As a result of this scandal, Gobby finds that the market value of his portrait of Christabel rises rapidly.

Happily, Ray eventually managed to extricate himself from Howard Hughes's plans for him to direct the mogul's anti-Red project, *I Married a Communist* (though it should perhaps be noted that the film, directed by Robert Stevenson after various figures – including Ray, Joseph Losey and John Cromwell – had expressed their dislike of the script, is not in fact the total fiasco of reputation, but a taut, visually striking *film noir* weakened by a simplistically propagandist narrative). Less happily, Ray then fell victim to another Hughes passion. RKO's owner was at the time enamoured of Joan Fontaine, who had for some years been keen to take the lead in a film of Ann Parish's novel *All Kneeling* – this Ray was finally asked to direct, under the working title *Bed of Roses*. As with *A Woman's Secret* – which also centred on a young woman whose angelic appearance concealed a ruthless, manipulative heart – he felt little affection for the material, but once again he demonstrated his professionalism by the sheer craftsmanship he brought to the film, despite not being allowed to change the script or the cast, the leading members of which (except Robert Ryan) had been selected by Hughes himself.

At least the screenplay, gradually knocked into shape by a dozen writers (including the gifted Jules Furthman), constituted a significant improvement on Mankiewicz's script for the earlier film. As it stands, *Born to Be Bad* is an enjoyably cynical and occasionally witty melodrama, which only succumbs to moralistic cliché in an embarrassing late scene written and tacked on, as the film was cut, by Hughes himself. Christabel (perfectly played by Fontaine, whose customary, rather sickly air of shy sweetness and innocence, familiar from films like Hitchcock's *Rebecca* and *Suspicion*, is here savagely undermined and shown as artificial) succeeds in exploiting the men around her only because they are vain, weak and blind to her true nature. Curtis, who seems never to have had to work for his money, is a fickle, complacent fool, and decides that he likes Christabel as soon as she flatters him with the reassurance that he is wise not to feel guilty about his wealth. Nick, on the other hand, has occasional insights into her mendacity, as befits a supposedly sensitive and brutally honest writer, but while he describes her as 'a cross between Lucretia Borgia and Peg o' my Heart', he is nevertheless so taken by her appearance that his obsession with her can only be seen as partly masochistic. Gobby, meanwhile, remains invulnerable to her sexual charms, armed with an objective, possibly gay, painter's eye and a money-minded cynicism that matches Christabel's. Even he, however, for all his protestations that he knows her, fails to realise that he serves a purpose in her schemes, not only in that he provides her with an alibi when she lies to Nick about meeting Curtis, but also in that his picture of her reinforces the impressions wrought on the other characters by her angelic external appearance.

Ray clearly felt little sympathy for any of his protagonist's victims, or for the sophisticated San Franciscan milieu in which they lead their quasi-Bohemian lives. (This being a studio-shot film, Ray makes little of the Californian setting, although the city does provide one visual pun, when he cuts from Chrisabel and Nick embracing with particular ardour in a bedroom doorway to a shot of Telegraph Hill's famous Coit Tower.) Donna is something of a dullard, in love with a worthless wastrel who is all too prepared to suspect the worst of her as soon as another woman turns up to flatter his ego; Christabel's aunt Clara is a timid if well-meaning simpleton, who despite having looked after the girl for many years is entirely unaware of her ambitions; and John Caine, who at times appears to see through his niece's deceptions, is too wrapped up in his own business to do very much about them. One cannot help feeling that Christabel's victims get their just deserts; certainly, one of the greatest pleasures when watching the film is to hear her insinuations and see her smiling to herself, safe in the knowledge that *we* understand far more about what she is doing than do the characters, because we, unlike they, are privy to her every word, action and expression.

Interestingly, Christabel's motivations for exploiting and deceiving those around her are not, in the end, financial. Money *is* of course a factor, but only insofar as it gives her *power*, which is the real object of her ambition; when she is married, she argues that Curtis should retain control of their finances, and most of her energies are devoted to gaining control of her many committees and charity organizations. The power she exerts over others is itself an end, rather than a means to an end; she actively *enjoys* the sensation of manipulating others, as is shown by the dreamy expressions of pleasure that

Invasion of space: Christabel (Joan Fontaine) takes measure of the relationship between Donna (Joan Leslie) and Curtis (Zachary Scott).

cross her face whenever someone succumbs to her strategies. It is therefore appropriate that Ray's direction is at its most telling and subtle in the way he reveals the extremely *methodical* nature of her rise to power, through his careful, almost symbolic deployment of objects, décor and dramatic situations.

Christabel's sense of her own power is partly suggested by the clothes she wears. For the first half of the film, she mostly dresses in white, which not only constitutes an ironic reflection of the unscrupulous ambitions that lie beneath her virtuous and self-effacing exterior, but also reveals the lengths to which she will go in order to deceive people; but once she is accepted by those whose lives she plans to control, once she has achieved enough to be more sure of herself, she begins to abandon white for darker hues, with the result that by the time she is married, she feels confident enough to be seen in more sumptuous black gowns.

Besides clothes, Christabel also uses objects and places to further her plans. It is while advising Curtis on what kind of jewellery to buy Donna as an engagement present that she is able to plant the idea in his mind that Donna may be marrying him for his money. (Jewellery figures heavily as a symbol of corruption and lovelessness: when Christabel tells her first lie – having deliberately arrived a day early at Donna's apartment in order to attend a society party – she nervously fingers the scarf on her neck; the gesture is often repeated at moments of deceit, but later the scarf is replaced by a necklace, showing her much improved status in a world largely devoted to material wealth.)

Even more telling is an emphasis in the film on telephones – and not only as used by Christabel. Gobby's selfish cynicism is initially established when he hangs up on a friend of Donna's after saying no more than hello; Nick's unconventionality is introduced when he breaks into a phone conversation between Christabel and her aunt, telling them to get off the line; while Christabel herself *uses* phones as tools of deceit, making secret assignations with Nick and Curtis and taking advantage of the fact that she cannot be seen by the listener. It is no accident, then, that she tells Curtis not to call her at her sick aunt's, when she is in fact going to see Nick; nor is it fortuitous that her deception is discovered when Curtis finds a bill for a call she had made to Nick, and visits the aunt himself, thus realising that Christabel is not even there. Indeed, in purely structural terms, one of Christabel's primary transgressions is that she is never where she is sup- posed to be, and is often where she is not wanted: when she deliberately arrives a day earlier than expected at Donna's, her disruptive presence is dramatically embodied and introduced when Donna trips over the baggage which the as-yet-unseen visitor has placed at the top of the stairs in her apartment.

If the telephone is an instrument of power for Christabel, so is any situation that pro- vides privacy or secrecy; that she is unusually concerned with her surroundings is shown in two crucial ballroom scenes. In the first, as she dances with Gobby she looks not at him but all around her, seeking out Curtis, on whose money she has set her sights; in the second, now married but unable to ignore the erotic attraction she feels for Nick, she dances with Curtis and, once again, looks not at him but around her, her eyes hun- gry for a glimpse of her former lover. The ball scenes are virtually identical, except that in each the object of Christabel's desire differs. In the first, she engineers a conversation with Curtis whereby he feels that 'we can't talk here', and she leads him away from the mansion's crowded terrace, down some steps, to a tree. Standing against this, she tricks Curtis into proposing to her, by hinting at her own loneliness and telling him that *he loves her*. At the second ball, *she* tells Nick, 'I can't talk to you like this', before leading him down the same steps to the same tree, where again she attempts to flatter and provoke the man to an admission of love by confessing to her own unhappiness. For Ray, it is not only the words spoken that matter, but the place: Christabel's trysts are deliberately removed from the gaze of the world (that they take place 'downstairs' shows that they involve a deeper, more secretive level of private communication). It is surely not by chance, then, that when we see her about to 'seduce' her lawyer at the end of the film, she mentions that she feels so alone and he replies, 'I think this office frightens you', before suggesting they go somewhere else to discuss her divorce over cocktails. Christabel's seductive methods are formularised to the point that history repeats itself, and Ray shows that environment and situation are key factors in her plans.

Because her strategies are planned in such detail, because her methods are virtually foolproof, we end up admiring her as an intelligent being surrounded by fools, and know- ing that she, not they, will ultimately triumph. At the end of the film, Nick has disap- peared from the scene, Gobby is left with a portrait worth $500 and Donna has returned to the man who humiliated her. In fact, thanks to Hughes's ludicrously moralistic rec- onciliation scene (in which Curtis lands in a near-trance after a flying trip – aviation was the mogul's greatest passion – and waxes mystical about how things can be seen in their true proportions up there), we can only surmise that Curtis, Christabel's most contemptible and complacent victim, is in danger of losing his mind! In which respect, *Born to Be Bad* might almost be seen as subversive; only in Christabel, who expresses remorse neither for the death of her aunt nor for the dissolution of her marriage to Curtis, do we encounter any real sense of purpose, achievement or happiness. The film has been labelled as misogynist, with one writer even suggesting that its cynicism may have been a product of the director's currently disastrous marriage to Gloria Grahame; but what misogyny there is was surely present in the script. Ray seems to have reserved most of his sympathies for the self-empowering Christabel who, while constituting (in the words of Mike Wilmington) 'a libel on the idealised image of woman Ray had presented in the delinquent films' (on Keechie and Emma, in other words), is by far the most positive character in the movie.

While it would be foolish to claim that *Born to Be Bad* is in any way a major Ray film (the passionate sympathies and scenes of almost Expressionist intensity that one finds in his best work are nowhere to be seen), it *is* witty, polished entertainment in which here and there, in the vivid performances and sensitive use of décor, one can discern its maker's hand. All too often, it has been dismissed as a studio chore with few redeeming features, but close inspection reveals a controlling presence at work. The script, tight and clever rather than profound, may not have been at all original, or even stimulating, but Ray was a sufficiently talented film-maker to bring it properly to cinematic life.

In a Lonely Place (1950)

SYNOPSIS: Dixon Steele, a down-on-his-luck Hollywood screenwriter with a reputation for violently losing his temper, is asked by his agent Mel Lippmann to read a novel with a view to writing a script. Dixon is not enthusiastic about the material and asks nightclub hat-check girl Mildred Atkinson to his apartment to summarise the story, which she has read. Early next morning, he is woken by Brub Nicolai, a former army colleague turned policeman, who takes him to be questioned by Captain Lochner. Dix is told that Atkinson has been found murdered and that he is a prime suspect for the crime. He claims that a neighbour saw the girl leave his apartment alone; when the witness, Laurel Gray, is brought in for questioning, she confirms his story. Dix and Laurel subsequently become lovers and Dix finds the peace of mind to work on the script. But Lochner is far from sure of his innocence, and when Dix discovers that Laurel has met the detective behind his back, he flies into a rage: in an argument with a driver whose car he has crashed into, Dix almost kills the man, with the result that even Laurel begins to doubt his sanity. When Dix proposes marriage she consents, but confides to Mel that she intends to leave town; she gives Mel the unfinished script in the hope that, if the producer likes it, her departure will be less painful for Dix. While celebrating their engagement, Dix discovers that the script is now in the hands of the producer, and angrily strikes Mel. Laurel rushes home to pack her bags and Dix follows to apologise, but when he notices that she has removed the ring he bought her, and takes a phone message confirming her reservation of a single air ticket, he attacks her dementedly, and is prevented from strangling her only by a phone call from the police, saying that Atkins's fiancé has confessed to the murder. As Lochner apologises to Laurel for the emotional pain she and Dix have suffered because of his suspicions, Dix leaves her apartment and walks out alone into the night.

Ray's second and last film for Bogart's Santana company is one of his most achingly romantic and thematically dense. Working from, and making a number of changes to, Andrew Solt's screenplay, which was based on a novel by Dorothy B. Hughes (in which, incidentally, Steele actually *does* commit several sex-murders), Ray was able to treat several themes close to is heart: the roots of violence, a love affair eroded by the pressures of society, the relationship between environment and emotion, and the painful vulnerability of the lonely and hyper-sensitive. Furthermore, the setting for the film was Hollywood, a 'lonely place' well known, of course, to Ray (who based Dix's home on his own first Hollywood apartment); although the story is a romantic thriller rather than a portrait of the movie business, one cannot but feel that Ray's characters reflect his less than entirely enthusiastic view of the world in which he was living and working. Indeed, the film may be seen as partly autobiographical. Ray felt less affection for Hollywood that Solt, and the unglamorous depiction of the milieu in which Dix and Laurel strive to sustain their relationship can probably be attributed to the director. Moreover, his marriage to Gloria Grahame had broken down – they kept their separation secret from the producers to ensure that the film went ahead as planned – and their real-life problems may have coloured Ray's exploration of the on-screen romance between Dix and Laurel.

Like *They Live by Night, In a Lonely Place* is a blend of *film noir* and love story, but it differs from the earlier film (and from *Knock on Any Door*) in that it concerns adults, rather than adolescents. Consequently, the sense of loss, loneliness and anxiety felt by its central couple is all the more poignant: that Dix and Laurel see their love as a last chance to find happiness cannot be dismissed merely as the pangs of youthful inexperience. Nevertheless, both are archetypal Ray creations, in that they are prone to the same romantic impulses and dreams and to many of the same confusions as their younger counterparts. Dix, for instance, besides being bitter, lonely and violent, is often nervous in the company of women. When Mildred summarises the book for him, Ray has her speak directly to the camera, which (mirroring Dix's wariness) pulls backwards, only to watch her step forward again, into almost oppressive close-up. Likewise when he asks Laurel if she will go out with him, Dix's intense gaze and fidgeting hands suggest his fear of disappointment and the excessive importance he places on being accepted by her. Seeing her as his potential saviour, he confesses that, 'I've been looking for someone for a long time. I didn't know her name or where she lived. I'd never seen her before. And a girl was killed, and because of that I found what I was looking for. Now I know your name, where you live, and how you look'; love and death, violence and redemption are, even at this early stage in their relationship, tragically interwoven in his mind.

Dix's capacity for violence is inextricably linked to this deeply romantic, hyper-sensitive approach to his own life. Full of self-pity and self-hatred, he externalises his emotions either through the scripts he writes (he tell Brub and Brub's wife Sylvia, 'I've killed dozens of people … in pictures') or through violent reactions to anything that might be construed as an insult: in the film's opening scene, he offers to fight a man who tells him not to pester his wife, and later he almost batters to death a motorist who calls him 'a blind, knuckle-headed squirrel'. But for the most part, Dix is reluctant to show his emotions: Lochner suspects him in part because he hardly reacts at all when told of Mildred's death; afterwards, however, away from the prying eyes of the cops, he visits a florist's to buy roses for her funeral.

Dix's problem, then, is primarily one of repression. When he does finally give free rein to his emotions, they are extreme and obsessive; when angered, he flies into violent rages, and when he is courting Laurel, he does so with such speed and intensity that she feels the need to warn him not to rush her. It is because of this fundamental lack of control and balance in his personality that he is forever on the brink of cracking up. He is a mass of contradictions – an intelligent, sensitive artist with generous, warm feelings for those less fortunate than himself (much is made of his friendship with a drunken has-been actor of the silent era for whom almost everyone else shows nothing but contempt), who at the same time can be cynical, flippant, self-pitying, withdrawn and murderously aggressive. Those sympathetic to him – Laurel, Mel and an ex-lover whom, we learn, he used to beat – tend to excuse his psychopathic tendencies by reference to his artistic temperament, whereas Dix himself, in his more lucid moments, knows better, acknowledging his precarious, uncertain sense of identity when children demand his signature: 'Who am I?' he asks, before agreeing when one of the autograph-hunters scornfully says, 'He's nobody.' Indeed, what Dix really fears and what provokes him to acts of violence is being treated as if he were 'a nobody'.

The writer's temper flares up when others discuss him behind his back or read his work without his consent; perhaps, too, he protects the has-been actor from insults and neglect because the man puts him in mind of what might one day be his own fate. Hollywood, depicted with uncommon honesty, is a place that rewards only the rich, successful and famous; when you are down on your luck, you might as well not exist. Dix, all too aware of this, feels that his love affair with Laurel offers an opportunity to become truly alive, so that his sense of identity and self-respect no longer depend entirely on his status in a philistine, profit-motivated film-making town. His sense of his own fragility is succinctly and lyrically evoked in lines he writes for his script, which he asks Laurel to repeat when they make up after their first argument:

I was born when she kissed me,
I died when she left me,
I lived a few weeks while she loved me.

As so often with Ray's heroines, Laurel offers Dix salvation and redemption, not only because she supplies him with an alibi, but because she diverts his attention away from the success ethic and social hierarchy of Hollywood, which are partly the reason for his paranoia and violence. Even she, however, is not strong enough to withstand the twin pressures of Dix's temper and a seemingly endless murder investigation, conducted by a cop whose ruthless determination to solve the crime goes as far as ordering Brub to inform on his old fried. (Lochner may be seen as almost the exact opposite of Dix; while the writer conceals his sadness about Mildred's death beneath a cool, flippant façade, Lochner is completely insensitive in his dealings with everyone, despite his humourless, self-righteous pretensions to humane warmth and moral rectitude.) Like Dix, Lauren has been emotionally scarred; when he meets her, she is in hiding from a former lover, and confesses that she prefers to get out of relationships before she gets hurt. Nevertheless, she is, in Dix's words, 'not cute or coy or corny; she speaks her mind and knows what she wants'. She resists the doubts sown in her mind by Locher's insinuations, which are repeated by her masseuse Martha, who advises Laurel to return to her former, wealthier lover. (Interestingly, Martha is shot and played in such a way as to suggest that she represents Laurel's subconscious; while she massages Laurel, whose back-lit face is shown from below is enormous close-up, Martha is barely visible behind her; her strangely passionless, monotonous voice is heard droning on, as if disembodied.) But it is only when Laurel herself *sees* Dix's violent temper, when she manages to stop him killing the motorist, that she begins to wonder about his sanity, and their relationship – regarded by each partner as a potential panacea for the ills of the world – begins to fall apart.

Seeing and being seen are, of course, what Hollywood is all about; its most famous contributions to the world are the movies and the stars we watch. It is perhaps appropriate, then, that seeing and being seen are here central to Ray's theme and method. In the context of a murder mystery, the act of seeing for oneself is related to empirical knowledge and truth (whereas hearsay is a matter of mere opinion and allows for falsehood); moreover, being watched (and the voyeuristic invasion of privacy which that implies) is a key factor in Ray's attempts to illuminate Dix's paranoia. The film's opening shot, beneath the credits, is of Dix's pained eyes reflected in his car mirror as he drives alone, by night, along a city freeway. Night, as we have seen, is a common Ray symbol for solitude, a motif reinforced by the cars that drift silently past Dix; but the focus on his eyes in the mirror prefigures further levels of meaning crucial to the film. Not only does Dix need to see himself as he really is, to come to terms with his violence and his self-regarding cynicism, but his problems derive partly from how he thinks he is seen by others; he *needs* Laurel's love and *needs* to be seen as a 'somebody' just to feel that he exists. At the same time, however, he shies away from the world, avoiding ex-lovers and answering the telephone only when it suits him, and it is because everyone (particularly the police) begins to watch him more closely after Mildred's death that he becomes more edgy and violent, so that his relationship with Laurel is doomed. And since seeing can be an invasion of privacy, it also becomes, for Ray, who was acutely aware of environment, an invasion of *space*.

This connection between space and visibility is apparent as soon as Dix takes Mildred back to his apartment. Unimpressed by the story she is telling him, and feeling vaguely threatened by her forwardness, he retires, away from her aggressively friendly gaze, into his bedroom, where, from his window, he first gains a proper view of Laurel, standing on the balcony of her apartment, on the opposite side of the courtyard. (That their homes are both linked and separated by the courtyard reflects the elements of attraction and repulsion in their relationship.) Having seen her *and* seen his own gaze returned, he decides to send Mildred home. Looking operates on one level, then, as an index of preferential loyalties, a function further demonstrated when Laurel is first brought in for questioning by Lochner: seated facing him, with Dix (whom she has never properly met) positioned behind her, she looks at Lochner until told that Dix is suspected of murder, at which point she turns around to study Dix's face. Trapped between the men, she is forced to choose which to believe; having decided the Dix is innocent, she then sits looking at him rather than at the cop who, to gauge *her* trustworthiness and regain her loyalty, is then forced to cross the room to position himself next to Dix. Nonetheless, his efforts are fruitless, since Dix and Laurel have made eye contact; although they answer Lochner's questions, they continue to look at, and address their replies to, each other.

As long as Dix and Laurel are able to look each other in the eye, their relationship remains strong and stable, but after they first argue (Dix complaining that she and Brub have discussed him with Lochner behind his back – in other words, that he had been an unwitting victim of a form of surveillance), they sit in the car, facing forwards, without looking at each other; distrust and deceit have entered their relationship. Henceforth, as her doubts about Dix's sanity grow, Laurel increasingly avoids his gaze, even to the

A matter of eye-contact: at the police interrogation the gaze signifies suspicion, surveillance and, for Laurel (Gloria Grahame) and Dix (Humphrey Bogart), the start of something good.

point of locking herself in her room – that is, out of his sight – as soon as she has decided to leave him. Mutual visibility is therefore an index of equality, affection and loyalty in a relationship; but seeing can also provide power and control. When Dix and Laurel first talk in private, he jokingly complains that she, because her apartment is built overlooking his, is able to see what he is doing, whereas he cannot look into her life; he is not only sensitive about being watched, but also knows that at this stage of their relationship she is in control, his fate is in her hands. The balance of power between them is conveyed very precisely by the locations in which Ray places their encounters. They first cross paths in the neutral, no-man's-land of the courtyard. Then, at the start of their love affair, Laurel visits Dix's apartment to reveal her interest in him, *allows* him to visit hers when she agrees to go out with him, and then more or less moves in with him to organise/take control of his life. Later, however, when doubt and fear enter her mind, the situation is reversed: she increasingly retreats to her apartment and he visits her (without, now, permission being granted or even asked for), taking control and invading her privacy to the extent that, in the final moment of crisis, just before trying to kill her, he threatens to break down her door.

Significantly, Dix's deranged attempt to murder her takes place when he forces his way into the inner sanctum of her bedroom, which not only makes plain the link between his violence and his sexual repression, but also reflects back on to his meeting with the dead Mildred. Whereas in the earlier scene, Mildred was dressed, Dix was in his bathrobe, and to escape her, retired to his bedroom (whence he caught a glimpse of Laurel in her negligée), now Dix is dressed, Laurel is in her negligee and she flees into her bedroom to escape him. Small wonder that Laurel, now worried that Dix might have killed Mildred after all, is afraid of history repeating itself.

That relationships (and cinema) are as much to do with space and seeing as they are to do with conversation is made explicit in a complex, ironic scene that occurs just after Laurel suffers nightmares which confirm her fear of Dix. She awakens to find him preparing breakfast in her kitchen, slicing a grapefruit. Instead of using the knife to threaten her as we half expect him to (and without plunging the fruit in her face as James Cagney did to Mae Clarke in *The Public Enemy*), Dix reiterates his love for Laurel by discussing romance in the movies, after she tells him how much she liked a love scene he has written: 'That's because they're not always telling each other how much in love they are. A good love scene should be about something else besides love. For instance, this one: me fixing grapefruit, you sitting over there, dopey and half-asleep. Anyone looking at us could tell we're in love.' The irony, of course, is that Dix is both right and wrong. On the one hand, the speech is virtually a statement of intent from Ray: film *is* about looking, and he was forever exploring the nature of love in films that appeared to be about something else; *In a Lonely Place*, for example, is primarily about a relationship, and only secondarily a 'whodunit' about Mildred's death. On the other hand, Dix makes his speech at the very moment when Laurel is beginning to question her love for him,

'Anyone looking at us could tell we're in love': Dix fails to notice Laurel is keeping her distance, in *In a Lonely Place*.

and *we* can see, as he cannot, that her 'sitting over there' (they are shown in profile facing each other from the extreme edges of the frame) is an acknowledgement of the emotional gulf that has grown between them.

Such ironies proliferate towards the end of the film. Dix is angry with Mel and Laurel because they have given his script to the producer without his permission; they took it hoping that if the mogul liked it, acceptance would diminish Dix's despair after Laurel's departure. News does arrive that the script has been well received, but only *after* Dix strikes Mel, making Laurel still more determined to leave. Similarly, because Dix ignores a phone ringing in his apartment in order to go directly to Laurel's, he attacks her *before* receiving Brub's long-awaited confirmation of his innocence. The call saves Laurel's life, but not her love for him; the revelation that he might kill her turns her doubts about his sanity into a terrified certainty that he is insane. The cops' delay in proving his innocence pushes him over the edge – as Laurel tells Lochner, 'Yesterday this would have meant so much to us; now it doesn't matter at all'; the realisation that Dix *could* have murdered Mildred is enough to bring about Laurel's complete withdrawal.

In an ending so bleak and ambiguous that it may be seen to prefigure that of Hitchcock's *Vertigo*, Dix descends the stairs from Laurel's apartment and, as she gazes after him (repeating to herself the words, 'I lived a few weeks while you loved me'), he walks away, without looking back, not to his apartment but out of the courtyard, into the darkness. Ray explained, 'You do not know whether the man is going to go out, get drunk, have an accident in his car, or whether he is going to go to a psychiatrist for help.' Whichever, Dix enters a dark void, his sense of who he is finally destroyed by his own lack of emotional control and by the pressures of living in a world beset by suspicion and betrayal.

In a Lonely Place is both a product of the years in which it was made (the paranoia, distrust and treachery that colour its portrait of Hollywood are surely linked to the mood prevailing in the United States during the anti-Red witch-hunts) and a characteristic Ray study of the destruction of an idealistic romance between lonely outsiders, by the harsh realities of the world around them. It is also one of the great Bogart movies, stripping away the insolence of so many of his roles to explore the insecurity, the romanticism and the repression that lay beneath a macho, violent façade. Gloria Grahame, too, gave one of her finest performances, freed from the conventions of the *femme fatale* to portray a woman at once strong, intelligent and vulnerable. But it is Ray's bleak lyricism, superbly complemented by Burnett Guffey's silvery-grey photography, and his vivid, subtle sense of detail that make it one of the most adult, poignantly affecting thrillers ever made.

On Dangerous Ground (1951)

SYNOPSIS: In their hunt for the killers of a fellow policeman, Jim Wilson, Pete Santos and 'Pop' Daly receive information that leads to Myrna, former lover of Bernie Tucker, a friend of the murderers. After 'persuading' Myrna to betray Bernie's whereabouts, Wilson thrashes the information out of him, and is cautioned by Captain Brawley, who applauds his results but abhors his methods. The next night, however, Wilson finds Myrna being beaten by two of Bernie's associates, and is only retrained from battering one of them to a pulp by Daly. Brawley then sends him upstate to the country, to 'cool off' and to investigate the murder of a young child. Wilson joins a hunt for the killer led by Walter Brent, the dead girl's vengeful father; the pair track their quarry through the snow to a remote farmhouse inhabited by the blind Mary Walden and her teenage brother Danny. While Brent continues his search, Mary confesses to Wilson that Danny, a shy, gentle boy who should have been institutionalised, is the killer and extracts a promise from the policeman that Danny will come to no harm. Wilson finds and confronts the boy in a nearby cabin, but just as he is about to disarm him, Brent arrives with his shotgun. As the men fight, Danny makes his escape, only to fall to his death from a cliff in the ensuing chase. When Wilson informs Mary of the accident, she rejects his offers of help, begging him to return to the city. On the road back, however, he recalls her words about his loneliness and Daly's warnings about his violence, and decides to return to Mary. Reunited, they embrace.

While making *In a Lonely Place,* Ray contacted John Houseman to ask if he would work with him on a film he hoped to make. It would be based on a novel he had discovered called *Mad with Much Heart*. Happily, Houseman, who was at that time under contract to RKO, agreed, and Ray was himself able to collaborate on the screenplay with A. I. Bezzerides, thus winning for himself a measure of control he had not enjoyed on any film since *They Live by Night*. Despite both the director's and the producer's subsequent misgivings about the result, which was renamed *On Dangerous Ground*, the film is amongst the finest of all Ray's work for RKO. Fascinated by the theme of an intelligent but violent man whose job it is to fight violence, he spent some weeks researching the project in Boston, accompanying policemen in their cars during the night shift; despite certain melodramatic elements in the plot (Mary's blindness and the romantic, reconciliatory ending which, incidentally, Ray himself never originally intended to shoot), the film is notable for the unglamorised authenticity of its depiction of police procedure, which is effortlessly integrated into the more schematic, lyrical study of a lonely, violent man who finds redemption through love.

In certain respects, *On Dangerous Ground* may be seen as an ambitious variation on traditional *film noir* motifs, the shadowy, Expressionist visuals of its early urban scenes reflecting both the city's menacing corruption and its protagonist's paranoia. At the same time, however, the film is quintessentially 'Ray': décor and environment affect and mirror the characters' states of mind; Wilson – an isolated, embittered individual – carries within him the seeds of his own destruction; the complex narrative structure centres on the motifs of the hunt and the spiritual quest; while many other recurrent Ray 'touches' (the concept of family, animal imagery, characters defined in terms of likeness and opposition) also figure strongly. Moreover, style is again entirely at the service of meaning; those who have criticised the film as broken-backed, its urban and rural episodes unconnected except by the figure of Wilson, have not only failed to notice the motifs that feature in both parts, but are blind to the fact that the structure *embodies* the torn, almost schizophrenic predicament of its protagonist.

As often with Ray, even the credits sequence is not without significance: the shots of the dark, wet city streets seen from a moving police car not only evoke *film noir*'s archetypal concrete jungle, but stress forward movement – a stylistic device recurring throughout the film that mirrors Wilson's uneasy restlessness and his need to reach out beyond himself, to establish communication with others. The opening shot proper also introduces a number of motifs that will enrich the basic plot: from a close-up of a black gun on white bed linen, the camera draws back as a woman places the pistol in a holster which she then straps on to her policeman husband, who is preparing to leave for work. Already, a visual contract of black against white has been made, foreshadowing the darkness of the city and the blinding white snowscapes of upstate; already, too, violence (the gun) is linked with sex and family (the bed), key elements in the drama that is about to unfold. As the scene shifts from Pete Santos and his wife to 'Pop' Daly's household, we see another family, significantly perhaps, watching a Western on television, the noise of gunfire drowning out all other sound; again the wife hands her husband his holster. These simple images of communal home life are then counterpointed by the introductory shot of Wilson, already wearing his holster (does he ever take it off?) and alone in his sparsely decorated room as he pores over mugshots of the cop-killers while hurriedly finishing his meal. Wilson later tells Santos that he was one of nine kids, but there is no evidence, in either his room or his conversation, that he ever sees his family: his job is his life, and Santos and Daly have become his surrogate family, just as Bowie was adopted by T-Dub and Chicamaw in *They Live by Night*.

As the three men tour the city in search of the cop-killers, Ray uses what at first seems an episodic, randomly ordered story to fill in the details of Wilson's character. That he is callous towards others in his pursuit of justice is shown by his off-hand treatment of an informer; that he is incorruptible, by his refusal of a bribe in a bar; that he is almost psychopathically violent, by his irate response to being called a dumb cop by an innocent he has roughly frisked under suspicion of armed robbery; that he is hyper-sensitive, by his being angry and upset when a friendly girl in a local drugstore jokes, 'That's all he [her boyfriend] would need to know! Me going out with a cop!' Even Daly, whose nickname 'Pop' and words of advice make him something of a father figure to Wilson, cannot penetrate beneath his colleague's tough protective shell; Wilson repeatedly turns down his invitations to dinner and refuses to discuss his own uncontrollable anger.

Wilson bears, in fact, a strong resemblance to Dixon Steele in *In a Lonely Place*: he is a wary, idealistic loner who cares not too little but too much; his violence is rooted in repression that is perhaps partly sexual. Certainly, when an attractive girl flirts with him in a bar, his distaste is so strong that he immediately has her thrown out for being under age, and when Santos asks when he will marry, he at once changes the subject. And when he tracks down Myrna, the undercurrent of sado-masochism in their encounter comes into the open when the girl, speaking of Tucker, shows him the bruises on her arm and says, 'He was real cute … you're cute too.' As he stands threateningly close to her, she continues, 'You'll make me talk, you'll squeeze it out of me with those big strong arms … won't you?' – to which Wilson, with soft-spoken menace, replies, 'That's right, sister.' Similarly, when he beats up Bernie, the scene carries vivid overtones of sexual sadism: bursting into the man's room, he finds him on his bed, and in the ensuing scuffle Bernie taunts him with the words, 'Go on, hit me, hit me.' Wilson complies, but only after voicing his rage at his own predicament: 'Why do you make me do it? You know you're gonna talk, I'm gonna *make* you talk. I always make you punks talk. Why do you make me do it? Why? Why?'

Because Wilson, in his solitude and his devotion to his job, has removed himself from any possibility of entering into normal relationships, he has become as tainted by violence as the 'crooks, murderers, winos, stoolies and dames' whom he is required to deal with. In a remarkably volatile sequence which includes a striking example of hand-held camera, he pursues Myrna's assailants down dark, claustrophobic alleyways, finally catching one and flailing at him like a madman. When Daly pulls him off the man and berates him for his violence, Wilson's confused, misanthropic paranoia is made absolutely plain:

WILSON: So I get thrown off the force! What kind of job is this, anyway? Garbage, that's all we handle: garbage!

DALY: Didn't you know? That's the kind of job it is.

WILSON: You've been doing it for sixteen years; you ought to know. How do you do it? How do you live with yourself?

DALY: I don't! I live with other people … When I go home I don't take this stuff with me, I leave it outside. But you! The way you carry it around with you, you must like it!

Wilson's violence, however, is so deeply ingrained after eleven years with the force that no amount of words, either from Daly or from Brawley, can change him; all too aware of how much cops are disliked, he wallows in the self-pitying knowledge that he has no friends to help him. He lives on the edge of sanity, in a nightmarish hell of his own making, superbly conveyed by Ray's rapid cutting, taut compositions, restless camera movements and shadowy visuals: we are almost half-an-hour into the film before there is a daylight scene (when Brawley first castigates Wilson for being free with his hands), and it is only when Wilson is sent upstate (to 'Siberia', as he calls it) that he is offered the chance of redemption in a complete change of environment. That his odyssey from the city to the countryside is not only geographical but spiritual is made clear by Ray's dreamlike use of dissolves to convey time, distance and change of climate as Wilson drives north (the mood is startlingly similar to that of Marion Crane's trip from city to country in Hitchcock's *Psycho*, a film on which *On Dangerous Ground* seems to have had some influence). But while the film now, as it were, starts again as a reverse mirror-image of everything that has gone before, Ray never succumbs to the facile, conventional moral polarity of evil city/pure countryside; what Wilson discovers in the Westham farmlands is far more complex and just as violent as anything he has left behind him.

Almost immediately upon arrival, he is forced to confront a form of righteous anger far more dangerous than his own. And yet Walter Brent's avowed intention to empty his shotgun into the belly of his daughter's killer derives from love for his family: he is, as Sheriff Larrey says, 'a real good man'. On one level, then, Brent stands as Wilson's *alter ego*: he wants no 'fancy trial' for the killer, just as Wilson was accused by Brawley of acting as judge, jury and executioner; on another level, however, Brent is, because of his family ties, Wilson's opposite, just at the empty snowy spaces of the Westham countryside are in counterpoint to the black streets of the city. And on yet another level, Brent becomes a surrogate father to Wilson, frequently chastising him for his lack of concern ('What do you care? It wasn't your kid'), and dragging the cop in his wake as the posse sets out, over the fields and mountains, to hunt the murderer with dogs and rifles.

Having expressed contempt for the man-made laws of the city and having transgressed them, Wilson now faces the more instinctive laws of nature, of unthinking bloodlust born of vengeance and passionate family love. Accordingly, the posse literally follows the tracks of the killer in the snow, and our first glimpse of the prey is when he drops – falling too quickly past the camera to be identified – from the boughs of a tree in which he has been hiding, like an animal. By the same token Mary Walden's home, invaded by Brent and Wilson, who suspect their quarry has taken shelter there, is filled with objects that evoke a life inextricably linked with nature: carved wooden statuettes, a Christmas tree, wind chimes and the massive branch of a tree. Mary's 'nature', however, is more 'civilised', more domesticated than Brent's predatory aggression, and Wilson is now forced to confront another, more protective embodiment of family love, which abhors violence. Horrified by the realisation that her brother has killed Brent's daughter, Mary is prepared to hand him over to Wilson as long as he promises to defend him from Brent's murderous lust for vengeance. At which point Wilson must choose between two contradictory, if connected, facets of natural family love; and in that choice lies his destiny, an opportunity to reject or accept forever a lonely life of hatred and violence.

Mary's blindness not only serves as a physical correlative to Wilson's moral myopia; it also teaches him the true meaning of isolation, and how to cope with it. When he tells her he would be lonely living in her country cottage, she replies that the city can be lonely too, and that 'sometimes people who are never alone are the loneliest'. Ironically, Mary 'sees' Wilson better than he sees himself (though she at first thinks he is used to dealing with blind people because his voice shows no pity), and, as usual with Ray's heroines, she offers advice that is essential to his salvation: when he says that being a cop means that he has come to trust no one, she points out that, being blind, she has to trust everyone. She can cope with her handicap because she cares for her brother, and the implication is that if Wilson were to break down the wall he has erected between himself and the outside world, if he were to learn to care for someone, his own moral blindness would be cured. It is only when Wilson, having understood this lesson, finally decides to protect Danny from Brent's wrath, that he is able to overcome his isolation and act not as an avenging angel of death but as a true defender of the law.

As depicted by Ray and played by his nephew Sumner Williams, Danny is a gentle, emotionally retarded teenager whose single act of murder stems from the fact that his desire to be liked by the victim has been frustrated. When Mary visits him in their fruit-cellar (another link with *Psycho*), his face is hardly visible; as she tries to persuade him to leave with Wilson, he remains in the shadows and his pitiful whimpering and long, soft hair reinforce the image of a caged, frightened animal. Indeed, he is almost the complete opposite of Bernie, who was betrayed by an ex-lover rather than protected by a sister; when Wilson finally confronts Danny, Ray explicitly reverses the situation of his brutal interrogation of Bernie. The dark-haired Bernie was in an upstairs room, and tauntingly encouraged Wilson to hit him; the blond Danny, conversely, we first (properly) see below ground. Wilson finds him later, in a cabin full of the wooden animals he has carved, and Danny advises the cop to keep his distance, or he will stab him. More significantly, Wilson's mood has also shifted from one of paranoid violence ('Why do you make me do it?') to caring protectiveness ('Who do you like, Danny? Who do you listen to?'). And it is clear, as the boy babbles pathetically about the little girl who would not smile at him (the sexual basis of the murder is made explicit by the phallic knife he

'He's just a kid': Brent (Ward Bond), Wilson (Robert Ryan) and Willows (Frank Ferguson) get their man (Sumner Williams).

holds erect throughout his unwitting 'confession'), that Wilson *would* be able to disarm him and take him away peacefully, were it not for Brent's arrival at the cabin, bursting through the doorway behind Wilson in much the same way as Norman Bates (another shy, nervy killer obsessed with animals and birds) erupts into the fruit-cellar behind Sam Loomis in *Psycho*. Brent's rifle is deflected by Wilson as it is fired, and Danny makes his terrified escape as the men fight.

Again, as before, they chase him through the snow, but this time we cannot but feel that Wilson accompanies Brent not to help him, but to prevent him from killing the boy. Again, too, the chase ends with Danny falling quickly past the camera, but this time the result is tragic; he has plunged to his death after losing his foothold on a sheer cliff, whose function in the story has already been foreshadowed, as if by destiny, when Wilson notices a painting on Mary's wall that shows an identical hill towering behind a cabin very like Danny's hideaway.

With Danny's death, Brent's rage is expended, and he sees for the first time, with a look of horror on his face, that, 'He's just a kid, that's all he is, just a kid.' He pushes Wilson aside to pick the boy up, *Pietà*-fashion, and carry him back to a nearby farm. Wilson, meanwhile, is filled with guilty remorse, and upon meeting Mary, who asks God to forgive her brother (Ray avoids excessive sentimentality by having her shed no tears), he in turn 'asks' for *her* mercy, offering to help her in her loneliness and in the search for a cure for her blindness. She, however, rejects his offer and, in words reminiscent of Laurel Gray's at the end of *In a Lonely Place*, asks, 'What difference does it make?' as Wilson tries to explain that Danny's death was an accident. For her, his remorse, his tenderness, have emerged too late, and she sends him back to the black, bleak city, after knocking over her furniture in confusion, and confessing that without Danny – her 'eyes' – she too feels afraid.

Wilson leaves with Brent, who now – in words that contrast with the insults hurled at the cop in the city – admits that Wilson *has* to be tough in his line of work. Wilson only snorts in contempt for himself, presumably aware that if he had dissociated himself from Brent's bloodlust earlier in the chase, instead of merely taking the bullets from his gun as he slept, Danny might still be alive. Had the film then ended as Ray originally planned, Wilson would simply have gone back to the city, chastened but likely to suffer a complete breakdown and/or return to his violent ways. Stars and studio, however, apparently wanted a more positive ending; as it stands, Wilson, recalling the advice of Mary and Daly as he drives into town, turns back to Westham, where Mary embraces him. Though this final scene may seem clichéd and contrived, it nevertheless carries considerable power and even has a modicum of credibility. Throughout the film, Wilson and Mary have been presented as complementary opposites who might, by coming together, escape private prisons built by blindness and solitude; and in a sense, everything that has gone before – Wilsons's repressed sexuality and desire to belong to a family, the fraught conflict between violence and love, the camera's restless forward motion – has been working towards such a resolution.

In style and execution, *On Dangerous Ground* saw Ray at his most confident to date. Not only is it his most suspenseful film (and one of his most virtuoso in its audacious cutting and camera movements), but his sense of composition, environment and structure is more precise and telling than in any film since his directing debut. Power and control in relationships are subtly suggested by the physical positioning of characters in the frame; the many reversals between the plot's two parts, even down to the way most of Wilson's hunting in the country is done on foot (as opposed to the cars used in the city), symbolise the cop's need for a complete moral and psychological turnaround.

Moreover, Ray was working with the most able team of collaborators he had had until that point. No actor was more suited to portraying an intelligent but embittered and inwardly tormented man on the verge of breakdown than Robert Ryan, whose Wilson is genuinely terrifying in his intensity, and no actor more potentially thuggish in his conservative commitment to the American ideal of family than Ward Bond, whose Brent makes the desire for bloody revenge all too plausible. Furthermore, the photography (by George E. Diskant, who shot *They Live by Night* and *A Woman's Secret*) transcends the *chiaroscuro* conventions of *film noir* to evoke, through its lyricism, the mesmerising, highly subjective nature of Wilson's voyage towards salvation, while the score by Bernard Herrmann, brought to work on the film by Houseman, is not only memorable in itself but perfectly complements the action with vigorous, racing crescendos for the hunt sequences and with the melancholy intimacy of a viola for Wilson's scenes with Mary.

The film is, in fact, beautifully realised on every level; as a result, it remains remarkably modern in feeling, anticipating not only *Psycho* but rogue-cop movies like Siegel's *Dirty Harry*, most of which are infinitely less complex in their examination of vigilante ethics. Consequently it was not only an important film for Ray (though it was not very successful at the box office), but a major contribution to the development of the police-thriller.

Flying Leathernecks (1951)

SYNOPSIS: In the summer of 1942, Major Dan Kirby, distinguished veteran of the battle of Midway, takes command of US Marine Fighter Squadron VMF 247, a group of fliers whose task it is to help to regain from the Japanese the island chain of Guadalcanal. The disciplinarian Kirby is frequently at odds with the military authorities because of his desire to implement close, low-flying air-support for ground troops. He also soon comes into conflict with his executive officer Captain 'Griff' Griffin, who objects to his superior's strict, apparently unfeeling attitude towards the young and largely inexperienced squadron pilots. The tension between the two men grows as a series of daredevil missions claims lives which Kirby seems to regard as expendable. Although Griff conceals his disaffection from the men, he takes Kirby to task in private for failing to bear in mind the squadron's youth. Kirby, relieved of command and posted to a desk job in the United States, tells him that he has recommended that Griff should not take over the leadership of the squadron. While back home, however, Kirby is asked to return to the Pacific to take command of a new squadron to supply close air-support for ground troops in a major operation, and Griff is once again appointed as his executive officer. During a dangerous air battle, a wounded Kirby is forced to bail out, but not before he has heard Griff giving firm instructions, over the radio, that result in the death of Griff's brother-in-law. Finally convinced of Griff's ability to make tough decisions, Kirby hands over to him the command of the squadron before returning home for a well-earned rest.

Along with *A Woman's Secret, Flying Leathernecks* is one of Ray's most anonymous and conventional films. It was a somewhat thankless task imposed on him by Howard Hughes; not only were patriotic war films very fashionable with the advent of the Korean War, but the studio head (then still tinkering obsessively with *Jet Pilot*) was always eager to make films that paid tribute to the glories of aviation. Hughes enlisted as his producer Edmund Grainger, who had scored a huge popular success with *The Sands of Iwo Jima*. For *Flying Leathernecks*, Grainger managed to gain access to documentary archive footage of aerial combat belonging to the US military. Ray, however, who was never very interested in patriotism or the spectacle of war, also suffered, according to his own admission, from a chaotic shooting schedule because there was never really a properly polished script for the film. The result is an almost entirely traditional and conservative war film, lacking a strong dramatic foundation and notable mainly for the efficient way in which the documentary footage is sewn, relatively seamlessly, into the story proper.

Nor did the fact that it was Ray's first film in colour seem to inspire him – surprising, perhaps, given his later adventurous use of colour symbolism. While the film is never less than adept, is it reasonably safe to assume that Ray was only concerned with mak-

Baptism of fire: Griff (Robert Ryan) learns the law according to Kirby (John Wayne) the hard way.

ing it as proficiently as possible under the circumstances, in order to remain in Hughes's good books. There is, admittedly, an uncommon emphasis on the wastage of human life involved in war, which makes it stand out from most other war movies of the period, but the film is still fundamentally a paean to the courage and determination of the US Marines, and the deaths that accompany every mission are included primarily to embody the fears and doubts encountered by Griff in his gradual transformation from a brave, capable pilot into a true leader of men, who understands not only the suffering of the individual but also the greater need of a nation at war. It is Griff, in fact, rather than Kirby, who is at the dramatic centre of the film, since it is he who develops as a character. (As incarnated by John Wayne, Kirby is far too solidly secure and heroic an officer to engage Ray's attention, and the depiction of his split nature – austere and pragmatic in public, sorrowing and sensitive in private – is wholly perfunctory.) Sadly, the constraints of a formulaic, episodic script prevented even Robert Ryan, often a mouthpiece for Ray's pessimistic confusion, from fully transcending the stereotypical dimensions of Griff's character, even though he is given two potentially illuminating and subversive speeches. In the first, he tells a young pilot why he joined the armed forces: 'Some guys take a look at the world when they're young and don't like what they see. And they realise that some of us are going to have to fight for the rest of us from here on in.' What might have become a characteristic Ray statement on youthful disillusionment and rebellion, however, is quickly turned into a hackneyed, less provocative variation on the 'why we fight' question when Griff continues, 'I'm a professional soldier, and I don't mind saying I'm kinda proud of it.'

Still more frustrating, in that it is never fully explored or developed, is Griff's embittered outburst when he attacks Kirby's apparent lack of feeling for his men: 'I got a bellyful of you, and I'm not buying the bill of goods you're selling. In my book it's easy to be internal, to put a shell between yourself and the rest of humanity. Four hundred years ago, a poet said it better than I ever could: no man is an island. When the funeral bell rings, it isn't just for the dead guy; it's a little bit for all of us. Each man's suffering belongs to everyone, or else why are we shooting off these guns?' This diatribe, spoken with great passion and conviction by Ryan, not only sends Kirby striding out of his tent speechless – perhaps the only sign of doubt he shows during the entire film – but suggests depths in Griff's character that remain obscure. It may be that his desire to be liked by his men is rooted in a hyper-sensitive awareness of his own solitude, and that his reluctance to decide which pilots must die in combat stems from an all-embracing inability to take responsibility for his actions. But any suggestion of existential anxiety, any idea that Kirby's defensive, authoritarian 'shell' is a failing, and any questioning of the very purpose of war are all swept aside as the film works inexorably towards its conclusions: Kirby's tough façade is vindicated, Griff becomes a carbon copy of his superior and the American armed services continue along their deathly but glorious route to honourable, heroic victory.

Flying Leathernecks is, finally, scuppered by the clichés of the genre to which it belongs. Kirby's admissions of fear, his writing of letters to the families of dead pilots, and his brief idyllic visit to his own brave wife and child; Griff's belated realisation that Kirby does in fact care about his men; Jay C. Flippen's cunning line-chief, forever stealing supplies from the artillery for his own squadron; the plucky, fun-loving Marines, in need of rest but prepared to fly to their deaths regardless of the fact that they are not wise enough to comprehend fully the harsh commands of men like Kirby: all are familiar from countless propagandist epics made in, and often after, times of war. If the film is often predictable, that may be because the war-film genre is somewhat limited in the characters and situations it tends to depict (revealingly, Ray's later *Bitter Victory* is a far better film precisely because war is merely the *backdrop* to a clash between its two central characters rather than the *sine qua non* of the film); and if the drama that unfolds between the many extensive aerial sequences lacks complexity and depth, that may be attributed to Hughes's consuming passion for aeroplanes. Ray elicited adequate performances from his cast, and never allowed the film to degenerate into excessively patriotic hogwash. But it is clear throughout that the material provided him with little of interest and his input was competent but insignificant; rather, the movie, if subjected to serious examination at all, is best regarded as an example of Hughes's own highly idiosyncratic, and in many ways marginal, contribution to propagandistic film-making.

The Lusty Men (1952)

SYNOPSIS: Veteran rodeo-rider Jeff McCloud, who has been wounded by a bull in a contest, hitches a lift to his childhood home, a run-down ranch which its present owner, the old Jeremiah, hopes to sell. While there, Jeff meets prospective buyers Wes and Louise Merritt, a young couple saving to purchase their own property. Wes is a rodeo fan and gets Jeff a job at the ranch where he works, asking that Jeff teach him how to become a rodeo-rider in return for half of any prize money Wes wins. Jeff agrees, much to the displeasure of Louise, who wants a stable home life and dreads her husband getting hurt. When Wes does well in his very first competition, however, she consents to his joining the circuit, on condition that he gives up the sport as soon as they have enough money to buy Jeremiah's property. Wes meets with great success but tensions mount between him, his wife and his friend: Louise is suspicious of Jeff's motives for managing her husband's career and is also dismayed when Wes, entranced by the fame and money he is winning, buys a trailer, proves reluctant to abandon rodeo and begins regularly seeing a young woman taken by his good fortune. Meanwhile, Jeff becomes increasingly enamoured of Louise and, after she argues with her drunk and philandering husband at a party, asks if she will leave Wes. She, however, for all her dissatisfaction with Wes's irresponsibility, still loves him, and begs Jeff to help protect her husband from his own high-flying ambitions. When Wes encounters the pair talking in the corridor outside the party, they kiss, and in the fight that ensues, Wes accuses Jeff of cowardice and of trying to take his money and his wife. The next day, Jeff, though out of practice, enlists for the rodeo competition and proves himself still a great rider, before catching his foot in his stirrup and suffering fatal injuries. He dies in Louise's arms, and Wes, chastened by the loss of a friend he has now forgiven, decides to give up his rodeo career and to go with Louise to buy Jeremiah's ranch, as originally planned.

Having made *Flying Leathernecks*, Ray was now in favour with Howard Hughes who, according to the director, invited him to become production supervisor at RKO. When Ray turned down the offer, he was asked to work on a number of films Hughes was having problems with (*Androcles and the Lion*, *Macao*, *Jet Pilot*, *The Racket* and *His Kind of Woman*). Mostly, this seems to have involved tidying up the films in the editing room, though he reshot a handful of scenes for *The Racket* (a film with which director John Cromwell had been none too happy) and about a third of the (reputedly incoherent) material shot by an unenthusiastic Josef von Sternberg for *Macao*. Despite the fact that the final version of the latter film is therefore in no small degree a work by Ray, his input was purely cosmetic; the plot's blend of light-hearted suspense and insolent erotic repartee was hardly, one may imagine, conducive to Ray's giving of his best, and the film is wholly lacking in distinctive personal touches, stylistic or thematic.

The Lusty Men, on the other hand, would seem to have been tailor-made for the director's special interests, even though he came to the project (originally entitled *Cowpoke*)
only after its producer Jerry Wald had hired and lost the services of Robert Parrish and
toyed with the idea of employing John Huston, Raoul Walsh and Anthony Mann. Once
engaged for the production, Ray, who had always been fascinated by American folk culture and groups of 'outsiders', immediately set about researching the lives, customs and
colloquialisms of modern cowboys, before working closely with novelist Horace McCoy
on the script. As the project proceeded, so (according to its star Robert Mitchum)
McCoy lost interest, with the result that David Dontort was hired as a second writer.
The film was finally completed in a quasi-improvisatory fashion, day by day, without any
proper screenplay to speak of. Nevertheless, the result constitutes a key development in
Ray's approach to narrative and genre; its relatively loose, ballad-like structure not only
enabled him to focus primarily on character and mood (as opposed to plot), but also
prefigured much of his later work.

Like the best of his earlier films, *The Lusty Men* is near-impossible to categorise into
any single genre: as a rodeo movie, it is closely linked to the Western, but at the same
time, the plot is at least partly a love story, while the semi-documentary style of most of
its rodeo scenes lends it the feel of a non-fictional sociological study. Indeed, the shots
beneath the opening credits of a typically American parade (featuring Indians as well as
cowboys and drum majorettes) are a hint that, on one level at least, the film may be seen
as being about America itself; this interpretation is justified by the account of independence, ambition, success and failure – in other words, of the American Dream – that is
at the core of the narrative. Ray himself described the film as, in part, a response to the
desire of many Americans during the postwar years to settle down with a family in a
home of their own, and it certainly exudes a mood of authenticity in its unromantic portrait of poverty, rootlessness and people's desperate dreams of a better life. At the same
time, as in *On Dangerous Ground*, this tendency towards downbeat realism is allied to a
lyrical poeticism verging on the abstract, and the depiction of everyday life in the rodeo
world is partly a framing device for a meditation on moral and metaphysical questions.

The opening shot proper, for example, of a billboard advertising a rodeo tournament
publicised as 'the wildest show on earth', is a suggestion that the sport, which serves as a
crucible into which Jeff and Wes pour their hopes of fame and fortune, is little more than
a sham built on false values. And while Ray never patronises his nomads of the rodeo
world, or denies their courage and needs, he does forestall any romantic view of the sport
by emphasising not only the hardship and risks involved, but also the extremely repetitive nature of the spectacles. Shown over and over again, the achievements of the com-
petitors are exposed as almost absurd: futile, foolhardy rituals performed for no purpose
other than to demonstrate the contestant's virile prowess to a crowd hungry for thrills.
Each time a rider is injured, he is quickly removed from the arena so that the show is
resumed with as little interruption as possible. So it is for Jeff McCloud who, after having
his ribs broken by a bull, limps alone at dusk across an empty, windswept arena filled with
debris left by the spectators who have already forgotten Jeff, despite his having been, during an eighteen-year career, several times world champion. With his career now seemingly

'I can git in outta the rain': Jeff McCloud (Robert Mitchum) tells his life story to old Jeremiah (Burt Mustin).

over, and injured spiritually as well as physically, he heads for the home he lived in as a boy, where (in a supremely simple, wordless sequence directed with beautiful under-statement by Ray) he crawls beneath the house, among the cobwebs, to find the last remaining treasures of a vanished childhood: a tobacco tin containing two nickels, a gun and a rodeo programme. The sequence's mood of melancholy nostalgia establishes Jeff's need to rediscover his roots and to overcome his feelings of solitude, ageing and failure; at the same time, Ray makes a connection between the sport and immaturity.

Jeff's lack of direction is further evoked in his encounter with Jeremiah, garrulous new owner of the homestead (''t ain't much to bray about', says the old man, when told that Jeff was born there). As the pair speak, the rodeo-rider's rootlessness, lack of money, loneliness and none too high opinion of himself are discussed, in dry, laconic dialogue as poetic and witty as it is naturalistic:

JEREMIAH: Yer got anythin' of yer own?
JEFF: What I started out with – a strong back and a weak mind.
JEREMIAH: A shack, some rocky ground, a horse an' a busted windmill, that's all I got.
JEFF: Still more than me.
JEREMIAH: Yeah, but you ain't 62 yet … You a thinkin' man?
JEFF: Oh, I can git in outta the rain, that's about all.

Jeff can probably see his future self in this old man, who then goes on to ask why books about success are never written by failures; and perhaps that is why, when he leaves ('Like

Two's company ... Jeff McCloud gets to appreciate the domestic life, thanks to Louise (Susan Hayward) and her fame-hungry husband Wes (Arthur Kennedy).

visitin' a graveyard,' says Jeremiah), he readily joins the Merritts, who still have hope in their young hearts.

The tensions that will define the Merritts' relationship with Jeff are subtly suggested by Ray's precise compositional sense, as soon as they offer Jeff a lift to the ranch where Wes works. First, as Wes gets out of their car to introduce himself to his hero, he and Jeff are reflected in the windscreen to the right of the frame, while Louise, who will at first be marginal to their plans, sits to the left of the frame, visually separated from them by the edge of the glass. Secondly, as they drive, she sits between them (suggesting that she will be emotionally torn), but a bar down the middle of the windscreen separates Wes from her and Jeff, implying that the husband's lust for independence will throw Louise and Jeff closer together. And finally, after Jeff has found employment at the ranch and has had dinner at the Merritts', his fundamental solitude is reasserted as he stands alone in the darkness, watching the couple walk arm in arm, back to the warmth of their small cosy cabin, and bed.

The narrative is structured around these shifts in the relationship between the three characters, with Wes initially mesmerised by his admiration for his surrogate father/teacher and Louise hostile to the influence exerted on her husband by Jeff's 'easy come, easy go' attitude towards life. Wes's need to emulate Jeff derives partly from immature hero-worship (Louise repeatedly refers to her having to protect and mother him), partly from his desire to find 'a short cut' to having enough money to buy a home, so that he will no longer have to obey any boss but himself. Jeff, for his part, agrees to help Wes become a rodeo-rider less for money than because the work will enable him to remain close both to the rodeo circuit and to Louise, whom he sees as a potential saviour. (At one point, after telling her how much money he has won and lost, he admits that maybe his life would have been different had he met someone like her.) Both men, in fact, as befits their work in a profession which thrives on fantasies about the freedom of the traditional cowboy life, attempt to live out dreams – Wes of wealth and glory; Jeff, belatedly, of marriage and security. Louise, meanwhile, is more lucid and pragmatic, explaining her position to Wes when he decides to leave the ranch for the full-time rodeo circuit: 'Look, buster, nobody's getting panicky. I'm just trying to keep us straight. And stop kidding yerself. You ain't the only guy who tried to take me from behind that counter in that hash-house and set me up in business. You ain't the biggest, you ain't the strongest. You ain't the richest and you ain't the prettiest. But you're the only one who wanted what I wanted. A decent steady life.'

Having embarked on their endless tour of trailer parks and arenas, the trio join a transient community whose individual members function as distorted reflections of themselves: riders repressing their fears of injury, death and failure through drink and gambling, and wives prematurely aged by anxiety. All of them, however, live in couples, and only Jeff is alone; even the talkative old-timer Booker Davis (himself something of a father figure to Jeff and, with his leg horribly scarred by a life spent in rodeo, a walking omen of the future to all around him) has his daughter Rusty for company. That the rodeo-rider's life is based on false values – on a degraded version of the pioneering spirit of the Old West – is emphasised, perhaps, by Booker's continuous recounting of tall and boastful stories about his past triumphs; the less glamorous reality is brought home when a rider, his face already disfigured by scars, alcoholism and fear of failure, dies in the arena, and his wife walks like a pale ghost into a drunken party to silence the revellers into guilt and bemusement with a recriminatory cry of despair: 'Dumb fools, calling this a sport!' For the most part it is the women, never participating in the arena but always expected to watch, suffer and furnish moral support, who are depicted as wiser about life than the men who are variously consumed by pride, insecurity, jealousy and a lack of self-esteem that strives to conceal itself, in company, beneath braggadocio and the purposeless activity of rodeo itself. The film may, in fact, be viewed as in part a melancholy critique of the immaturity of the male psyche.

Jeff, at least, is man enough to acknowledge the dangers of his profession; despite his nostalgic comments about his years of fame and money, he also longs to leave the circuit to settle down with the woman he has come to love. Wes, however, is childlike in his reckless, irresponsible attitude to the sport and his wife, and Jeff points out his immaturity by questioning his ability to hold his drink and advising him not to enlist for the bull-riding events. It is Jeff, finally, who by sacrificing his life will reveal to Wes the error of his ways. When he and Louise follow Wes to yet another party, they find him covered in lipstick after being kissed by predatory fortune-hunter Babs (whose submissive nature is symbolised by an introductory shot in which she is seen being lassoed by a reveller), and pathetically courting flattery by asking the girls, 'Who's gonna be champion bull-rider this year? Who can bronc-ride longer, bull-bronc better, an' calf-rope quicker than any man in this room?' Louise, having told the girl to stay away from her husband and having poured a jug of water over her, is thrown out of the party, accompanied by Jeff, who asked Wes to leave too. Wes refuses, and outside in the corridor, in a scene played with heart-rending tenderness, Jeff at last respectfully professes his love for Louise. She, however, cares only for Wes, and asks Jeff not to let Wes end up crippled, like him. At which point Wes and the rest of the guests emerge from the party, and Jeff says, 'I do think I ought to kiss you for all the times I won't.' When Louise consents, Wes – hypocritically, given his behaviour with Babs – accuses him of trying to steal his wife, and of being too afraid to ride himself; unwittingly invoking Jeff's destiny, he complains that he is tired of him 'dragging your foot in my stirrup'. Jeff's immediate response is to knock him out, and the next day, against the advice of everyone except Wes, who wishes him good luck, he enters the rodeo, and displays his superior skill before catching his foot in his stirrup, being thrown from his horse and having his ribs knocked into his lungs.

Jeff's death – which, ironically, given the fact that he has devoted his life to the great outdoors, occurs in a dark, cramped cabin interior – is virtually an act of self-sacrifice which he carries out to prove his love for Louise; when Rusty Davis asks if Jeff signed up 'to show Wes' or for the money, Louise replies No. At the same time, however, the fatal ride will give his life meaning; when Booker says, 'Everybody knows Wes ain't in the same class as you', Jeff replies, 'Everybody but me.' But, besides being a last attempt to prove his worth to himself, Jeff's enrolment in the rodeo serves to humble the arrogant Wes, who is forced to admit that, 'He's the best.' In so doing, Jeff obliges Wes to question his own future on the circuit, and when he dies in Louise's arms (explaining, 'I used to make my own money, buy my own whisky, take my own falls. A fellow just likes to know if he can still do it. Isn't one man enough for you to worry about?'), the loss of life makes Wes decide to give up rodeo entirely. Out of love, Jeff has answered Louise's plea for help: to her he has given the security she wanted; to Wes the salutary lesson that allows him to become a mature, responsible man; and to himself, tragically, a peace of mind and restfulness denied in life. In death, Jeff at last finds a home.

As the Merritts leave the arena for Jeremiah's, followed by Booker and Rusty, who will be their farm-hands, they pass beneath a massive sign marked 'Exit'; Jeff, too, has found a way out from his solitude. But Ray was seldom one to soften an unhappy ending, and with dark irony, he cuts from the departing group back to the arena, where another young rider is making his first stab at fame and fortune; for humanity at large, the show, sadly, must go on.

Arguably the most elegiac of Ray's films – thanks partly to Lee Garmes's spare, sombre monochrome camerawork – *The Lusty Men* also pointed the way forward, with its ballad-like structure, to the loose, less conventional plots of films as diverse as *Johnny Guitar*, *Rebel Without a Cause*, *The True Story of Jesse James*, *Wind Across the Everglades* and *The Savage Innocents*. The long, repetitive rodeo sequences function as a kind of ironic, rousing chorus that alternates with the more developmental verses that are the quieter, contemplative scenes of life outside the arena, many of which are shot at dusk, night or dawn. The careful balancing of these scenes (wrecked, unfortunately, in a mutilated short version distributed in some countries, including Britain) is achieved not merely by Ray's assured, leisurely pacing, but by the consistent excellence of the three central performances. Ray effectively used and probed Susan Hayward's aggression and Arthur Kennedy's cockiness, and found new dimensions in Robert Mitchum's moody, masculine taciturnity to uncover an aching vulnerability: watchful, sensitive, tough, but never once stereotypically macho, Jeff McCloud is perhaps Mitchum's finest role ever, certainly his most moving and dignified, thanks largely, one suspects, to the director's ability to empathise fully with loner figures. At every turn, Ray and his actors appear to understand exactly what they are doing (surprising, perhaps, given the circumstances of the film's making): as painted through images, dialogue, décor and performances, the portrait of rodeo life is never less than completely plausible, while the deeper themes – of love, loss and redemption, of self-respect and self-sacrifice – are allowed to emerge naturally, almost organically, from what is for the most part a relatively undramatic plot about men wanting to exchange their lives with one another. The film's beauty, in fact, derives from the deceptively simple way in which Ray examines, through the unusual, colourful context of the rodeo world, a universal predicament: the need for love, respect and a home; the need, in other words, to feel that one belongs.

Johnny Guitar (1954)

SYNOPSIS: Johnny 'Guitar' Logan, a gunslinger who now prefers to go unarmed, is summoned by his former lover Vienna. She wants him to help protect her saloon, and her plans to build a rail-station, from the violent opposition of the local community. Soon after his arrival, a group of men led by a woman, Emma Small, whose hatred of Vienna is almost psychopathic, bursts into the saloon carrying the corpse of Emma's brother, the victim of a stagecoach hold-up. Emma accuses Vienna of being part of a gang led by the Dancing Kid, whom Emma loves but who himself loves Vienna. When the Kid arrives, accompanied by Black Bart, Corey and Turkey, full-scale conflict is averted only by Johnny's pacifying presence. Emma's ally McIvers then gives Vienna and the gang twenty-four hours to leave town. When the Kid and his companions – not outlaws, in fact, but silver-mine prospectors – return to their hideaway, they plot to rob the town bank as revenge against their persecutors. The next morning, Vienna and Johnny, who have now put aside the bitterness caused by their separation five years ago, are at the bank when the gang arrives for the robbery; although Vienna tries to dissuade the Kid from the crime, she is later visited by a posse headed by McIvers and Emma, whose empty promises of forgiveness trick Turkey (hidden in the saloon after being wounded during the gang's escape) into a false admission of Vienna's guilt. The mob hang Turkey, but Vienna's life is saved by Johnny, who cuts the noose and then accompanies her by way of a mineshaft to the Kid's mountain retreat. Vienna averts a fight between her rival suitors, but Bart, tired of following the Kid's orders, lets the posse into the hideaway and kills Corey, before being shot by Johnny while trying to kill the Kid. In a showdown, Emma kills the Kid, and is herself shot dead in self-defence by Vienna. Allowed to go free by McIvers, Johnny and Vienna embrace.

In February 1953, Ray finally left the studio he had been with for seven years; he had failed to persuade RKO to let him make *No Return* (a project about modern American gypsies, based on research done by his ex-wife Jean Evans, which later served as the basis for *Hot Blood*). Through his friendship with agent Lew Wasserman, he was almost immediately able to start work, together with Joan Crawford and the highly literate screenwriter Philip Yordan, on a film for Herbert J. Yates's Republic, most successful and prestigious of the minor studios. The movie, *Johnny Guitar*, was Ray's first proper Western (though some critics have claimed that it is too eccentric to be included in that genre), and his second film in colour. Unlike *Flying Leathernecks*, it engaged his attention sufficiently for him to make full use of the larger palette at his disposal; and thereafter, with the sole exception of *Bitter Victory*, he would always work in colour. Indeed, the film may be seen as something of a turning point in Ray's career; henceforth, much of his work would be more flamboyantly stylised, more headily melodramatic in tone and less constrained by generic conventions than his earlier films. *Johnny Guitar* is also, arguably, his most complex film, functioning on so many levels that an entire book might be written to do it full justice. Clearly, any such exhaustive analysis is here impossible, given the intent and scope of the present study, but I hope, at least, to demonstrate the film's remarkably rich texture and to outline a number of its thematic and stylistic aspects as material for further research.

Ray himself regarded the film as baroque, and it is this tendency towards excess, towards elaborate ornamentation, that has alienated *aficionados* of the more traditional Western; even its admirers have admitted to its weirdness. François Truffaut, in a much-quoted review, called it 'a fairy tale, a hallucinatory Western' and 'the *Beauty and the Beast* of Westerns, a Western dream', thus touching on its fundamentally non-naturalistic feel. One may go further, and make references to opera, myth, Greek tragedy, romantic melo-drama, even surrealism, all of which sound echoes through what is a florid but surpris-ingly coherent film. What gives the film its unity, as it veers between violent hysteria and melancholy lyricism, is Ray himself, not only in the sense that both the story and char-acters are, once again, close to his deepest concerns, but also in that he was one of the very few directors able to take the various devices by which meaning is expressed in film (plot, dialogue, performance, music, colour, composition, movement, cutting, décor and so forth) and make them work together in complete, if sometimes strange, harmony. Certain elements in *Johnny Guitar* – painted backdrops, costumes, lines of dialogue – might seem, to a viewer barely acquainted with his highly synthetic style, to be pur-poseless, accidental flourishes; close examination, however, reveals a skilful, organising mind at work that is finely attuned to every detail in a complex tapestry of meanings. Hardly surprising, then, that the film has been examined not only in terms of its relation-ship to Ray's work and the Western but also as an anti-McCarthyite political allegory, as a Freudian fable and as a proto-feminist variation on what is traditionally regarded as a 'masculine' genre.

After the opening credits, which show an appropriately romantic landscape of high mountains and valleys, Johnny enters the frame, lazily riding with his guitar on his back. Immediately, a series of unexplained explosions rocks the mountains (only later do we learn that the railroad is coming to town), serving to introduce not only the theme of a peaceful man faced by forces of a deadly violence, but one of the main strands of sym-bolism in the film: the natural elements. Then, even before the explosions have died away, Johnny sees a stagecoach robbery far below him in a valley; his lack of response to the attack and his lofty viewpoint reveal his sense of detachment, his reluctance to involve himself in any violent situation. Within seconds, a dreamlike mood of mystery, a sugges-tion that what we are about to see concerns strange, barely fathomable primal forces has been established, a sense intensified by the next shot of Johnny descending into a windswept desert and galloping through the swirling dust towards a bizarre, isolated building hewn into the sheer side of a massive cliff. It is the saloon they call Vienna's.

Inside, the place is equally unreal: the ochre stone of the cliff forms one wall; two croupiers, a barman and Tom, the ageing kitchen-hand, stand silently, having no cus-tomers to attend to; everything is immaculately neat and ordered, a sanctuary from the

howling chaos of the world outside, the embodiment of its owner's desires to bring civilisation to the West and to control her own destiny. When Vienna appears, having heard
Johnny ask for her, she looks down on the men from a balcony (just as Johnny was first
seen looking down from the cliff), dressed in a dark blue shirt and jeans; as one of the
staff tells Johnny (and us, for he addresses his remarks directly to camera), 'Never seen
a woman who was more like a man; she thinks like one, acts like one, and sometimes
makes me feel like I'm not.' In her attempt to tame the wilderness, Vienna has inten-
tionally become 'masculine' and a potential castrator in the eyes of others. Her secret,
real self may be gauged from the soft blue paintwork, silver tableware and bust of
Beethoven that adorn her private quarters, where she entertains a businessman, hoping
that he will support her plan to build a railway station. Her determination, the fact that
she gained her power through ruthless planning, is shown when she says that she learned
of the railroad company's project by exchanging confidences (the sexual nature of which
is implied by Crawford's smile) with a surveyor, and also when she replies to the businessman's blessing with the assertion that she is 'not trusting to *luck*'.

Their conversation is suddenly interrupted by the thunder of galloping hooves; as if
out of control and blown in by the storm, Emma whirls into the saloon, accompanied by
McIvers, the marshal and sundry male townsfolk, to confront Vienna with the accusation that she is guilty of the stagecoach robbery and, therefore, of the death of Emma's
brother. All at once, various themes crowd in on the narrative, and Ray weaves them
together seamlessly. On one level, the scene offers a sardonic study of lynch-mob mentality, as Emma and McIvers, ignoring the warnings of the marshal, try to implicate
Vienna in a crime nobody saw her commit. On another, the scene introduces the theme
of repressed sexuality, as Vienna reveals that Emma's real reason for hating her is envy,
and that Emma is ashamed of her desire for the Dancing Kid, who loves only Vienna.
Emma's actions, rooted in guilt and frustration, are less those of a grieving sister than
of a fanatical puritan bent on destroying a woman whose complete control of her own
sexuality has won her both power and the admiration of men. And on yet another level,
we see a further example of Ray's fascination with the predicament of the outsider, in
Vienna's determination to preserve her independence in the face of a destructive, malignant society. When told to put down the gun she has pulled on the mob to stop them
coming up to invade her private quarters, she warns, 'Down there I sell whiskey and cards;
all you can buy up these stairs is a bullet in the head.' The threat of death is her only
effective response to a world in which violence means the power to curtail the freedom
of the individual.

As the daunted mob is about to depart, the storm blows Dancing Kid and his cronies
into the saloon, their laughter and firing of guns setting them in sharp contrast to the
dour party that brought in Len's body. Immediately, a deafening silence falls upon the
place, and a battle between the rival groups is averted only by the sudden reappearance
of Johnny, who has hitherto been confined with Tom in the kitchen (thus revealing his
servile, 'feminine' function in Vienna's plans), and whose conciliatory, pacifying ways are
made plain by his taking a cigarillo from the Kid and a light from McIvers. Both factions
are confused by the stranger's unfrightened humility – he claims that all he needs is a

smoke and a cup of coffee, calls everybody 'sir' and, when asked why he wears no gun, replies, 'Because I'm not the fastest draw west of the Pecos.' After Emma and McIvers depart, having told Vienna and the Kid's gang to leave town within twenty-four hours, the Kid is further mystified by the tender glances between Vienna and Johnny, and Black Bart picks a fight with Johnny, to test his mettle. Johnny wins, establishing that his peacefulness is a matter of choice, not of cowardice, but further light is shed on his reason for not carrying a weapon when the young Turkey, determined to prove that he is 'man' enough to stay and look after Vienna, begins shooting at glasses to show her his prowess. Johnny, thinking he is firing at Vienna, rushes crazily from the kitchen and shoots the gun out of Turkey's hand, prompting Vienna to accuse him of still being gun-crazy. For her, violence, unless carried out in self-defence, signifies immaturity (she tells Turkey, 'That was good shooting, *for a boy*'), and a lack of self-control:

VIENNA: You haven't changed at all, Johnny.
JOHNNY: What made you think I had?
VIENNA: In five years, a person should learn something.
JOHNNY: Five years ago, I met you in a saloon; now I find you in one. I don't see much change.
VIENNA: Except I *own* this one.

Vienna is not only Johnny's ex-lover and potential saviour, but also, in a sense, a mother-figure, to Johnny, Turkey and the Kid, all of whom she advises, chastises, and give orders to; Johnny therefore becomes in his turn a kind of father-figure to Turkey and the Kid, who, true to Freud's Oedipal theory, need to destroy him in order to banish him from Vienna's affections. Indeed, all the characters are related, not only by the plot, but by patterns of similarity and contrast: the Kid and Johnny both have musical, faintly 'feminine' names; Bart's aggressive bluster mirrors what Johnny might become were he to succumb to his violent instincts; Vienna's past as a dance-hall prostitute is in direct opposition to Emma's repressed desires; and the group that works and lives at the saloon resembles the Kid's gang in that they are viewed as unwanted outcasts by the townsfolk. Most important for Ray, however, is the bond between Johnny and Vienna, both loners new to town and striving to make a better life for themselves at the same time as minding their own business.

While the gang's response to McIvers's threats is to avenge itself with a bank robbery before leaving town, Vienna chooses to stay and fight the bullying townsfolk with the help of a 'family' consisting of Johnny, whose skill with a gun she hires to protect her, and her other staff: she cannot act alone. Accordingly, she and Johnny must cast away their bitter memories of the past, when his reluctance to settle down taught her not to love, for fear of being hurt. At night, therefore, unable to sleep and dressed in a scarlet dress that reflects the promiscuity of her years without Johnny, she descends the stairs, spins the roulette wheel with an ironic laugh that reveals her low opinion of trusting to chance, and finds Johnny drinking, morosely, alone in the kitchen. Then, in what are perhaps the most beautifully poetic lines of dialogue in any of Ray's many tender, feint-and-parry scenes of courtship, the couple attempt to come to terms with their years apart:

Prelude to a duet: Vienna (Joan Crawford) visits Johnny (Sterling Hayden) as he drowns his sorrows.

JOHNNY: How many men have you forgotten?
VIENNA: As many women as you've remembered.
JOHNNY: Don't go away.
VIENNA: I haven't moved.
JOHNNY: Tell me something nice.
VIENNA: Sure. What do you want to hear?
JOHNNY: Lie to me. Tell me all these years you've waited.
VIENNA (*coldly and mechanically*): All these years I've waited.
JOHNNY: Tell me you'd have died if I hadn't come back.
VIENNA: I would have died if you hadn't come back.
JOHNNY: Tell me you still love me like I love you.
VIENNA: I still love you like you love me.
JOHNNY: Thanks. Thanks a lot.

Paradoxically, Vienna's flat, unemotional intonation reveals to us, if not to Johnny, the profound love she still feels for him; the repression of her emotions is such that when she does at last admit to her love, the dramatic effect is all the more cathartic. Thus, when the couple, happily reunited, visit the bank the next morning, their witnessing of (and, therefore, in the eyes of the xenophobic townsfolk, their involvement in) the gang's robbery is all the more tragic. It is not enough, for Emma and McIvers, that Vienna tries to stop the Kid from taking the money or that Johnny – unarmed – simply observes their escape, saying, 'I gotta lotta respect for a gun; besides, I'm a stranger here myself.' Emma's campaign against Vienna has nothing to do with the truth, and her jealousy is only exacerbated when the bank teller, forced by Emma to say that Vienna was part of the gang, mentions that he saw the Kid kiss Vienna before making his escape. The hunt is on, and anybody who stands in Emma's way as she seeks Vienna's death becomes fair game. Urged on by this vengeful harpy, the townsfolk turn into a posse (or, in Johnny's words, an animal), their murderous purpose embodied by the black mourning clothes they are still wearing, fresh from Len's funeral. (That Emma's grief is subsidiary to her bloodlust is shown in the way she casts off her veil as the mob ride, like Furies, out of town in a cloud of dust.)

Meanwhile, the Kid's escape route is blocked by further dynamite explosions in the mountains; Turkey, injured when his horse rears in terror, is reluctantly abandoned by the gang, and while they return to their secret hideout, he is found by Tom and taken to Vienna's. She, having dismissed her staff and Johnny (who has shown himself less than trusting in his enquiries about her presence at the bank robbery), is alone in the saloon, playing her piano in a full white dress that both emphasises her innocence and contrasts with the black clothes of the lynch mob that storms in out of the night. Vienna angrily insists on her innocence and refuses to betray the whereabouts of the Kid's hideaway, but once Turkey is found, she is betrayed; the boy – who once adoringly offered to look after Vienna – is bullied and duped with hints that, if he speaks up, he might go free. He agrees to say that she was one of the gang, Tom and the marshal are shot trying to save the pair from a lynching, and Vienna and Turkey are dragged out into the night. Emma then returns to shoot down the saloon's chandelier, which produces a conflagration as uncontrollable and destructive as the bloodthirsty madness revealed on Emma's ecstatic face while she stares, entranced, at the leaping flames.

At the hanging tree, Turkey's betrayal of Vienna counts for nothing, and he is sent to his death, but none of the men in the posse is prepared to hang Vienna, so the task falls to Emma. Too late, however: hidden nearby, Johnny cuts the noose as Emma whips Vienna's horse, and the pair – her white dress matching his white steed – take flight together through a mineshaft tunnel, Vienna changing into less conspicuous jeans and shirt while explaining to Johnny the need for mutual trust in any relationship. By morning, they reach the waterfall that conceals the entrance to the Kid's retreat; he welcomes them with a display of aggressive jealousy towards Johnny, urging him tauntingly to draw the gun he now carries. This time, however, Johnny does not fire – the long-awaited showdown between the two men that should, by tradition, take place never occurs – and although the Kid insinuates that Johnny is still gun-crazy, Vienna can see that he has learned his lesson. Moreover, Johnny then saves the Kid from being shot in the back by the treacherous Bart, who has already killed the loyal Corey and let the posse in through the waterfall in return for Emma's promise that he will be allowed to ride away a free man. With Bart dead, the posse fires on Johnny and the Kid, but when McIvers sees Emma walk through the hail of bullets to the cabin, he orders a ceasefire, and the inevitable showdown is left to the women. First, however, in a final act of guilt-ridden repression, Emma kills the Kid, before being killed in her turn by Vienna, who throws

away her gun in disgust at the violence she has seen, suffered and been forced to per-
petrate. Then, as Victor Young's melancholy theme song rises on the soundtrack, Vienna
and Johnny descend the stairs from the cabin, make their way past a shamefaced posse,
and pass through the waterfall to embrace in the bright, clean light of freedom.

If the above description of the plot suggests little more than a faintly unusual Western,
that may be because Ray's style, at once direct and metaphorical, lyrical and bravura,
subtle but visceral, is very hard to evoke through mere words. One can mention the sophisticated nuances in characterisation: the complex web of likeness and contrast that links
the characters; the ambiguity of motivation (the Dancing Kid, for example, seems basically decent, and, at least before the robbery, hardly deserves to be treated as an outlaw,
yet at the same time he includes among his partners the malicious Bart); the ingenious
casting of actors, with Ray drawing upon Crawford's almost masculine toughness, Ward
Bond's reactionary boorishness (McIvers is reminiscent of his Walter Brent in *On
Dangerous Ground*), Sterling Hayden's gentle-giant menace, and Crawford and
Mercedes McCambridge's off-screen dislike of one another. But that still does not
account for Ray's acute attention to detail (the asthmatic Corey, for instance, is seen
enjoying books, most unusual in a Western), or for the sense that many of the characters
exist not only as real participants in the tale being told but also as socio-political, psychological or mythic ciphers.

Witch-hunt in the West: Emma (Mercedes McCambridge) and McIvers (Ward Bond) head the mob as
they inspect the fruits of their endeavours.

The scenes in which Emma and McIvers threaten, bully and make empty promises to the innocent victims of their self-righteous fanaticism immediately evoke an America gripped by fervent anti-communist hatred, just as the emphasis on betrayal, loyalty and the need for trust mirrors the paranoia induced by the McCarthyite witch-hunts. Equally, the various quasi-Oedipal relationships and the rooting of Emma's hatred in sexual repression are backed up by a Freudian equation of gunfighting skill and firepower with masculinity. Indeed, Vienna's likening of irresponsible gunplay to (implicitly sexual) immaturity, her castigation of male egoism and double standards (while a man has his pride, she says, he is still a man whatever he may have done, but if a woman slips once, she is a tramp), and the fact that she and Emma dictate the men's actions all conspire to lend the film an almost feminist critique of masculine behaviour.

At the same time, *Johnny Guitar*, with its primal, heated emotions, its unrealistic sets and painted backdrops, its poetic dialogue and its stark conflicts played out in clashing, symbolic colours, recalls the monumental simplicity of myth, even of Greek tragedy. While Destiny itself is never invoked, Vienna's refusal to trust to luck, her systematic stopping of the roulette wheel's turning whenever she decides to take control of events, her methodical mapping out of her future ('Luck had nothing to do with it') all suggest a character inexorably driven by a sense of her own fate. Johnny, on the other hand, in changing his name and abandoning his guns, tries to change his destiny, linked as it is with violence, while Emma, leader of the Furies who hound Vienna to within an inch of losing her life, seems motivated by natural forces beyond her control.

Indeed, the elements themselves assume a major role in the drama. Vienna and Emma are fighting, partly, for possession of the land; Vienna points out to her rival and to McIvers that they 'don't own the earth ... not *this* part of it'. More intriguingly, wind, fire and water take on symbolic powers as the story proceeds: in the first part of the movie, all the characters are, as it were, hurled into Vienna's saloon by a raging dust storm, the turbulence of which matches the blustering violence of the emotions inside. Then in the middle section, fire – symbol of destruction – comes to predominate: Vienna speaks of how her love for Johnny was burnt to ashes, anticipating, as if by premonition, the way that Emma's wanton actions will raze her saloon to the ground and the way that her own white dress (in other words, her attempt to regain her lost innocence) will catch fire as she escapes through the burning mineshaft. And finally, at the film's climax, water becomes a symbol of safety: the waterfall that both conceals and protects the Kid's hide-away from a predatory outside world, the streams through which Vienna and Johnny take flight, hiding their tracks, and the final shot of the waterfall and the river against which the couple, safe at last, embrace.

It is perhaps this elemental, mythic aspect of the film that makes it strangely timeless in its appeal; certainly, it was one of Ray's most financially successful movies, and may be seen as an influence on numerous later Westerns, including Leone's self-consciously mythic *Once Upon a Time in the West*. Those who see its appeal as primarily camp, citing its bizarre theatricality, blind themselves to the complexity of Ray's direction, and in so doing, to the full riches of one of the most extraordinary films ever to emerge from Hollywood.

Run for Cover (1954)

SYNOPSIS: Matt Dow and Davey Bishop, who have only recently met each other, are mistaken for bandits by train guards, who in their panic toss a bag of money to the pair as they pass. En route to Davey's home town of Madison – where Matt plans to return the money and settle down – they are met by a posse, who shoot Davey in the leg before taking Matt to town to be lynched. The guards confess their mistake, however, and Matt is set free. He visits the crippled Davey on the Swenson farm, and decides to remain there, working for Helga and her father until he manages to get the boy walking again. The townsfolk offer Matt the post of sheriff as recompense, and he accepts on condition that Davey be made his deputy and that there will be no more lynchings. But after bandits rob the town bank, Matt returns from catching Morgan, one of the bandits, to find that the townsfolk have overpowered Davey and lynched the other bandit. Matt, keen to give the boy a second chance, dispatches Davey to escort Morgan to a fair trial in the county seat, but when Davey returns wounded, claiming to have lost Morgan in an ambush, Matt accepts his resignation. After a second bank robbery (during which Helga's father is killed and it transpires that Matt, once wrongly mistaken as a bandit, has served a jail sentence), Matt leads a posse in pursuit of the gang; by the time they reach the desert, however, only Matt and Davey are left to continue the search. Failing in an attempt to kill Matt, Davey admits to having joined Morgan's gang and to having helped organise the second robbery; he then manages to make his escape while the two men are fleeing Indians. Matt finds Morgan and Davey in their ruined Aztec hideout; he wounds the bandit and vows to take his former deputy back for trial. When Morgan pulls a gun on Matt, Davey kills the bandit, while Matt – believing the boy is about to shoot him – kills Davey. Back in town, he returns the stolen money 'with Davey's compliments', and tells Helga that Davey died a hero's death.

After the baroque, mythic complexity of *Johnny Guitar*, Ray's next film was an altogether simpler, more straightforward kind of Western. While Harriet Frank Jr. and Irving Ravetch (who wrote the original story of *Run for Cover*) would later be lauded for lending the genre a downbeat realism with *Hud*, *Hombre* and *The Reivers*, and while Ray and his star James Cagney – coming out of a temporary retirement for the film – were keen to create something a little different from the traditional heroic cowboy film, the ambitions of Paramount and the film's producers were rather more routine. William H. Pine and William C. Thomas (who had hitherto specialised in producing 'B' Westerns) appear to have got on amiably enough with Ray, but they effectively held out against any idiosyncratic touches he wanted to insert (notably in the detailed depiction of everyday life on the Swensons' Swedish-immigrant farmstead), generally preferring a more clichéd account of Western life.

At the same time, however, despite Ray's later complaint that the film's story lacked any real conflict, one may discern, in the relationship between the middle-aged Matt Dow and the embittered young Davey Bishop, his characteristic fascination with the gulfs that can exist between father and son, teacher and pupil. Indeed, in many respects the film looks both backward, to *Knock on Any Door* and (to a lesser extent) *Johnny Guitar*, and forward, to *Rebel Without a Cause*. From the first of these three films, it reworks the mood of suspicion and betrayal between Morton and Nick Romano (the latter, particularly, evoked by the casting of John Derek as Davey); from the second, the idea of innocent outsiders threatened by a lynch mob masquerading as a 'respectable' citizenry; while *Rebel*'s study of a confused adolescent – which itself would be a refining of *Knock on Any Door* – is also anticipated.

As incarnated by Cagney, Dow is not a typical Ray outsider, even if, in certain respects, he fits the category. Divorced by his wife, sceptical about society's claim to justice after being wrongly imprisoned by a hasty crowd for a crime he did not commit, and the recipient of a less than warm welcome as he approaches a town he intends to inspect with a view to settling down, he also has within him a capacity for violence, as is shown in the first scene, when he pulls a gun on Davey simply because the boy comes up behind him without warning. (Davey's justifiable claim that he might have been shot 'for doing nothing' introduces, already, the theme of innocence hounded and punished.) But it is significant that Matt does *not* fire: his turning on Davey is an act of self-defence (he is wary of surprises, understandably enough given his earlier experiences), and he has

Good men and trigger-happy: innocent Matt (James Cagney) suffers a pre-emptive strike by a posse led by an over-zealous sheriff (Ray Teal).

learned to control his trigger-finger. Indeed, Matt's suffering, his imprisonment and his son's death have made him unusually strong and stable: though the past hangs heavily on him, he has determined to live in a way that never compromises his dignity or humanitarian ethics. Thus, he agrees to become sheriff for a community that nearly lynches him on condition that there will be no more lynchings; thus, too, in spite of having been left by a wife who 'just hated' him, he has sufficient faith in human relationships not to draw away from the clearly interested Helga. Matt's attitude to his life is far more positive than that of most Ray heroes, which is why he takes upon himself the task of educating and caring for Davey Bishop.

It is Davey, in fact, who more closely fits the mould of an anguished, self-destructive Ray outsider. On the brink of manhood (he is the same age as Matt's son when he died), Davey is morally torn between Matt's sense of honour and self-respect, and a more cynical response to the injustices perpetrated by an uncaring and hypocritical world. Davey, an orphan who spent his childhood being shunted from guardian to guardian, is already dangerously arrogant and eager for an easy life when Matt first meets him. He tells the older man that he needs no lesson in how to behave like an adult, and is tempted to keep for himself the fortune that is tossed by the cowardly guards from the passing train. But it is only after the posse shoots and cripples him for 'doing nothing' (other than riding back to town with Matt and the money) that this arrogance turns into a genuinely contemptuous hatred of the world. Like Tommy Farrell's in the later *Party Girl*, Davey's lameness is ethical, spiritual and physical: feeling that society owes him something for the suffering it has inflicted upon him, he wallows in an unforgiving, self-pitying desire for revenge.

Typically, however, Ray takes plot and characters beyond the simplistic level of good, wise older man meets foolish, vengeful adolescent. For Matt's desire to help and educate Davey is never completely altruistic. In Davey, he sees not only his son (whose death he regards as a personal failure), but his own youthful and rebellious self; and by the boy's limp he is reminded of the fact that he made Davey ride in front of him as they returned to town, thus accidentally ensuring that it was the boy, not himself, who was shot by the posse. Matt's caring for the boy, then, is partly a means of assuaging his sense of guilt, partly a reflection of his need to keep his own capacity for violence in check. Nor are his methods of instilling the boy with the courage, stoicism and rectitude he himself has learned always kind (even if they are necessary). When Davey falls on to his bedroom floor, shocked and afraid to find he can barely walk, Matt's response is to bully him until he drags himself up to a standing position, snarling, even as the boy succeeds, 'That's the last time I wanna see you crawl.' (Angrily, Davey then hurls the chair with which he has hauled himself up at a mirror, smashing – and so rejecting – the image of father and son Matt offers.) And when, later, Davey, ashamed that he was too weak to stop the townsfolk lynching his prisoner, asks for a second chance, Matt complies, but in so doing knowingly sends him off alone with a dangerous and cunning outlaw who has already attempted to bribe Matt to set him free. When Matt turns down Morgan, who claims that, 'Nobody'll know the difference' if he accepts the bribe, he is sufficiently assured of his own worth to reply, 'Nobody but me'; but to expect a young, desperate boy, already filled with resentment at his lot, to abide by that code of honour is blinkered, and only puts temptation in his way.

Davey is certainly no mere victim, however. He deliberately uses Matt's guilt and trustfulness in order to win his pity and help, and several times tries to kill the older man. He clings to Matt partly out of a genuine if inconsistent desire to make good, and partly out of a need to justify his criminal deeds: in Matt, he senses a dissatisfaction with the hypocrisy and rough justice of society, a dissatisfaction which he himself espouses as an excuse for his failure to live within the law. If Davey is a product of an unjust society, he is so consciously, playing on that fact with profit in mind, and completely careless of his responsibility to others; and it is to some extent Matt's blind faith in him that allows the boy the opportunity to turn to crime and, in so doing, to destroy himself.

To both 'father' and 'son', however – this, like many Ray films, is a kind of Oedipal drama – Ray grants a form of redemption. For Matt, keen to find a new family and home and to preserve the peace he has managed to discover within himself, his relationship with Helga is crucial. Though she herself is tactfully rebellious against the strict Old World Puritanism of her father (refusing, in her relationship with Matt, to be guided by a Swedish sense of propriety, rather than by her emotions), her kindness and common sense represent, for Matt, stability and peace; indeed, from the beginning, she is able to see through both Matt's desire to atone for his son's death in his relationship with Davey, and Davey's deep antagonism to the world, pointing out, when Matt makes the boy his deputy, that putting a gun in his hand will not cure his heart. It is not, finally, Davey's welfare but the love that Matt and Helga have for one another which makes Matt settle down in Madison and thus achieve a sense of belonging; for without her love, Matt would again, presumably, be riddled with guilt after Davey's death, and return to his life of wandering. Put simply, Helga's love ensures Matt's salvation.

Davey's redemption, on the other hand, is more complex and tragic, and comes only at the moment of his death. Despite Matt's continuing faith in his ability to make good, the boy repeatedly betrays him, not only out of a desire to hit back at society but also because Matt's strength, compassion and moral rectitude serve as a chastening reminder of his own shortcomings. (In Oedipal terms, Davey may be seen as envious of Matt's authority and his success with Helga, and thus driven to kill his surrogate father out of a profound filial hatred; interestingly, his jealousy is contrasted with Matt's willingness to bow to the stern authority of Helga's possessive and protective father.) Only when Matt catches Davey red-handed with Morgan, and renounces all faith in his 'son' even as he refuses to kill him there and then (he abides in his conviction that everyone deserves a fair trial, however strong his personal feelings in the matter), does Davey finally see and come to terms with the error of his ways: he kills Morgan in order to stop the bandit (a 'bad father' as opposed to Matt's good example) killing Matt. But too late: because Matt's trust in Davey has been eroded by repeated betrayal, he assumes that the boy is about to fire at him, not at Morgan, and so, in misguided selfdefence, he kills him.

Run for Cover is primarily a character study, a portrait of a relationship between two individuals entangled as much by their differences as by their (potential) similarities; its plot, for the most part, is functional, a series of fairly conventional Western situations. But besides giving the characters of Matt and Davey considerable complexity (by pointing to the contradictions, ironies and Oedipal elements in their father–son relationship), Ray also manages to lend extra depth to the story by means of his direction. The society in which they live is evoked with a vivid sense of detail which, apart from often serving a metaphorical purpose, succeeds in showing how people really lived in the West when they were not robbing banks and shooting one another. At the Swenson farmstead, Helga's father plays chess with Matt when the latter comes to ask for her hand in marriage, and Matt asks that Davey be given books to read during his convalescence; even the Indians Matt and Davey encounter during their pursuit of Morgan never actually attack the two men but are shown playing a form of polo, using a boot instead of a ball. Moreover, Davey's taste for violence is made perfectly understandable by the characterisation of the Madison townsfolk, who, even after Matt's arrival, are all too ready to shoot before asking questions and to hang a man without trial. (Interestingly, it is the sheriff who leads them against Matt after the alleged train robbery; again, as in Ray's earlier films, one may discern elements of anti-McCarthyite allegory in the depiction of irresponsible figures holding authority.) But as ever, it is in Ray's use of symbolism, camera movements, environment and colour that his ability to enrich a narrative is most clearly in evidence.

Time and again, for example, night provides an opportunity for intimacy, whether it be the hesitant courtship of Helga and Matt, or Davey's confession of his real distrust of Matt as they camp down by a river. Water, too, as in *Johnny Guitar*, has a quasi-symbolic function, evoking not only peace, safety and sustenance, but also the need to make a choice (which, after all, is the theme of the film as far as Davey is concerned). When Matt and Davey meet and decide to ride together rather than fight each other, they do so by a river where Matt is watering his horse; after they have taken refuge from the Indians in a riverside campsite, Davey makes his last attempt to kill Matt by trying to drown him; and when, at the end, Matt returns to town with the stolen money and news of Davey's death, meeting the townsfolk as he crosses a river, he confirms his loyalties by tossing them the bag with a contemptuous 'With Davey's compliments', before walking away with Helga, whom he tells 'Davey did fine'.

Environment is, in fact, used systematically throughout: the tranquillity of the Swenson farmstead – Matt's haven of peace – is contrasted with the drunken and hysterical violence of the scenes in town, while the low-point in Matt's relationship with Davey – the moment when the boy first pulls a gun on him – occurs as they cross an arid, windswept desert. Most remarkably (and prefiguring Ray's use of the Berber caravanserai in *Bitter Victory*), Matt finally admits to the wreck of their friendship amid the ruins of an Aztec citadel, which Davey and Morgan have made their hideout; Matt's search for them, through crumbling corridors and into an inner sanctum, reflects the tortuous, labyrinthine nature of his voyage of discovery leading to the core of his relationship with the boy. Crucially, when Matt first finds Morgan and Davey, he stands on a gallery looking down at them, as if to assert his superior moral worth and his consequent position of control, just as, earlier in the film, he had stood over the crippled Davey, bullying him into finding the courage to stand up and walk again. Significantly, in that scene, the camera adopted Davey's point of view, rising with him as he pulled himself from the floor, to make us identify with him rather than with his harsh taskmaster; in the later scene, however, the camera descends with Matt as he climbs down to face Morgan and Davey, whose manifold betrayals have forced us to shift our sympathies to Matt.

Small details, perhaps, but like the moment when Matt hands over a wooden gun he has just finished carving to a small child, while Davey bemoans the lack of excitement in his job as a deputy, they lend depth and complexity to what otherwise might be a simple and hackneyed story. *Run for Cover* transcends its origins as a fairly formular tale of a stranger bringing law and order to a corrupt and violent township, to paint a soph-isticated portrait of two potentially alienated individuals striving to benefit, in entirely opposite ways, from their relationship with each other. Davey, as played by John Derek, exhibits all the confusion of inflamed and embittered youth that one has come to expect in Ray's films; but Matt, played by a James Cagney fruitfully cast against type, is one of Ray's most positive characters, never sentimentalised but endowed, despite his need to draw private strength from what is a profoundly ambiguous desire to help Davey, with enormous dignity. And as if shaped by Matt's mature acceptance of life's injustices, the entire film is paced and shot in such a way as to achieve a convincing final serenity: the gentle natural tones of landscape, the relaxed spontaneity and respectful tenderness of the scenes featuring Matt and Helga, and Ray's uncluttered compositions – all lend the film an unusually mellow atmosphere which, while lacking the anguished intensity of the director's finest work, certainly exudes a charm and mood of quiet resignation all its own.

High Green Wall (1954)

SYNOPSIS: Henty – sole survivor of an American expedition – stumbles ill and exhausted into a clearing in the Amazon jungle. He is taken into care by McMaster, an Indo-American who has spent his entire life there and who treats the local Indians as his servants. When, after four days, Henty awakens, he learns that his host – who is unable to read – adores the works of Charles Dickens; these he gratefully agrees to read aloud to McMaster until he is fully recovered. But time passes, and he not only discovers that a previous reader died before he could leave the settlement, but also becomes suspicious that McMaster intends to prevent his return to civilisation. Refused the use of a boat, the desperate Henty secretly gives a message about his plight – in the form of a page ripped from a volume of Dickens – to Aubert, a French prospector who passes through the settlement; but when McMaster learns of the imminent arrival of two men looking for Henty, he has the American drugged during a night of Indian celebrations, and tells the search party that his guest died of jungle fever, deliriously believing that he was a character from Dickens. By the time Henty regains consciousness, his potential saviours have departed, and so, resigned to the fact that in the eyes of the outside world he is no longer alive, he returns, at McMaster's command, to his reading from Dickens.

In 1945, two years before *They Live by Night*, Ray had directed for television a version of Lucille Fletcher's radio play *Sorry Wrong Number*, starring Mildred Natwick. (Sadly, since parts of the transmission were live, no prints of the programme survive.) Produced and co-scripted by John Houseman, the half-hour thriller had been a critical success, and so it was perhaps not surprising when in 1954 Ray responded favourably to an invitation, from MCA TV's Jennings Lang, to direct a programme for the company's 'GE (General Electric) Theatre' series, apparently on condition that he could use a crew and actors who had never before worked in the still relatively new medium.

To all intents and purposes, this condition was met – his cameraman was Hollywood's acclaimed Franz Planer, his lead actors Joseph Cotten and Thomas Gomez. Even more crucially for the success of the film, the material (an adaptation of Evelyn Waugh's 1933 short story 'The Man Who Liked Dickens', which the following year Waugh integrated into his novel *A Handful of Dust*) seems, in retrospect, to have been unusually well suited to Ray's own preoccupations and sensibility. Indeed, if proof be needed that at this time (also to be looked back on as a Golden Age of American television drama) the director was at the peak of his powers, one need only examine his handling, in *High Green Wall*, of what was to him an unfamiliar medium with restricted technical resources. Shot (on 35mm) in three or four days, after a week of rehearsals, the film never quite transcends its lowly budget; its single jungle-clearing setting now looks all too obviously like the product of studio artifice. But within these constraints, Ray made full, expert and expressive use of the tools at his command, so that the film – though only half-an-hour long and having only two main speaking parts – is rich in both resonance and detail, constituting yet another stage in Ray's development as an artist.

The opening shot even anticipates that of Ray's next film, *Rebel Without a Cause*, with Henty staggering weakly into frame out of the depths of the jungle, in much the same way that James Dean's Jim Stark will collapse drunkenly into the gutter of a dark street in a concrete jungle. Immediately, Ray cuts to McMaster, lazing regally in his hammock surrounded by Indians, a rifle cradled in his arms. McMaster then approaches his unexpected visitor with gun at the ready. The economy of the two central characters' first exchange of words ('Anderson died … My name is Henty'; 'You're very ill, my friend') is not only dramatically forceful, but suggestive of what will follow: Henty's struggle to retain a sense of identity in the face of death, and McMaster's sinister pretensions to friendship with Henty, which have as their aim the controlling of his 'guest' through references to his vulnerability.

After this introductory prologue, the first scene proper, in McMaster's cabin, enriches these twin theses by supplying further details about each man's life and by introducing a number of motifs and sumbols that will recur throughout the film. When Henty awakens after what turns out to be four days asleep to find McMaster smiling genially over him, he at once puts his ear to his wristwatch and exclaims in surprise: 'Still running; but I've lost track of time.' When the appropriately named McMaster admits that he took the liberty of re-setting the watch each morning during his guest's convalescence, one may be forgiven for surmising that the watch symbolises a bond of friendship between the pair (as it did, in part, for Bowie and Keechie in *They Live by Night*), but such an idea is merely what McMaster wants to implant in Henty's mind; in reality, it is the slow passing of time in McMaster's jungle dominion that will actually threaten Henty's sense of identity, and in controlling time, McMaster will manage to control the American.

Indeed, the fact that the latter has lost track of time suggests that, like so many Ray protagonists, he is somehow already 'out of time'; certainly, as he presently confesses to his host, 'I was fed up with the jungle of the civilised world, so I thought I'd explore the real jungle.' Like Ed Avery in *Bigger than Life*, James Leith in *Bitter Victory* and Walt Murdoch in *Wind Across the Everglades*, Henty has been driven by a sense of personal failure (here, it transpires, with regard to his wife) to feel completely disenchanted by and alienated from Western 'civilisation'; McMaster, by contrast, who was born in the jungle, the son of an American missionary and his Indian wife, feels entirely at home in the settlement he has made his kingdom, and which he has never left. Some of the natives are McMaster's relatives, and all of them consider themselves his 'children' – that is why they obey him and, of course, his rifle. McMaster, in fact, prefigures Cottonmouth in *Wind Across the Everglades*, lording it over his surrogate family in a primeval wilderness through a combination of threatened violence and paternalistic, seemingly benevolent tyranny; and like the Everglades, the jungle is at once lethal and fertile, beautiful and horrific, providing, as McMaster tells his patient somewhat ominously, medicines 'for everything: medicine to make you well, to make you ill; plants to

Trading places: McMaster (Thomas Gomez) and Henty (Joseph Cotten) engage in a power struggle in the jungle.

cure you or make you mad'. In fleeing 'civilisation', Henty has clearly leapt from the frying pan into the fire.

McMaster, when told by Henty why he joined the expedition, replies that perhaps it was God's will that brought him to the jungle; in evoking destiny (a theme that will recur when it is later implied that the American is following in the footsteps of Barnabas, the Venezuelan 'guest' who used to read for McMaster until he died), McMaster contrives to turn the conversation to the subject of his beloved Charles Dickens, who, he tells Henty, believed in God. Explaining that he himself cannot read – as a child, he refused to allow his father to teach him, preferring instead to be read to aloud – McMaster climbs a stepladder to fetch down his complete set of Dickens, from which position he subtly begins to dominate Henty by appealing to his gratitude; he lures him ('Do you like to read aloud, Mr Henty?') into offering to read for his host. At which point McMaster climbs down from the ladder, as if in humility, then, still servile, makes Henty comfortable in his own hammock, before seating himself on the verandah floor. Here he listens enraptured as the American begins to read aloud the opening words of *A Tale of Two Cities*: 'It was the best of times, it was the worst of times. It was the age of wisdom, it was the age of foolishness. It was the season of light, it was the season of darkness. It was the spring of hope, it was the winter of despair.' And as the image then fades on Henty's face, a beast of the jungle howls off-screen, as if forewarning us of Henty's own journey into foolishness, darkness and despair.

For Henty *is* foolish, almost stubbornly refusing to perceive and act on the signs that reveal his destiny. When he finds the grave of Barnabas, McMaster tells him that he intends to erect a cross to commemorate *both* the Venezuelan's death *and* Henty's arrival; but instead of taking issue with his being linked to the dead man and determining to make his escape, Henty merely looks down, puzzled, at his watch (memento, for him, of his having been saved by McMaster) and then goes back to reading from *Oliver Twist*. Even before he starts this, his perilous predicament is further illuminated not only by McMaster's flattering remark, 'You read beautifully; it's almost as if my father were here again' (evidently, he is seeking a substitute for the parent he made his servant), but also by McMaster's resumption of his place in the hammock while Henty takes a subservient position on the verandah at his host's feet. Earlier McMaster appeared to be tending to Henty's needs; that situation is now reversed, and the latter's condition is evoked by the passage he reads from *Oliver Twist*: 'He was alone in a strange place, and the boy had no friends to care for him. And he wished as he crept into his narrow bed that it were his coffin.'

After Henty, still more or less compliant in his bizarre imprisonment, asks McMaster's mute, inscrutable Indian 'children' to build him a boat, he readily acquiesces when McMaster, once more making use of time, tells him he cannot possibly leave until the rainy season begins. Simultaneously, in being made to wait for his hoped-for departure, Henty begins to realise the worth of all that he left behind him; it is, somewhat ironically, Dickens's writing which finally reveals to him that 'our civilised world *does* produce some wonderful things', and that he now feels strong enough to face his wife once more. Too late, however; even when the rains start, and Henty runs ecstatically into the night, McMaster claims that Indian superstition forbids the building of boats during the wet season. Belatedly, Henty sees his plight and complains to his keeper that he is being held against his will, to which McMaster replies, with more than a little justification, that he is free to go. Then, in a shot taken through the imprisoning gauze of the cabin door, Henty objects that he can only leave with McMaster's help, to which the latter responds that Henty had best do whatever he asks, and leaves. The American, irate at his own impotence, hurls a book after him, at the door, and so tears the gauze – a futile gesture, since he is kept there less by McMaster's rifle than by his own lack of courage and determination.

Despair sets in; since Henty refuses to read, he is refused food by McMaster. Inevitably, Henty relents; he starts reading, 'And I have been seized with great violence and indignity, and brought a great journey on foot; now held here against my will, I suffer beyond hope.' After McMaster orders an Indian to bring him food, he continues, 'For the love of heaven, of justice, of generosity, I supplicate you to succour and release me from this prison of horror, where I find every hour nearer to destruction', before hearing, as if by divine intervention, an answer to his prayer: a stranger's voice outside the cabin. It is Aubert, a Frenchman who remembers, from a visit to McMaster nine years previously, a Venezuelan who 'always had a book in his hand, too'. Again, Henty is likened to the dead man, and when McMaster advises Aubert that he should move on as soon as he has eaten, Henty says he will go, too. But McMaster insists he is not well enough to leave ('If you left now, you'd never survive'), and so Henty, too timid to resist this veiled threat, tears out the page of Dickens he was reading ('release me from this prison of horror'), and presses it into Aubert's hand, away from McMaster's prying eyes.

Now, for Henty, comes a brief spring of hope, and McMaster's suspicions are aroused not only by his more cheerful rendition of passages from *David Copperfield*, but also by news brought by one of the Indians that men will soon arrive, looking for his 'guest'. Cunningly, McMaster keeps the news from Henty, announcing instead that they are to attend, that night, a tribal celebration, which the American gullibly welcomes as a break from routine. Given Henty's suspicions about McMaster, his reaction is surely foolish: as he sits watching an Indian woman perform an exotically erotic dance (not altogether dissimilar from that danced by Vicki Gaye in the later *Party Girl*) in a strangely seductive but sinister gathering that prefigures Cottonmouth's drunken manipulation of Murdoch in *Wind Across the Everglades*, he should perhaps expect the drink McMaster offers him to be drugged. He accepts it, however, and claiming that he now knows how to cope with the civilised world, and (like Murdoch) weakening to the point where he admits, 'In an odd way, I shall always think very fondly of this place, at least of the way I feel right this moment: good and drowsy and at peace', he gives in to oblivious sleep. Then, after McMaster removes his watch, he is carried off by the Indians into the enveloping darkness, as a cackling bird proffers cruel and ironic comment on his dreams of release and somnolent claims to nostalgic, blissful well-being.

When the two strangers arrive at the camp, the man they seek is nowhere to be seen, and McMaster, with sadness in his voice, tells them that he died of jungle fever, often believing himself a character out of Dickens (this explains the page given them by Aubert). Then, to forestall the men's doubts as to his honesty, McMaster shows them the cross on Barnabas's grave, saying he dug it for Henty, and gives them, as further evidence, Henty's watch to take to his widow. Again he has re-wound it daily, but while the men accept this as a symbol of his fond memories of the dead Henty, in reality he is merely using time once more to manipulate and control others (interestingly, his duplicitous deployment of the watch for emotional blackmail foreshadows similar strategies used by Farrell in *Party Girl*). No wonder, then, that when (to our surprise) Henty emerges dazed from a hut, only to learn that men came looking for him but have already left thinking him dead, McMaster contemptuously describes them as having been 'very easily pleased'. Though products of an apparently sophisticated civilisation, they – like Henty before them – were too gullible to see through the illiterate McMaster's clever performance, and one cannot but sense that here, as in the later *Wind Across the Everglades* and *The Savage Innocents*, Ray felt considerably more sympathy for the native cunning of the 'primitive' world than for the feckless self-pity and easily flattered vanity of modern Western society.

Henty's hopes of rescue are shattered (though, of course, were he made of sterner stuff, he could still try to brave the jungle and his keeper's gun). He wanders defeated back to the cabin where his despairing face is shown in close-up from behind the gauze on the door, while McMaster's voice is heard off-screen, offering him a day without Dickens but promising that he shall read 'tomorrow, and the day after that, and the day after that, and the day after that. And then we'll begin *A Tale of Two Cities* again. There are certain passages in that book I can never hear without the temptation to weep.' Then, as the camera cranes up and back from Henty's face to an overview of the settlement, full of Indians going about their daily work, and with the sound of a pig squealing in the background, the American's voice is heard again, reciting the opening lines of *A Tale of Two Cities* in a dead, flat, echoing tone of voice. As the passage moves towards the words 'It was the winter of despair', Henty's blank face is superimposed over the long shot of the Indians, and gives way in turn, with the sound of thunder, to shots of a storm blowing up in the forest, and a falling tree hit by lightning. The high green wall that divides McMaster's domain from the outside world *can* be toppled, but for Henty, so deep in his despair that he has lost both his sense of identity and his will to live, it is too late.

Not only does *High Green Wall* show Ray working through a number of his recurrent themes (master/servant and father/son relationships; the conflict between civilisation and 'primitive' or alienated outsiders; the effect of destiny on human actions), and making highly inventive use of composition, sound, décor and symbolism; it also remains an unusually pessimistic and powerful example of television drama at its best. For one thing, Waugh's fable is greatly enhanced by the script's precise, evocative use of specific passages from Dickens (absent in the original story) to delineate Henty's predicament and state of mind; for another, the film's narrative economy makes both for enormous dramatic and emotional intensity, and for a sense of inexorability which is entirely in keeping with the material – Henty's downfall would not occur were he not the kind of person to court such disaster. Furthermore, in casting Cotten and Gomez, Ray once again revealed his sensitivity regarding actors, with the former's rather soft, dreamy and morose passivity (already explored by Orson Welles in *Citizen Kane* and *The Magnificent Ambersons*) wholly suitable for Henty, and McMaster perfectly served by the latter's sweaty, corpulent, unsettlingly polite blend of joviality, pompousness and menace. If one can forgive the somewhat wooden Indian extras and the less than extravagant studio sets, *High Green Wall* not only contributes to our greater understanding of Ray's artistry, but stands out as a superb example of short-film-making, the like of which is these days all too rarely seen.

Rebel Without a Cause (1955)

SYNOPSIS: Late at night, three adolescents are hauled, separately, into the juvenile department of a police precinct station: Judy, mistaken for a streetwalker while wandering around town, is convinced that her father hates her; Plato was found shooting puppies in despair after his absent, divorced parents forgot his birthday; and Jim Stark, new in town, depressed by his parents' frequent arguments, and confused about what it takes to become a man, was found drunk in the gutter. The next afternoon the three strangers (all pupils at Dawson High) go on a school trip to the planetarium, where Jim befriends Plato before being provoked to a knife fight with Buzz, who is Judy's boyfriend and leader of a teenage gang. The fight deemed inconclusive, Buzz challenges Jim to a 'chickee run', to be held that evening on a nearby coastal promontory. As the pair drive their cars towards the cliff-edge, watched by the gang, Jim jumps out to safety, but Buzz catches his sleeve on the car door handle and plunges to his death. Jim comforts Judy and drives her home, before arguing with his parents, who advise him not to confess to his role in the incident. He goes, nonetheless, to the police station, where, however, no one is prepared to hear his story. He collects Judy to take her to hide from the gang (who think he has informed on them) in a remote, dilapidated mansion often visited by Plato. The latter, having been beaten up by the gang, presently arrives to warn Jim that the youths are looking for him. When the gang turns up at the hideaway, a terrified Plato shoots one of them, before making his escape to the planetarium, pursued by the police. Hoping to avoid further bloodshed, Jim follows Plato, tricks him into allowing him to remove the bullets from the gun, and persuades the police not to fire as they leave the building. In a moment of confusion, Plato is shot, but his death reconciles Jim with his own anxious parents, to whom he introduces his new friend Judy.

Partly because it was Ray's most commercially successful movie, partly because of the cult surrounding the late James Dean, more has been written about *Rebel Without a Cause* than about any other Ray film. Even now, it is popular amongst teenagers, not only because Dean has become something of a legend but because its sympathetic treatment of adolescent anguish remains both attractive and relevant.

The director himself considered it the finest of his films, and spoke enthusiastically of its making. The story and characters were essentially his own (despite the many writers – Leon Uris, Irving Shulman, Stewart Stern, Clifford Odets – who contributed to the script); David Weisbart proved to be a helpful producer; and in Dean, Ray encountered not only a highly talented young actor (whose gifts had hitherto been properly explored only in Elia Kazan's then unreleased *East of Eden*) but a willing and able collaborator whom Ray saw, to some extent, as his *alter ego*. Furthermore, Warner Bros. were so pleased with his early rushes that the film, originally intended to be shot in black and white, was made in colour and CinemaScope – the wide-screen process for which Ray, with the interest in horizontal lines he inherited from Frank Lloyd Wright, came to hold a special affection. Indeed, the film was a career landmark in several respects: even more so than in *Johnny Guitar*, Ray's use of stylised composition and gesture seemed to take him closer towards the non-naturalistic forms of the musical; his casting of young, often unknown actors, who besides Dean included Dennis Hopper, Nick Adams, Corey Allen, Sal Mineo and Natalie Wood (who had until then appeared only in child roles), was his most adventurous to date; while his fondness for complex, unusual narrative structures was given free rein.

On the one hand, the film, partly inspired by *Romeo and Juliet*, adopts the temporal and geographical unities of classical tragedy, since it is set in a handful of locations over a period of little more than twenty-four hours; on the other hand, however, despite its frequently melodramatic plot, it exists as a partly improvised sociological study of American middle-class youth, complete with a schematically balanced cross-section of leading characters. In fact, Ray based his potentially controversial story – originally entitled *The Blind Run*, and softened somewhat (for reasons of censorship) for the finished film – on research he had carried out at juvenile detention centres into contemporary delinquency. His desire to make a fiction film, however, was such that the finished movie bears no resemblance what-soever to the book that gave it its final title, a case history about a working-class delin-quent written by psychiatrist Robert M. Lindner; Ray felt he had already dealt with such people in *Knock On Any Door*, and was reluctant to repeat himself. None the less, despite the fresh approach, the film remains characteristically 'Ray', and it is in that light, rather than as an example of Dean's brilliant if short-lived genius, that it will be examined here.

After the opening credits, in which Jim falls drunkenly into a gutter and plays with a toy monkey (a symbol of his fundamental innocence and immaturity, and one of the film's many allusions to animals), Ray cuts to the precinct station. Here, a virtuoso scene takes place which cleverly introduces the three principal characters, at the same time as suggesting, concisely, the reasons for their 'anti-social' behaviour – typically for Ray, this derives from a lack of love and understanding in the family.

As Jim is brought into the building, Ray also shows, in passing, Judy and Plato (the use of the extra width of the 'Scope format is masterly even in this first scene), and deploys the office's glass partitions to create frames within a frame, simultaneously to separate the three strangers from one another *and* to connect them. Each of them, when interrogated (Judy and Jim by a sympathetic officer named, suggestively, Ray), explains his or her various problems: Judy's father, resisting her new maturity, calls her 'a dirty tramp' when she dresses up and puts on lipstick; Plato's parents simply ignore him, leav-ing him with a kindly but ultimately powerless black nanny; and Jim's parents – who come from a party to collect him, stiffly garbed in formal dinner-wear – bicker all the time, his mother too concerned with keeping up an appearance of respectability, his father too weak to give Jim the guidance he expects. The boy's expectations are an aspect of his immaturity, and his violent expression of his needs is ultimately self-destructive: after screaming at his parents, 'You're tearing me apart', he is taken into Ray's office where he attacks the man himself, and then pummels a desk with so much crazed energy that he ends up in tears. Jim's anguish arises from his naïve confusion about what it means to be a man: he has frequently 'messed up' other boys who have called him 'chicken' – thus prompting his parents to move from town to town – and he feels contempt for his father because he will not dominate his mother. Jim is basically peaceful, but ashamed to be thought a coward, and it is only at the end of the film, when he does his utmost to avert violence, rather than give way to it, that he finally, through an acceptance of both himself and his parents, becomes adult.

The morning after this interrogation at the police station, when Jim leaves home for his first day at Dawson High (his dad advising him to be careful when choosing his pals and not to let them choose him), he sees Judy, whom he recognises from the Juvenile Hall, and tries to make conversation with her, in one of Ray's now familiar courtship dialogues:

JIM: I know where it was.
JUDY: Where what was?
JIM: Where I first saw you. Everything okay now? You live here, don't you?
JUDY: Who lives?
JIM: Hey, where's Dawson High?
JUDY: At University and 10th.
JIM: Mmm. Thanks.
JUDY: You wanna carry my books?
JIM: I got my car. You wanna go with me?
JUDY: I go with the kids.
JIM: Yeah. I bet.
(*The gang's car screeches around the corner*)
JIM: All right.
JUDY: You know, I bet you're a real yo-yo.
JIM: I love you too.

Though simple, this blend of duel and duet evokes not only the pair's hesitant attraction towards one another (although Judy is stand-offish, she never tells him to go away), but also their awkward predicament, trapped between childhood (carrying books) and adulthood (cars), between solitude ('who lives?') and peer-group pressure (going with the kids). Indeed, for all their need to belong, Jim, Judy and Plato seem to feel most at home when far from the madding crowd; each is a creature of the night, and it is no accident that their happiest moments will be when they are alone, together, as a new, chosen, surrogate family in Plato's run-down, almost Gothic mansion.

That Plato (who, as played by the dark, boyish Sal Mineo, is visually reminiscent of Farley Granger's Bowie and John Derek's Nick Romano and Davey Bishop) has retreated into a fantasy world is apparent when he opens his school locker to reveal a fan photo of Alan Ladd; that he views Jim as a potential hero, saviour and father figure, from the way he stares at Jim's reflection in a mirror mounted next to the pin-up. At the planetarium, therefore, he deliberately sits behind Jim, who in turn is happy to find that he is seated behind Judy, Buzz and the gang; as the lecturer points out the constellation Taurus, Jim moos in the hope that his joke will endear him to the group, who respond by calling *him* 'Moo' and betting that he fights cows. This animal symbolism prefigures the knife fight outside, which Ray shoots in a highly artificial, choreographed style evocative of a bullfight; likewise, an omen of the future is given as the planetarium show depicts the cosmos exploding in a cloud of red gas, which foreshadows the explosion of Buzz's car as it plunges over the cliff, and which so disturbs the doomed Plato that he hides, terrified, on the floor behind Jim's seat. The effect of the sequence is both to chasten the hitherto indifferent, disrespectful pupils, and to warn them, and us, that life is cruel: as the lecturer opines that, 'The earth will not be missed', and that, 'Man himself seems an episode of little consequence', we are not only forewarned of the characters' less than wholly traumatised reactions to the deaths of Buzz and Plato, but shown exactly what it is – the injustice, the transience and the ultimate solitude of existence – that Ray's characters are vainly rebelling against.

From the disquieting darkness, the artificial night, of the planetarium, Jim and Plato emerge into the bright, harsh sunlight of the afternoon, there to face the hostility of the gang. Like Johnny Guitar, Jim is reluctant to involve himself in violence, and only after Buzz has slashed his car tyres, called him 'chicken' and tauntingly tossed a flick knife at his feet does he enter into physical conflict. Though shot with considerable and stylish bravura – with Ray using a variety of close-ups, medium-shots and distant overhead shots, and exploiting to the full a real feeling for tension and the quasi-ritualistic nature of the action – the fight itself is of little dramatic significance other than to reveal various loyalties (Plato attempts to defend Jim with a chain, while Judy remains steadfastly with the gang) and to pave the way for Jim's next scenes with his father.

In the first of these he arrives home to find his dad kneeling on the upstairs landing, looking ludicrous in a frilly apron as he clears up the food he has dropped while taking a meal to his wife, who is in bed with a headache; patriarchal in his conception of what constitutes masculinity, Jim feels ashamed of and for his father, just as, in a brief cutaway scene, Judy is humiliated when her father chastises and slaps her for kissing him at the meal-table (he is embarrassed because she is too old). More crucially, in the second scene with his father, Jim – thinking of the 'chickee run' that lies before him – asks him whether a man should risk his life over a question of honour. The answer, evasive and typically tidy (his father proposes making a list of pros and cons), is at once sensible, caring and exactly what Jim, who wants to grow up immediately, does not want to hear. As a result, he puts on a bright red jacket that he will wear for the rest of the film – a symbol of his urgent rebellion against the comfortable, conservative greys and creams that decorate his parents' home – and storms downstairs and out into the night.

The precipitous cliffs at Millertown Bluff – venue for the 'chickee run', in which the first driver to leap from his car as it hurtles towards the edge is deemed 'chicken' – are the perfect location for Jim's moral and psychological vertigo as he teeters on the brink of manhood: will he survive the experience in one piece, or plunge into an abyss of genuine delinquency? Using all the tools at his command, Ray heightens the ritualistic mood of the scene to convey a wealth of meanings. Jim's red jacket not only establishes a link with Judy, who wore a red coat while at Juvenile Hall, but differentiates him from Buzz; where Jim wears red and drives in a black car, his rival wears black and is first seen in a

car with red seats. They are like opposite sides of the same coin, and it is hardly surprising, therefore, when Buzz tells Jim that he likes him. 'So why do we do this?' asks
Jim, to which comes the reply, 'You gotta do something, don't you?'

Where Buzz's response to adolescent confusion is to indulge in any form of action,
however (self-)destructive, Plato – who, ironically, will prove to be the most dangerous
member of this lost generation – dreams of family and friendship, fantasising to Judy that
Jim, who he claims is really called James or Jamie, is his best friend, and pointing out the
importance of sincerity. And it is finally the three characters who value sincerity (Jim, Judy
and Plato) who will be led by Buzz's death to divorce themselves from the tribal ethos of
their peers. As Buzz and Jim rub dirt on their hands and Judy instructs the gang/specta-
tors to line up the cars on both sides of the driveway and shine their headlights on to Jim
and Buzz, the staging of the 'chickee run' becomes almost theatrical, its ritualistic trappings serving to make the danger of the 'game' somehow unreal. But Buzz does die, and
whereas the gang leaves to nurse its desire for revenge against the one they – quite unrea-
sonably – hold responsible for their leader's death, Jim, Judy and Plato are united, at last,
by their shocked sense of loss. In confronting their emotions and forgetting about the
demands of the gang – which, like the adults, cherishes its own brand of conformism –
Jim and Judy, at least, are offered the opportunity of becoming fully responsible adults.

The trio's reaction to Buzz's death is to become a surrogate family: as they stand alone
looking over the edge of the cliff, Jim extends his hand to Judy, and Plato stands in the
background between them. Almost immediately they begin acknowledging their affinity
to, their connections with, each other: when Jim drives Judy home, he gives back her
compact-case, which he found at Juvenile Hall, and which he kissed before beginning
the 'chickee run'; and when Plato leaves Jim to go home, he confesses, 'If only you
coulda been my dad.' First, however, before they can attempt to begin a new life
together, Jim must try to come to terms with the part he has played in Buzz's death. At
home, he discovers his father asleep (in other words, morally complacent), and settles
down on the couch before being roused (in a remarkable shot that makes a 180-degree
vertical turn to show, subjectively, his point of view) by his mother coming downstairs.
Speaking openly about Buzz's death, Jim asks his father to confirm that he should go to
the police, but his parents advise him to keep silent and not to get involved. Jim, however, is determined to be honest, if only with himself, and after a lengthy quarrel on the
stairs – a recurring location for indecision and crisis in Ray's films – be drags his father
to his feet and is only prevented from strangling him by his mother. As he storms from
the house, he kicks a hole in a painting that lies on the floor – an action that symbolises
his contempt for his parents' useless, perfunctory pretensions to respectability.

After being noticed by the vengeful gang on the steps of the police station, where the
desk sergeant is too busy to listen to him, Jim finds Judy, who apologises for her earlier
treatment of him and tells him not to believe what she says when she is with the rest of
the kids. To get away from the 'zoos' that are their homes, they go to hide in the mansion
Plato pointed out to Jim from the planetarium. Plato, meanwhile – having been beaten
up by the gang (who find Jim's address on him and go on to hang a live chicken above
Jim's parents' door), and finding a cheque in his room from his father, bluntly inscribed

Domestic violence: Jim (James Dean) tries to get a rise out of dad (Jim Backus) while mom (Ann Doran) watches in horror.

'For support of son' – has reached the end of his tether; armed with the revolver he keeps under his pillow, he joins Jim and Judy at their hideaway. As the gang and the various parents search for the trio, Jim, Judy and Plato find brief peace in make-believe imitations of the adult world: Jim and Judy, who soon confess their love for each other, pretend to be newlyweds, and Plato alternates between playing the part of a real-estate agent selling them the property, and falling asleep like a baby while Judy sings a lullaby. Removed from the compromises of the real world, they are able to live out an idealised version of family life; crucially for Jim, Judy confides that she wants her lover to be brave, strong and *gentle*. His more peaceful instincts thus having met with approval, he no longer feels it necessary to equate masculinity with violent rebellion; when, later, Plato flees to the planetarium after shooting in panic one of the gang (on a staircase!), Jim adopts a protective rather than an aggressive role and does everything to prevent violence, even though Plato – feeling betrayed by Jim, just as Jim feels betrayed by *his* father – accuses Jim of leaving him alone to the mercy of the gang and screams, 'You're not my father!'

It is certainly not Jim's intention to betray Plato; he does so, unwittingly, when in the planetarium he tricks the boy, with a sincere reassurance of his friendship, to give himself the chance to remove the bullets from Plato's gun. The act is as foolhardy as Wilson's unloading of Brent's rifle in *On Dangerous Ground*: if Jim had simply taken the gun away from Plato, he might have lost his love and respect, but the police would not have seen the boy's gun as he emerged from the planetarium, and so would not have shot him. In thus killing Plato with kindness – he even gives the boy his red jacket before they leave the building, just as he offered him another jacket at Juvenile Hall before they had prop-

erly met – Jim is put in virtually the same position as his own father, who, seeing Plato
die in Jim's jacket, initially believes that he has lost his son, and so is himself required
to confront his own misguided if well-meaning attempts to look after Jim. Forced, therefore, to face the almost insurmountable problems involved in taking responsibility for
another human being, both Jim and his father come, belatedly, to an understanding of
one another: as Jim kneels, hysterical, over Plato's body, his father says to him, in a reversal of his earlier scenes at home with the boy, 'Stand up, and I'll stand up with you.' A
fruitful balance has been achieved, Jim now knows what it means to be a man, and he
and Judy are accepted by his parents. But Ray, who himself makes an enigmatic, mute
appearance beneath the closing credits, walking towards the planetarium at dawn as
everybody leaves, is all too aware of the great human cost of the enlightenment and reconciliation of father and son; he cuts from Jim's smiling parents to show, in the film's
final close-up, the tears pouring down the face of Plato's distraught nanny.

Just before Jim persuades Plato to leave the observatory, promising to 'fix' things with
the cops, he sets the planetarium show going, and Plato asks him if the end of the world
will come at night. Jim replies, 'Uh-uh. At dawn.' It is as if he has been visited by an
omen of Plato's tragic destiny. But the exchange also calls to mind their earlier visit to
the building and the lecturer's comments on the transience of human life. Plato's death,
then, may be seen as symbolic, emblematic of all needless human suffering. Without
love, without someone to take proper responsibility for us, Ray seems to be saying, we
are all doomed to lives of loneliness and confusion. Jim was lucky; it could easily have
been him, rather than Buzz and Plato, who died during this long night of the soul.

Ray's direction in *Rebel Without a Cause* is at its most polished, above all in the way
it integrates symbols and metaphor into the plot without ever disrupting the narrative
flow. The extraordinary dynamism of many of the scenes arises both from the physical
intensity of Dean's extremely tactile performance (before punching Ray's desk, he
caresses it; even his drinking from a bottle of milk seems to evoke his internal turmoil),
and from the way Ray precedes every moment of violence with a period of unnerving
stillness. There is a flexibility in the editing – ranging from long, complex takes to fast,
fragmented montages – that is particularly rare in films shot in CinemaScope (which tend
to avoid quick cutting), and his compositions, often lit with an almost theatrical
Expressionism, extract every ounce of mood and meaning from the wide frame. The performances, too, are successful examples of his willingness to cast against type, nowhere
more so than in the case of Jim Backus – otherwise best known as the voice of the car-
toon character Mr Magoo – who brings wit and pathos to the role of Jim's kindly but
ineffectual father. If the film is flawed (its treatment of Jim's mother verges on misogyny,
the last scene is rather hasty, not to say contrived, and various points are made with an
explicitness rare in Ray), its emotional punch is none the less powerful, thanks to the
richness of detail in both script and direction and to the evident commitment to the project of all involved. Few films have examined the confusions of an entire generation with
such fervour or insight; it is by far the best film of Hollywood's rebellious-teens genre
which, with *The Wild One* and *The Blackboard Jungle*, it established, and it remains for
many *the* American movie of the 1950s.

Hot Blood (1956)

SYNOPSIS: When Marco Torino, king of an urban gypsy tribe, learns that he is seriously ill, he decides that his younger brother Stephano must succeed him at once. He plans Stephano's marriage to Annie Caldash, daughter of a Chicago gypsy family, and sabotages his brother's plans to become a dance teacher by implying to Swift, head of the dance school, that Stephano is a thief. At this point, however, he is informed by Stephano (who has partly forsaken gypsy life for the ways of *gajo* – non-gypsy – America) that he has no intention of marrying or becoming king. Annie then tricks Stephano into going through with the ceremony, reneging on her promise to turn him down, and confounding her family's plans to swindle Marco out of a wedding gift of $2,000. Cheated, Stephano leaves Annie for *gajo* dancing partner Velma, but when he learns that Swift will not employ him, he throws the man through a window and is arrested. Secretly, Marco pays his brother's bail and tells Annie of his own illness; she, meanwhile, plans to make Stephano love her before she in turn deserts him, and accordingly gets him drunk. After another argument with Marco, Stephano goes on tour with Velma, but their act is a flop and he returns home, only to find Annie, whom he has come to miss, dancing with Marco. He hears gossip that she may be pregnant, and jealously visits his brother, beating him in a fight, but, after discovering papers in which Marco's illness is revealed, he seeks out Annie, who demands a divorce. At a tribal council hearing, Stephano, appointed judge by Marco and admitting his errors, agrees to Annie's request that their marriage be annulled. She leaves with her family, Stephano tells Marco to set out for the gypsies' promised land and Marco, in turn, persuades Stephano to act like a *gajo* and follow Annie. The couple are reunited, and Stephano consents to be made king.

As early as 1951, Ray had worked with the writer Walter Newman on a first draft of a script about urban gypsies, based on research carried out by Ray's first wife, journalist Jean Evans. The project, then entitled *No Return,* had been cancelled by RKO, even though Jane Russell had shown an interest in playing the lead. Nevertheless, Ray – whose interest in ethnic minorities, folklore and outcasts made him unusually suitable for the project – never entirely abandoned the script, and some years later Columbia agreed to make the film, which now went under the title of *Tambourine*.

The production was fraught with problems, however: the studio insisted that the script be rewritten (Ray collaborating with Jesse Lasky Jr.), and shooting commenced before the new draft was polished to Ray's satisfaction. He himself was barely given time to recover from making *Rebel Without a Cause*; Russell was tired after her work on *Gentlemen Prefer Blondes*; leading man Cornel Wilde's relationship with Ray proved less than cordial; and producer Harry Tatelman was somewhat inexperienced. Moreover, in the heat of the moment, Ray – forced to make the film before he felt ready – chose to adapt his material, which he had hitherto valued for its authentic depiction of contemporary gypsy life, to the style of a musical. The result, though far from an artistic disaster, was nonetheless not as well executed as one might have hoped. The director himself did not even stay to edit it; the day after filming ended, he left for Europe to oversee the release of *Rebel* and to think further about *Heroic Love*, one of several projects he envisaged making with James Dean. As a drama, *Hot Blood* – as Columbia retitled it – appears to lack the intense emotional commitment Ray brought to most of his films, and large parts of it seem underwritten and almost arbitrary in their relation to the whole. That said, it nevertheless features sequences of terrific *brio*, with colour, décor, music and joyous movement all adding up to a lively and vivid account of gypsy life.

It is easy to see why Ray was attracted to a film in which he could portray the customs and experiences of a gypsy minority living in a contemporary American city: like the rodeo community in *The Lusty Men* and the Eskimos in *The Savage Innocents*, the gypsies are both wanderers and outcasts who adhere to traditional tribal rituals and who are viewed with suspicion by 'respectable' *gajo* society. Throughout the film, Ray's sympathy remains firmly with the gypsies: while their customs (notably their attitude to marriage, with male infidelity condoned, its female counterpart frowned upon) may appear strange, unreasonable, even reactionary, they are always treated with respect, so that even their faith in magic never becomes the object of condescension or knowing humour (though the film does include moments of deliciously wry comedy). Rather, the gypsies are seen as victims of social injustice; when the Caldash family are jailed en route from Chicago, Marco points out that gypsies are always being arrested precisely because they *are* gypsies. At the same time, however, Ray never glamorises them; instead, avoiding stereotypical generalisations, he simply acknowledges that like any other group of individuals, they range from good to bad: while Marco is a man of honour and integrity, Annie's father and brother plan to take his money and run, as soon as the wedding is over.

What Ray seems to have admired most about gypsy life, besides its thriving traditions, is its sense of community and its *joie de vivre*, superbly evoked in the vibrant scenes featuring ensemble dancing and action. And it is this fecund community that Stephano longs to escape, in order to join a more stolidly WASP, conventionally 'American' society where dance is something taught in academies and regarded as commercial entertainment (when he is on tour with Velma, he sells himself short by appearing under the name of 'Gypsy Steve'), rather than indulged in spontaneously and naturally by all and sundry.

Like most Ray heroes, Stephano is a romantic (he rejects Marco's advice that 'a gypsy marriage is nothing to do with love; that comes later', and will not marry a stranger for money), torn between the 'family' to which he belongs – through blood, history and temperament – and the *gajo* world he aspires to (not only for its riches and respectability but because he is wary of the bonds and responsibilities that go with being part of the gypsy tribe; he objects to their 'deep laws'). He is, then, an outsider on two counts, not to mention a would-be traitor to his own kind (Marco considers Stephano 'so stubborn, he double-crosses himself'), who voices his need to become a man, independent of Marco, by denying his roots: unwittingly subscribing to *gajo* ideas about gypsies, he even accuses Marco of stealing Annie from him, and money from the family, in order to pay for his mobile home (christened with telling irony 'The Promised Land').

Stephano, eager to win independence, also denies his own desires: while he readily admits that he finds Annie beautiful, he refuses to submit to the arranged marriage, prompting her to note that, 'To turn down your brother, you turn me down.' Unsurprisingly in a Ray film, it is through a wiser, more pragmatic woman that he finds redemption and a sense of belonging. While Annie is by and large happy with the traditional customs of gypsy life, a belief in her own worth drives her to reject both the male-chauvinist double standards associated with gypsy marital practices, and the money-motivated duplicity of her father and brother: her deceit serves merely to win her man. She marries Stephano not only because she loves him, but also because she is tired of wandering, deceit and the prejudice she has suffered with her family; like Stephano, she too is to some extent a rebellious outsider, but unlike him, she recognises and accepts her true nature and destiny, never feeling impelled to pretend to be anything but herself. (It is surely not accidental that Stephano becomes a 'performer' and that Annie is a fortune-teller – which is to say, she can see her own destiny.)

The development of Stephano's relationship with Annie (and, through her, with his own tribal destiny) becomes, as in many Ray films, a matter of tested faith, of aggression turned to mutual understanding, of duel and duet. (When Stephano, back from his trip with Velma, accuses Annie of infidelity, their recriminatory dialogue is strangely reminiscent of the hesitant exchange between Vienna and Johnny in *Johnny Guitar*.) Through experience, Stephano must learn to be faithful and trusting, to recognise the existence and worth of the emotions of others; only when he discovers the truth about Marco's illness does he understand why he has been asked to take over as tribal king and why, consequently, he should abandon his *gajo* pretensions, accept himself as a gypsy, and marry Annie. (Though the film is lighter-hearted than most Ray movies, Marco's incurable illness still serves as a kind of 'sacrifice' by which Stephano achieves enlightenment.)

Where the film differs from Ray's earlier work is in the way the courtship of Stephano and Annie becomes almost *literally* duel and duet, through the use of dance and music: once tricked into marriage, Stephano punishes Annie (and expresses his desire to dominate her) by performing at the reception a 'whip dance' in which he angrily whips her too hard; later, while Annie watches him wash during a brief truce in their hostilities, her realisation that 'I could learn to love you' is expressed in musical lyrics, sung by Russell in off-screen voice-over, the lines of which are alternated with the pair's spoken conversation; later still, when Stephano suspects Annie of being unfaithful, he jealously watches her dance in a park with Marco; and their final reconciliation is celebrated by a joyous, massed dance performed by the whole tribal family.

Here dance and music are not mere interludes but exact indexes of emotion, situation and character, completely integrated into the narrative; one of the most notable scenes features a vigorous street dance in which Stephano, angry at Swift for having refused him a job, and ironically playing up to the gypsy stereotype in which the dance

A question of control: Stefano (Cornel Wilde) uses the whip dance in an attempt to teach feisty bride Annie (Jane Russell) a lesson in marital duty.

professor believes, dances to an accompaniment of bangs on cars and garbage cans, the percussive effect expressing his rage. Indeed, even the non-musical scenes are virtually choreographed: when Stephano and Marco fight each other with belts (echoing the former's earlier 'whip dance'), their actions are staged and shot in such a way that the sequence becomes, as it were, a ballet of violence. The effect of this formal artificiality is not merely decorative, but highlights the ritualistic nature of gypsy life, simultaneously lending the film an almost abstract sense of cultural tradition as well as vital, profoundly physical immediacy.

Linked, inevitably, to this expressive use of movement and music is Ray's characteristically vivid deployment of colour and décor. With their highly ornate drapes and carpets, the gypsies' rooms seem almost tent-like, symbols of the now settled people's nomadic past, while their gaudily coloured costumes not only lend an exotic, sensual vibrancy to their characters, but offer a visual correlative to their temperaments. Annie, for the most part, is clothed in whites and reds that reflect her moral purity and fierce independence (one character says she has 'fire in her feet'); even at her wedding, her white dress flies up, as she dances, to reveal a scarlet petticoat. Red, in fact, is used primarily to suggest marital warmth, passion and *unity*; at the wedding ceremony, to mark their 'love', Stephano (wearing a carnation, red cravat and sash over his white shirt) and Annie share red wine before having their wrists bound together by a red scarf and slit to mix their blood; later, in the wedding suite (where a white nuptial bed lies beneath a scarlet canopy), Stephano tosses the sash, symbolically, on to the floor as he announces his intention to abandon Annie immediately without consummating the marriage; and later still, when Annie gets her husband drunk in an effort to soften his heart, she undresses behind a translucent scarlet curtain.

Conversely, Stephano – most of the time refusing to acknowledge that unity – usually dresses in browns, blacks and oranges (Marco, in fact, makes the contrast explicit by referring to the newlyweds as like 'positive and negative', and therefore able to create electricity together); and so it is only logical that when Annie finally petitions for divorce, she comes to court dressed in an orange blouse, her adoption of a colour frequently worn by her husband signifying her agreement with him that their marriage should be annulled. Her change of mind, however, is also a form of compromise, and Stephano, no longer feeling threatened by her indomitability, and at last recognising the virtues of gypsy life, decides after all to take her as his wife; their attitudes (like their colours) clashing no more, the pair are finally united.

While this exotic visual symbolism has its roots firmly in real-life gypsy culture, the repeated colour-coding, centred on notions of harmony and contrast, is also typically 'Ray'. Equally, one may see the delirious, cluttered 'Scope compositions as proof of the director's sympathetic belief in the spiritual fecundity of gypsy culture: though social injustice is mentioned, and though the sick Marco quotes his doctor that it is unhealthy for gypsies to live in cities, Ray never *shows* the squalid poverty that is so often their lot in real life. Ethnological authenticity was merely used by Ray as the starting point for a typically personal, visually and formally extravagant hymn to the gypsies' determination to survive in an uncaring *gajo* world. Conventional dramatic naturalism is abandoned in favour of a more poetic, semi-allegorical fable about a magical, mythical people's search for a home and a sense of identity; Stephano's predicament might be seen as that of any minority caught between a desire to integrate itself into a dominant culture and the need to remain true to itself.

At the same time, this tension between artifice and historical realism is perhaps what ultimately makes the film somewhat uneven in tone and achievement. The baroque exoticism of the imagery militates against the fundamental seriousness of the film's social dynamics, while the fact that Ray never had enough time to transform it into a fully fledged dance-musical makes for occasional uninspired scenes and less than satisfactorily rounded characters; either way, one never cares as deeply about Stephano, Annie and Marco as one does about most of Ray's creations. Although the acting is for the most part impressively muscular (with Jane Russell's forthright, witty performance amply compensating for Cornel Wilde's rather wooden playing of Stephano), and while Ray June's lavish Technicolor camerawork, Les Baxter's gypsy-inspired score and Ray's superbly fluid, pacy handling of the crowd scenes provide a sensual feast for the eyes and ears, the film finally suffers from a lack of depth, and is best seen as evidence of its director's growing assurance with colour.

If all concerned in its making had given *Hot Blood* more attention, it might have been a truly great original. As it stands, it looks rather like half-completed sketches for a movie, an impression reinforced by the presence of several deeply idiosyncratic Ray touches, including a subjective shot, conveying a drunken Stephano's view of Marco as the latter enters a room, that turns 180 degrees from upside down to upright (recalling a similar shot in *Rebel Without a Cause*), and a characteristically economic indication of Stephano's arrest after he has thrown Swift through a window, in which the arrival of the police is suggested simply by the wail of sirens and a circle of light shone on to the gypsy (a 'shorthand' effect previously used in both *They Live by Night* and *Knock on Any Door*). Shots such as these are typical of Ray at his best, and give an idea of what might have been, had the circumstances of the film's making been happier. As it is, the film is a far from negligible achievement, but its main point of interest lies, perhaps, in that it gave Ray an opportunity to experiment with ever more delirious images, and thus paved the way for the non-naturalistic splendours of *Bigger than Life* and *Party Girl*.

Bigger than Life (1956)

SYNOPSIS: Teacher Ed Avery, unbeknown to his wife Lou and son Richie, moonlights several afternoons a week as switchboard operator for a cab company. Overworked, he begins suffering dizzy spells, and hospital tests reveal that he is likely to die within a year from an inflammation of the arteries, unless he begins taking a newly developed drug, cortisone. Though warned that the drug can cause severe depression, Ed agrees to the strictly regulated regime and at once starts feeling far healthier. Very soon, however, to cope with depression, he begins to exceed the prescribed dosage: as a result, his behaviour becomes increasingly unpredictable, arrogant and aggressive, particularly towards his wife, whom he now considers too stupid to understand his 'revolutionary' theories about education, and towards Richie, whom he cruelly punishes for being too lazy to pay attention to the demanding private tuition Ed gives him. Finally, Ed finds the upset boy about to throw away his medication. Inspired by a church sermon relating the story of Abraham and Isaac, he informs Lou that he intends to kill Richie (whom he now considers a thief) and that he and she should then commit suicide. As he visits his son's room, however, he is overcome by dizziness; Richie escapes, and in a fight with Wally, a fellow teacher and close friend whom Lou has summoned for help, Ed is subdued. At the hospital, where he is heavily sedated, the doctor warns Lou that Ed may have lost his mind completely, and that whatever happens, he will have to keep taking the cortisone. Fortunately, however, when he awakes, Ed is able to remember all that has occurred, and is happily reconciled with his family.

After completing *Hot Blood*, Ray made his first trip to Europe, to promote *Rebel Without a Cause*; it was there that he heard the deeply upsetting news of James Dean's fatal car crash (the pair had hoped to make several films together, notably *Heroic Love*). It was also in Europe that Ray read a *New Yorker* article by Berton Roueché, entitled 'Ten Feet Tall', about a teacher who becomes mentally disturbed after taking a course of the new 'miracle drug', cortisone. Ray – who was, apparently, indignant about the low wages paid to American teachers – was fascinated by the report and persuaded 20th Century-Fox, with whom he now had a two-film contract, to make a film on the topic. The actor James Mason, who was also intrigued by the idea of working on such a film, agreed to play the part of the teacher and to serve as producer, which he did intelligently and sympathetically. The result, based on a script by Cyril Hume and Richard Maibaum, which was then rewritten by Ray, the English critic-turned-screenwriter Gavin Lambert and Clifford Odets, was the director's last entirely happy collaboration with Hollywood, and though most critics of the time found *Bigger than Life* too melodramatic and exaggerated, the film is now widely regarded as one of his very best. Indeed, its emotional intensity – a result, partly, of the taut economy of the narrative, which runs only 95 minutes – its thematic depth and its wholly convincing analysis of the social ills of middle-class America in the 1950s are such that it may justifiably be seen as Ray's masterpiece.

With an even more all-embracing sense of disenchantment than before, Ray dissects the American Dream and finds it a nightmare. Ed Avery (certain French critics have likened his surname to the word 'average') is, according to first impressions, a completely ordinary, mild-mannered, middle-class and middle-aged teacher and family man; in a sense, he is an archetypal all-American male, and the unwary viewer might think that he becomes a monstrous, megalomaniac patriarch *only* because of the cortisone. Ray, however, did not intend the film to be about cortisone *per se*, and explained that its real subject was the danger and folly of believing in any kind of miraculous panacea, whether it be drugs, drink, money, psychoanalysis or religion. Cortisone, then, is less cause than catalyst; it simply serves to clarify, in that it brings to the surface and accentuates, what was already wrong with Ed's state of mind and, by implication, with the world he inhabits. It is, ironically, Ed's whole-hearted endorsement of the conservative middle-class values to which he aspires that, in the end, nearly leads him to commit the most anti-social act imaginable to that same middle-class world: the murder of his family.

Indeed, the film is full of such ironies: Ed's devotion to the idea of education drives him, eventually, to feel nothing but contempt for the intelligence of his pupils and to treat his son with terrifying cruelty; his growing insistence on the need to be rational and to avoid fuzzy-minded sentimentality coincides with his increasing madness; his ambitious plans for the future of civilisation transform him into a fascistic tyrant convinced of his superiority over the rest of mankind; and his disdain for the trivia of 'petty domesticity' turns him into an irresponsible wastrel obsessed with keeping up an appearance of being wealthier than he really is. In fact, although the film is, generically, a prime example of the Hollywood domestic melodrama, it bears a strong resemblance at the same time to tragedy, in that Ed suffers from *hubris*, an arrogantly deluded sense of his own worth that is also the immediate cause of his attempted destruction of himself and of those close to him. And it is Ray's rigour, in both moral and narrative terms, in demonstrating the tragic inevitability of Ed's descent into murderous dementia that makes the film so very powerful in its pessimism.

Even in the early scenes of the film, Ray reveals the facets of Ed's personality that will turn him – when they are exaggerated by the lethal blend of paranoia and overweening self-confidence catalysed by his medication – into a grotesquely mutant paradigm of middle-class conservatism. As he leaves school at the end of the day, he phones his wife to say that he will be home late due to a board meeting; explaining to the principal why he has not told Lou he works extra hours at the taxi firm – she would think the job was not good enough for him – he reveals both his underlying, chauvinist suspicion that his wife does not understand him and his acute sense of class. Clearly, Ed himself does not consider the switchboard job worthy of his talents: he only does it for the cash (to keep up with the Joneses?), and as he arrives at the taxi garage, the garish yellows of the cabs that suddenly fill the screen, in total contrast to the quiet greys and browns of the school, suggest not only the shock and distaste he feels in shifting from a 'respectable' environment to one that is more obviously working-class, but also the sickness that overwork and leading a secret double-life are creating for him. Unsurprisingly, then, it is just as he is changing his clothes, before taking his seat by the telephone, that we first see him bend over in pain.

That Ed is reluctant to accept the economic realities of his life becomes still more apparent when he arrives home. The house, decorated in pastel colours with rather too great a show of 'good taste', embodies his dreamer's dissatisfaction with his lot; the maps and travel posters on the walls, significantly, become more exotically foreign as one proceeds upstairs (France and Italy, as opposed to the Grand Canyon by the front door): as often for Ray, upstairs evokes the possibility of privacy and aspiration (in his own words, 'of refuge, serenity and joy'), downstairs a communal, more down-to-earth reality.

Ed's high-flown ambitions, and his contempt for the situation in which he finds himself, are further shown by the disapproval he expresses as Richie watches a Western on television (a genre, we may recall, in which Ray had worked several times, and which would include his very next film), and by his telling Lou, after a bridge evening, that they, like their guests, are dull, totally lacking in wit and imagination. Half confession, half accusation, this provokes a small rift in their marriage and Lou, already made suspicious by his coming home late and now wondering if his boredom has driven him to infidelity, moves away to the opposite side of the landing so that the staircase forms a chasm between the couple. This gulf immediately closes when Ed collapses on the floor, as if his despair about his life were too much to bear; Lou crosses to take him in her arms and tells Richie to call a doctor. Before Ed leaves for the hospital, however, we are given further insights into his psychic malaise: he tells Richie he must now become a man and look after his mother (Ed clearly has little real respect for Lou), and gives the boy his prized football from the mantelpiece. At the same time, he reminisces about his own youthful achievements on the sports field, thus gently hinting at his disappointment over the way his life has failed to live up to his dreams. Then, as he is driven away by Wally to the hospital, he forgets to take the slippers Lou brought downstairs for him: already, subconsciously, he is preparing to put his life of 'petty domesticity' behind him.

In narrative terms, the scenes at the hospital serve only to introduce Ed's 'Catch 22' predicament: in order to remain alive, he must adopt a lifelong regime of taking cortisone every six hours, but the success of the drug is not assured, and there is every chance that the treatment will produce unpleasant side effects. Stylistically, however, the hospital scenes shift the movie into the realm of nightmare, and introduce several visual motifs that will inform the rest of the film. Interestingly, Ray stresses not only Ed's physical pain, but his humiliation at the hands of doctors who, while well-meaning, are coldly dispassionate in their conversations with him (François Truffaut, pointing to the fact that they were usually shown in groups of three, likened them to gangsters!): this humiliation fuels Ed's insecurity about status (he complains that he cannot afford a private room) and contributes to the paranoia which will eventually turn him into a megalomaniac. Even more tellingly, Ray uses Expressionist images to evoke a life in danger; frequently (when Ed is X-rayed drinking a barium meal, and when he awakes in a darkened room at night contorted in agony) blazing red dominates the frame. At the same time, Ray diminishes the frame – to create a claustrophobic sense of entrapment – by filling large parts of the screen with blocks of black. The horizontal compositions that have so far suggested a sense of security are replaced by diagonals that convey an idea of chaos, tension and instability. These motifs will return again and again as the film progresses. Indeed, even as Richie awaits, with his mother and Wally, his father's return from hospital, the boy is first shown in a bright red jacket (like Jim Stark's in *Rebel Without a Cause*), which he will wear for most of the rest of the film, symbolising the (perhaps Oedipal) threat Ed sees him as; and on Ed's first day back at school, teaching painting to the infants, he asks a small boy whether a grotesque picture in red and black is of a spaceship, only to be told that it is of a man who is 'as *mad* as mother'.

Even before Ed has left the hospital, his tendency towards intellectual arrogance is shown when he rejects a nurse's gift of crosswords by complaining that, these days, they are far too easy for him. Far more disturbing is the aggression he shows when he insists on taking Lou and Richie on a shopping expedition at the end of his first day back at work. Having seen a colleague in a smart outfit, Ed is determined not to be outdone, and decides to buy Lou a dress from the most expensive couturier's in town. Here he loudly objects (admittedly with some justification) to the snooty, high-handed attitude of the staff, and forces Lou to parade before him in a series of increasingly extravagant gowns, sweeping aside her reservations about the cost. (Significantly, he chooses a red dress, which he will later insist that she wear, against her will, because he likes bright colours.) Rapidly, the shopping trip becomes less treat than torture, just as later, his games of football with Richie will turn into a form of punishment by means of which Ed, under the guise of trying to 'improve' the boy, is able to wield sadistic power over him.

As Ed becomes more erratic, taking more and more tablets in order to escape from

Makeover mania: Ed (James Mason), desperate to remodel his life, begins his grand plan with wife Lou (Barbara Rush).

his worries (about his health, his dullness, his status) into a fantasy world of euphoric self-confidence, so Lou and Richie become increasingly resentful of his unreasonable demands; they find themselves trapped by the knowledge that he cannot stop taking the cortisone. Horribly aware of his weak, vulnerable, mortal body, hating his lower-middle-class lifestyle, Ed becomes obsessed with power, mind and money to the extent that he begins to abandon all idea of responsibility to anyone but himself; even when he speaks grandly of his plans to become a revolutionary educationalist, he is prepared to abandon his family, and his desire to civilise the world is only a dream of re-creating it in his own god-like image. In a parents' meeting at the school, when he describes his pupils as intellectual morons and moral midgets, his advocacy of hard work, discipline and a sense of duty is not only so conservative as to sound fascistic, but also a shocking ploy by which he shows his own sense of superiority over his audience; he encourages one lone parent to express the gratifying sentiment that he, Ed, should become school principal. Likewise, at home he is insulting about Lou's 'trivial' intellect, treats her like a slave, accuses her of flirting and plotting with Wally behind his back, berates the milkman for rattling bottles too loudly out of envy for his mind and deprives Richie of food until he has mastered a risibly complex maths problem.

On the level of script, the film is subtle and entirely realistic in its portrait of Ed's growing psychosis; in visual terms, it achieves an altogether more complex form of accuracy, with precise compositions, clashing colours and Expressionist lighting combining to take the film into a realm of nightmarish Gothic horror which matches the family's *subjective* experiences. When, for instance, Ed stands complacently looking at himself in the bathroom mirror, pretending that his bathrobe and towel are an expensive morning-gown and cravat, while Lou is expected to make endless trips downstairs to fill his bath with a kettle, her justifiable anger at his tyranny is expressed as she slams the bathroom cabinet shut and breaks the mirror: the image is telling, not only because, as Ed continues to stare into the shattered glass, the fragmented reflection of his face symbolises his broken mind, but also because Lou's battle will be not against Ed himself but against a distorted double he imagines himself to be. Similarly, when Ed is forcing Richie to do the maths problem over and over again, his shadow on the wall behind him – diagonally disfigured to resemble a terrible, preying monster that towers, ready to pounce, over Richie – is an exact embodiment of the boy's fears about his father.

Father–son relationships were usually presented by Ray as problematic, and while Ed's delusions of grandeur drive him to reject Lou, saying that in his mind he has already divorced her, the film gradually comes to focus most sharply on Ed's conflict with Richie, who (understandably under the circumstances) comes to side more and more with his mother. On one level, in fact, the film becomes a typical Oedipal drama, with father and son feeling so threatened by one another that murder offers the only possible resolution to their battle.

On another level, however, Ray widens the relevance of the story by introducing a religious motif, which he integrates beautifully into the narrative. In a scene immediately following Ed's irate announcement, in front of Richie, that as far as he is concerned he is no longer married to Lou, the family are seen in church, listening to a lesson about

Abraham. Then, at home, Ed complains about the 'feeble-minded' sermon, which now makes it necessary for him to take on the task of giving Richie moral as well as academic guidance. Richie, meanwhile, tries to find the cortisone tablets, planning to destroy both them and the father who is torturing him and his mother. Just as he finds the pills, however, he is discovered by Ed, who locks him in his room. Now convinced that his son is a thief and murderer beyond redemption, Ed walks slowly down to the foot of the stairs, reading from the Bible, in which he traces with a pair of scissors the words of the story of Abraham and Isaac. Standing terrified below him, Lou divines his intentions, and cries, 'But Ed, you didn't read it all. God *stopped* Abraham.' To which her husband, all-consumed by Oedipal hatred and hubristic sense of his own wisdom and power, simply replies, in one of the most remarkable and subversive lines in the history of Hollywood cinema, 'God was wrong!'

Ed's deranged plans for Richie's redemption have a strange, terrible logic: if his son is killed before he can commit a sin, as Ed is sure he will, then the boy will remain innocent, and his parents – who must then kill themselves in a suicide pact – will assume his damnation and guilt. Naturally, Lou is unconvinced by this argument, and after she tries to appeal not to Ed's sense of logic but to his emotions – by showing him photos of Richie as a baby in which Ed is kissing him – he pushes her into a cupboard, locks it, turns on the television at full volume, and returns upstairs to Richie, breaking the scissors to create a dagger and, symbolically, knocking the Bible to the floor as he does so. As a futile peace offering, Richie holds up the football (reminder of happier days) to his father as he enters the room. Then suddenly Ed's vision is clouded by a red mist – the retributive but protective hand of God, or a cerebral haemorrhage, according to the level on which one interprets the film – and Richie makes his escape to free his mother. In the nick of time, as Ed recovers his sight, he is met on the stairs by Wally, whom Lou had earlier phoned for help, and in the fight that follows, Ed is knocked out.

Hollywood has always liked happy endings, and Ray's pessimism was here also compromised by the American medical industry's insistence that cortisone should not be shown in too unfavourable a light. Nonetheless, *Bigger than Life* ends in bleak ambiguity, with doctors reminding Lou that Ed, even if he wakes up with his sanity restored, will still have to take the cortisone in order to remain alive. After she reasserts her faith in her husband's ability to be more careful with his dosage in the future, they enter Ed's room: he wakes, and his words at first suggest that he has indeed lost his mind. Quickly, however, it transpires that he had been dreaming of walking with Abraham Lincoln (ironically, given Ed's earlier fascist tendencies); then, remembering another Abraham, he recalls his attempted murder of Richie, and in facing up to his insanity, proffers a glimmer of hope that his recovery will be complete. The doctors leave him happily hugging his wife and son (in a balanced, equilaterally triangular composition that suggests some semblance of stability); symbolically, the doctors turn off the red light outside his door. However hurried and false this scene may appear, its brevity and artificiality serve to keep in mind all that went before; after all, Ed's fundamental dissatisfaction with life was only enhanced by the cortisone, and there is every indication that the nightmare will begin again.

Because Ed feels himself alienated from the kind of life he has to lead, he resorts –

like so many Ray protagonists – to aggressive rebellion. At the same time, however, he is unlike Bowie, Nick Romano, Dixon Steele and others in that he *has* a family, friends and material comfort; since he rejects what other Ray protagonists dream of, he is more complex than they, and the film is all the more subversive, since it fails to find consolation from despair in an ordinary, middle-class lifestyle many of its audience would either lead or aspire to lead. While many of Ed's ideas and deeds are those of a madman, it is nevertheless true that Ray shows great sympathy for his basic predicament: Ed's pupils do *not* seem interested in learning, the bridge evenings in his immaculately tidy home *do* seem dull and he is perfectly justified in his desire to travel. What concerns Ray, rather, is that Ed's need to feel important entails a complete abrogation of his responsibilities to his family; in dwelling on his own despair, in wanting to take a kind of short cut to wealth and happiness, Ed ignores the needs and feelings of those around him and so alienates himself still further. For Ed, the cortisone *is* the short cut, a reputed panacea which increases both his self-confidence and his distaste for the world; the means becomes the end, and the cure only aggravates the sickness that is Ed's sad inability to recognise and accept his own mediocrity. He, far more than Jim Stark, really is a rebel without a cause.

Bigger than Life is simultaneously Ray's most pessimistic and most perfectly realised film. The Expressionist flourishes – wonderfully conveyed by Joe MacDonald's camerawork – are fully appropriate to the subject matter, while the film works equally well as an accurate depiction of a family torn apart by mental illness and as a withering examination of the hopes and dreams of lower-middle-class life. Notwithstanding James Mason's excellent performance (and he is more than ably supported by Barbara Rush, Walter Matthau and young Christoper Olsen), the film's emotional and intellectual intensity derives above all from a simple, direct and pacy narrative which, while extremely detailed, focuses throughout on essentials: everything (dialogue, composition, colour and décor) is meaningful, nothing is superfluous. Its various levels of plot – Oedipal (in a sense, the son *does* kill his father, or at least the 'evil' part of him), allegorical (Ed as Satan who challenges God's power), tragic (Ed as a mortal who sees himself as divine), psychological horror (Ed as a monstrous id threatening a repressed, repressive household), and Hollywood melodrama – are seamlessly interwoven, so that they enrich each other with a wide, complex tapestry of allusions.

Many of the basic elements of Ray's story were already present in embryonic form in Berton Roueché's case history of the New York teacher he calls Robert Laurence: the sudden shifts between paranoia, depression and ebullient feelings of moral and intellectual superiority over people obsessed with petty domesticity; the extravagant shopping sprees; the bullying of wife and child; the sense of being involved in a mission to lead the world into a new era of education. But Roueché's article was primarily intended to reveal the potentially dangerous side effects of cortisone ('it was not a cure … only an alleviative'), whereas Ray was concerned with diagnosing and analysing the more insidious ills affecting American life in general, and enlarged the scope of his film accordingly, by using to the full every tool at his command. And it is here, therefore, more than in any other Ray film, that the truth of his dictum, 'if it were all in the script … why make the film?', is most gloriously evident.

The True Story of Jesse James (1957)

SYNOPSIS: Missouri outlaws Jesse and Frank James are trying to make their way back home after seeing most of their gang killed or captured in a disastrous raid on the bank at Northfield, Minnesota. As their journey proceeds, Jesse's gradual transformation from quiet farm-boy to notorious bandit is recalled by his mother, his wife Zee and Frank. Jesse, already incensed during the Civil War by the invading Yankees' callous treatment of Missouri farmers, had joined his brother as a member of Quantrill's Raiders; but only after being shot while surrendering, and then being persecuted by Yankee sympathisers, had he assembled a group of local farmers to rob Yankee-owned banks. Despite Zee's desire for a tranquil family life, Jesse had become increasingly entranced by ill-gotten booty, killing and taking revenge against traitors to the South – to the extent that he had continued in his life of crime far longer than originally intended. The forces of law and order, including Pinkerton's Detective Agency, had proved largely ineffective, thanks to widespread local support for his exploits, but Jesse's audacity had finally driven him to move out of familiar territory in order to conduct the raid on Northfield. The raid, however, had not been a success: the gang had become lazy and disorganised, while Jesse had underestimated the courage of the Northfield townsfolk, who had immediately routed the robbers and given chase. Now, while escaping, Jesse and Frank fall out with each other and separate. Back home, Frank hears that his brother has been killed, but just as Zee is about to collect the body, Jesse arrives wounded, exhausted and finally resigned to giving up his criminal ways (the dead man was another gang member in whose pocket Jesse had planted his watch). As Jesse prepares to leave to start a new life with Zee and their children, however, he is shot in the back by his cousin Bob Ford. Frank, chastened by Jesse's death, decides to give himself up.

After *Bigger than Life* Ray had been invited to Europe to make *Bitter Victory*, but he first needed to fulfil his contract with 20th Century-Fox. They suggested that he make a new version of their successful 1939 Western *Jesse James*. Though reluctant to do a mere remake, he complied, intending to structure the familiar story of one of America's best-loved anti-establishment figures along the lines of a traditional folk-ballad he had heard during his years working with the Lomax Brothers, and which is now heard at the end of the film in extremely truncated form. He planned, he said, to forego any notion of 'realism' and 'to do the whole film on the stage as a legend with people coming in and out of areas of light, making it a period study of … the effects of war on the behaviour of young people'. Unsurprisingly, Fox was less than happy with this idea, and the film was made in a more conventional style. Nevertheless, Ray still shot it in such a way that company executives found a first cut confusing, so that when Ray went into hospital after shooting was finished, the film was re-cut by Fox, with several scenes removed and a number of shots of swirling red mist added to introduce flashback sequences.

Ray was never happy with flashbacks, and was further upset by the smoky inserts. Consequently he preferred to dismiss the film as routine. Nevertheless, while one may sympathise with his displeasure at yet another example of studio interference, the completed film is far from negligible; as it stands, it is immediately recognisable as a work by Ray, especially if one compares it with other Hollywood films about the James brothers. Henry King's *Jesse James* (1939) – the first major bio-pic – is imbued with a romantic nostalgia that views the pair as heroes righteously resorting to crime in reaction against Northern carpetbaggers; Fritz Lang's sequel, *The Return of Frank James* (1940) is similarly celebratory in tone; Sam Fuller's *I Shot Jesse James* (1949) presents Bob Ford's betrayal of Jesse as a fatal error; and two much later versions, Philip Kaufman's *The Great Northfield Minnesota Raid* (1971) and Walter Hill's *The Long Riders* (1980), are both self-consciously modernist analyses of genre traditions, the first a witty, politicised debunking of the heroic myth, the second an austerely stylised study in kinship. Ray's film, on the other hand, is mostly a historically accurate (if inevitably condensed) re-creation of the brothers' lives, while remaining a characteristic study in adolescent anguish and violence, inflamed by confusion, alienation and social injustice. Indeed, if the film *is* flawed or disappointing, it is because, rather like *Rebel Without a Cause*, it is too obviously a Ray film; its arguments are rather too explicitly mounted, its themes too familiar, with the result that it may be seen as the product of a brief period in the director's career when he was marking time.

First, Jesse himself is an archetypal Ray hero: immature, fatherless, disillusioned by the cruelties of adulthood after the experience of being shot at by the Yankees while surrendering, unarmed, with a white flag. He turns to rebellion (that is, bank robbery) out of a fervent sense of injustice. An opening pre-credits caption characterises him as 'a quiet Missouri farm-boy' who came to embody the curious mixture of good and evil spawned by the Civil War; as played by Robert Wagner, the adolescent Jesse is certainly gentle rather than a vicious sociopath. He is, however, hot-tempered and proud, as is shown by his reaction to a beating he suffers from Yankee sympathisers who are searching for his brother: he rushes off immediately, despite his mother's protests, to join Frank in Quantrill's Raiders. Yet, for all his courage and determination, he never becomes a fully matured adult – not, at least, until the moment just before death, when he at last sees the effect his exploits have had on his own children.

Sexually, he remains shy and repressed (it is Zee who courts him, rather than vice versa, and when they move into their new home, he demands that a print of Rubens' 'Venus and Mars' be removed from the wall, on the grounds that it is 'indecent'); and emotionally, he is so insecure that any criticism of his methods of leading the gang, even by Frank, immediately provokes threats of violent retribution. Moreover, despite his initial claims that his outlaw life is a reaction to the iniquities perpetrated by the victorious Yankees against poor Southern farmers, Jesse really acts out of a private, irrational desire for revenge (he kills an informant in the service of Yankees, who is indirectly responsible for his half-brother's death and his mother's loss of the use of her arm, in the full knowledge that it will ruin any chance of an amnesty for Frank and himself). Furthermore, as Frank points out after the raid on Northfield, Jesse actually comes to enjoy killing. His innocence, then, is ambiguous and ambivalent; on the one hand, he moves from righteous anger to a delight in crime for crime's sake (thus he becomes, eventually, a rebel without a cause); on the other, he is innocent throughout in the sense that, until death, he is unable to understand either the world around him or himself.

In many other respects, too, the film fits snugly within the Ray canon. Zee – pure, kind, level-headed and supportive of Jesse whatever his sins – is seen, like so many women in Ray films, as Jesse's potential saviour from himself; she understands his true nature, that he is 'lost', since by her own admission, she is 'as much of a stray as he is'. Frank, on the other hand, is to Jesse what Jim Stark was to Plato, or Andrew Morton to Nick Romano: an older father-figure, a would-be restraining influence who will go along with Jesse's plans, but only so far. And, as often in Ray, the world around Jesse is cruel and more than a little venal; the Northfield posse persists in its hunt for the robbers only after Pinkerton has raised the reward (the marshal himself admits that he would not turn his back on the money), while Jesse, having been wounded by the Yankees, is given shelter by Rufus Cobb (a distant relative) only when Frank promises to work Cobb's farm in return for hospitality (Cobb also demands a decent endowment when Jesse asks for Zee's hand in marriage).

Jesse's predicament stems partly from his own lack of control and self-knowledge, partly from the fact that – like Bowie, Jeff McCloud and others before him – he is simultaneously repelled and attracted by the society from which he is excluded. He distrusts adult ways, and only really feels safe when he escapes to the artificiality of the enclosed little home he sets up with Zee under the pseudonym of Mr and Mrs Howard (not surprisingly Jesse, in true Ray fashion, also appears to feel most secure at night); at the same time, he apes normal life with a household that is almost a parody of bourgeois respectability – the plans he excitedly makes with Zee for their future sound very similar to the childlike fantasies of adulthood indulged in by Bowie and Keechie, Nick and Emma, Jim and Judy.

In scene after scene, the film echoes moments in earlier Ray movies. After the opening sequence of the Northfield robbery, the posse's frantic pursuit (with hunting dogs!) of the gang recalls the 'hunt' scenes in both *On Dangerous Ground* and, more especially, *Johnny Guitar.* The various characters' premonitions of Jesse's death – his mother distrusts Bob Ford, and Frank keeps telling Jesse he should watch out behind him – evoke a sense of destiny almost ubiquitous in Ray. Similarly, the emphasis on the need for loyalty and trust in times of betrayal recurs frequently in Ray's 1950s work (interestingly, Ray does not altogether condemn the treacherous quisling Askew, who explains that he aids the Yankees against the Confederate sympathisers because he does not 'hold with slavers'). And Jesse's naïve, vain belief in the romantic Robin Hood tales printed about him by the press – these drive him to help an old woman by giving her $600 to pay off a mortgage, which he promptly retrieves from the bailiff – recalls Chicamaw's anxiety about his public image in *They Live by Night*. Even the self-destructive side of Jesse's nature, which amounts to a kind of death-wish (he gives Bob Ford his gun, before turn-

A race against time: the raid on Northfield, Minnesota.

ing his back on him, saying that he cannot trust anybody and expects someone to put a bullet in his back to win the reward) has its precedent in Bowie, Nick Romano, Jeff McCloud and Plato.

Although, therefore, *The True Story of Jesse James* offers nothing particularly fresh or original in Ray's thematic concerns, the film is of rather more than passing interest, partly because he radically re-interpreted a popular, almost legendary, historical figure in the light of his own views on the problems faced by contemporary youth, partly because he refused to portray Jesse either as a romantic hero or as a black-hearted villain. Like Welles's *Citizen Kane*, whose investigative flashback structure it borrows, the film uses the reminiscences of various witnesses both to build a complex, multi-faceted picture of Jesse, and to refute, finally, the notion that there might be one 'key' to his character (the film even resembles *Kane* in showing a journalist who, in trying to put together an obituary for Jesse, expresses his contempt for the hackneyed clichés so far written about him). On one level, then, the film is about perceptual problems, and it is no accident that it includes two very different scenes showing the Northfield robbery. The first, at the beginning of the film, is chaotic, confusing, and shown largely through the eyes of the townsfolk who, taken by surprise, do not really know exactly what is happening or why; the second, towards the end of the film, is far more complex and comprehensible, and shows the event as it is experienced by the gang, whose members we have by now come to know and recognise, so that we ourselves can gain an insight into what, exactly, went wrong.

Jesse's fatal error is that he has become so sure of his invulnerability that he is no longer able to judge either his own capabilities or those of his colleagues (in which respect he faintly resembles Ed Avery). In believing the stories printed about him, he not only considers himself powerful enough to mould reality (he repeatedly refers to the Northfield raid as the best robbery he ever planned, as if his plans could never fail), but he stubbornly ignores Frank's advice, as well as the doubts and fears of his gang, about the folly of robbing a bank so far from home. For the historical Jesse, the Northfield raid, executed in 1876, was a disaster, but he continued his life of crime until he was shot in 1882; for Ray, however, working from a script that condenses time, the raid carries a greater significance, coming as it does immediately before Jesse's decision to change his ways, and his death. Typically for the director, Jesse's transgression is seen in spatial terms: he literally overreaches himself by making a foray into unfamiliar terrain where there is no local support for his outlawry (in Missouri, he is a 'spokesman for everyone whose life is quietly desperate'). And though the Northfield townsfolk are actually unprepared for the robbery, Ray's superb staging of the raid and its deadly aftermath treats it as if the gang had walked into a trap: even as they ride into town, their long, white linen-duster coats (worn to suggest they are cattlemen?) at once differentiate them visually from the inhabitants; as soon as the alarm is raised at the bank, their escape routes are blocked and the townsfolk shoot down from roofs and balconies on to the gang below. The shattering of Jesse's dreams of invulnerability is given vivid, poetic expression when he and Frank, seeking a means of escape, are forced to ride their horses through a shop window.

Ray's direction is characteristically precise in using visual means to delineate character and situation. While the Northfield scenes use fast cutting, low angles and cluttered compositions to evoke the chaos that enters Jesse's life as his plans fall apart, the rest of the film is notable for its symmetry, clarity and its sense of balance. When, for example, Jesse and Frank first gather together local farmers in a barn to announce their plans to rob a Yankee bank, they are seated respectively to the left and right of a vertical wooden beam, as if presenting the assembly with a clear choice. Cole Younger, chief spokesman for the farmers, is at first sceptical of Jesse's hotheadedness, and stands to the right of Frank, whom he considers more mature and sensible; then, when Frank expresses his approval of Jesse's plan, Cole moves to a position in front of the beam between the two brothers, still undecided about whether to join them; finally, convinced by Jesse's plans and ready to accept him, rather than Frank, as gang leader, he moves to the left of Jesse, to show his loyalty.

Equally expressively, the gang's first train robbery, in sharp contrast to the confusion at Northfield, reveals Jesse's clear, determined thinking; the camera follows him, in a magnificent tracking shot, along the roofs of the train carriages, his steady forward progress suggesting his cool, calm mastery of a dangerous situation. Such moments recur throughout the film, as do a number of visual and verbal references to water and fire. The former is a symbol of purity (Jesse being baptised in the river with Zee) and safety (the gang repeatedly make their escape from robberies by galloping through rivers and streams); the latter is a symbol of Jesse's passion (Zee speaks of his 'hidden fires' when she first kisses him) and his tendency towards violence (the burning fields, set alight by

Yankee sympathisers, that drive him to crime; the fire a lawyer says he kindles in the public's hearts; the smoke behind him as he looks down on the driver of the train he will rob; exploding safes stolen from banks). Just as Frank's caution is balanced against Jesse's volatile temper, so fire and water are precariously balanced in Jesse's nature which, like those of so many Ray characters, is torn by inner conflicts between love (for family, friends and the South) and hate (for traitors, Yankees, and any gang member who somehow fails him).

When, after the catastrophic visit to Northfield, Jesse is at last able to return home to Zee, he decides to abandon crime, and a fragile peace and balance are temporarily restored. As the couple pack to leave for a farm in Nebraska that Frank is buying for them, Bob Ford warns Jesse – who is still masquerading as the respectable Mr Howard – not to go outside wearing his guns; Jesse, figuring he will not need the weapons any more, gives them to Ford. Then, having stopped his children playing 'Jesse James' (they do not know his true identity, and he is visibly upset by their game), he returns indoors where he is left alone with the Ford brothers, who seem annoyed at not being allowed to join his gang as they had hoped and disillusioned by his comment that in the last few years he has no longer enjoyed being a wanted outlaw. (Nevertheless, Jesse is still sufficiently proud of his infamy to boast, with an arrogant smile, of the massive price on his head.) Climbing precariously on to a chair to adjust a wall sampler embroidered, ironically, with the motto 'Hard Work Spells Success', he confesses to the boys that he expects someone to try and kill him for reward or reputation; when Bob Ford says, 'They'll never get a chance,' and Jesse, with his back to him, asks, 'What makes you so sure?', Bob fires and kills him. He thus achieves the notoriety denied him by Jesse's decision to go straight. Immediately, after Bob has run into the street proclaiming his treacherous deed, the house is filled by morbid onlookers and souvenir-hunters stealing trinkets from the scene of Jesse's murder: a petty, pathetic end to the life of a folk hero, which is at once transformed into the stuff of legend by a passing blind beggar, who begins singing the 'Ballad of Jesse James' to the shocked townsfolk in the street. The sign around his neck ('Help the poor') is a cruelly ironic reminder of Jesse's compromised ideals and the falsity of his reputation.

Ray's version of the Jesse James story, then, is impressive for his refusal to iron out the ambiguities of legend; he allows us partly to understand why Jesse may have turned to crime, but never implies that there is a single, easy answer, and never resorts to the romanticised rewriting of history to be found in other film accounts of the outlaw's life. As suggested above, the film breaks no new ground in stylistic or thematic terms for Ray himself, but his dynamic editing, his taut, evocative compositions (once again in a CinemaScope frame) and his subtle use of symbolic motifs, décor and colour ensure that this is the richest and most complex of the many different variations on a much-told story.

Bitter Victory (1957)

SYNOPSIS: In Libya during World War II, Major David Brand and Captain James Leith are placed in command of a special force sent on a dangerous mission, behind enemy lines; its task is to steal important documents from German headquarters in Benghazi. The two men's already strong dislike for one another, inflamed by Brand's realisation that his wife Jane knew Leith before the war, reaches a crisis point when Leith, seeing his superior hesitate to kill a German sentry during the raid, dispatches the man himself. Thereafter, during the long and difficult trek back to base through the desert, Brand does his utmost to rid himself of Leith, chief witness to his cowardice: he leaves him behind – easy prey for German patrols – to tend men wounded in a skirmish with the Nazis, and later neglects to alert him to the presence of a scorpion which climbs up Leith's leg to sting him as he sleeps; when Mokrane, the platoon's Arab guide and Leith's friend, who witnessed Brand's silence during the scorpion attack, tries to murder Brand, Brand shoots him. The next morning, as Brand prepares to leave the now gangrene-stricken Leith alone in the desert, a sandstorm arises, and the dying man saves Brand's life by covering his body with his own. The storm abates, and the platoon are rescued by a search party, but not before a German they have captured has tried, with only partial success, to burn the stolen documents. Back at British headquarters, Brand is awarded the DSO by his commanding officer General Patterson but, Jane having left him after being told of Leith's death, and the platoon having displayed their contempt by watching the award ceremony in cynical silence, he pins the medal on to the chest of a dummy used for bayonet practice.

After the problems Ray had encountered with Fox during the making of *The True Story of Jesse James*, he was keen to work in France on an adaptation of René Hardy's novel *Bitter Victory* with producer Paul Graetz. Sadly, the making of this film proved no easier than many of his unhappiest experiences in Hollywood: Graetz gave Hardy script approval, employed Paul Gallico to modify the script produced by Ray and Gavin Lambert and, against Ray's wishes, cast the German actor Curt Jurgens as Brand (Ray wanted Richard Burton, who eventually played Leith, for the part, and Mongomery Clift – who became unavailable because of his car accident – or Paul Newman as Leith). To make things worse, Jurgens proved reluctant to play Brand as the 'unmitigated heel' that Ray envisaged, and tensions during shooting – much of it in harsh conditions in the desert near Tripoli – were such that, after filming was completed, Graetz wrote to a number of American producers complaining about Ray's drink problem. Nonetheless, the film remains remarkably powerful, even though Columbia, from whom Graetz obtained the greater part of his production money, and who distributed the film, released it to most territories in severely mutilated prints that can only be described as a betrayal of Ray's original intentions.

The war film is, generally, a rather limited genre in its dramatic and moral thrust; all too often, clichéd stories are deployed simply to propose either a patriotic celebration of individual heroism, or a pacifist, anti-war message. In *Bitter Victory*, however, the trappings of war itself are hardly seen; they function primarily as a metaphorical backdrop, a context in which Ray can explore his abiding themes of anguished alienation, confusion and violence. First and foremost, the film is an almost abstract study of conflict, not between Britons and Germans, but between two men whose quest for happiness and meaning in life has led them along somewhat different paths. For Ray, war is simply a crucible in which the masks men don to conceal their true selves fall away, just as the cortisone in *Bigger than Life* exposed Ed Avery's latent megalomania and paranoia. And for that reason, the desert in *Bitter Victory* – its blistering heat, blinding light, burning sand and howling storms – serves as a central character, stripping away from the protagonists their thin veneer of 'civilised' behaviour to reveal the frayed, raw nerves that lie beneath; at the same time its massive, timeless impassivity dwarfs and throws into perspective the petty human rivalries to which it bears mute witness.

Simplistically viewed, Brand and Leith might be regarded as conventional opposites, descendants of Kirby and Griff in *Flying Leathernecks*: the by-the-book, stuffed-shirt major and his rule-breaking, popular captain. Each, however, is a far more complex creation than any such cliché suggests; each is filled with doubts, self-loathing and contradictory impulses. Neither man is emotionally or spiritually concerned with the war effort *per se*; both see the dangers of the mission to Benghazi as proffering an opportunity to escape and overcome their moral weakness and inertia. Their rivalry, particularly their jealous battle for Jane's affections, is, in fact, partly a pretext; the real conflict is internal, with and within themselves. Leith, at first sight, may seem to be the braver of the two – it is he who kills the German sentry, he who exposes Brand's cowardice – but his courage verges on masochism, while his desertion of Jane before the war and his preference for the past, embodied in his archaeological interests, suggest that his pragmatic, intellectual attitude to life is a defence against the demands and needs of those around him. Brand, conversely, is a coward less because he is afraid of being killed (after all, he volunteers for a mission that all acknowledge as being fraught with danger), than because he fears both fear itself and the act of killing; he too has retreated into a shell (of regimented military status, as opposed to Leith's cynical nihilism) to protect himself from the chaotic, confusing realities of life. Each man, indeed, is a typical Ray protagonist: lonely, lost, self-destructive and apparently dependent on the respect of the woman he loves for redemption.

After the opening credits – which, with a directness of expression typical of Ray, show soldiers filing between bayonet-practice dummies with hearts painted on their chests – the film begins with a nervy Brand being interviewed by General Patterson, who is considering putting Brand in charge of the mission against the Nazis' Benghazi headquarters. Patterson, portrayed as a prig and a fool (he dislikes Leith just because he is 'bad-mannered', an intellectual and Welsh!), unwittingly acknowledges the reason for Brand, hitherto involved only with paperwork, wanting to take command; the general points out that the mission offers 'a great opportunity to *show* [my italics] what you can do … and a chance for quick promotion, too'. Eager to impress, Brand offers no comment on the chances of the mission's success whereas Leith, questioned immediately after Brand (whose exact position in the frame he at once assumes, thus foreshadowing their rivalry), estimates that the operation has a million-to-one chance of succeeding. But this apparent pragmatism is, perhaps, only a mask for Leith's suicidal tendencies, since he at once insists that, despite the odds, he is not against the project. For Brand, then, the mission offers the chance of glory, of proving himself to others; for Leith, the likelihood of death.

Precisely why the two men cherish these ambitions becomes apparent when Brand's wife appears in the mess bar (where an extended close-up of a soldier's hands childishly acting out a battle serves to imply that war is little more than an absurd game); Brand proceeds to introduce Leith to Jane, ignorant of the fact that they were once lovers. On one level the sequence introduces a human element into the men's moral and existential conflict, with Ray carefully positioning Leith, as a divisive, disruptive force, between the married couple, and underlining and undermining the meanings of their seemingly innocent words with a subtle array of significant glances: Leith and Jane searching, reproachful, warm and intimate, Brand confused, then jealously suspicious. As in *In a Lonely Place*, looks are of prime importance as an index of loyalty and esteem; Brand is forced to interrupt the eye-contact between his wife and her former lover by proposing a toast ('To *us*, Jane'), while later, in the desert after the raid on Benghazi, he will deliberately 'perform' before the collective gaze of the platoon in an attempt to prove his courage and steer their loyalty away from Leith to himself. For Brand, courage and virtue are a question of appearances, of being *seen* to be brave; his very leadership of the mission is assumed simply because he wants Jane to respect and love him. Leith, conversely, seems not to care what others think of him (as was clear from his frank, even insolent response to Patterson's interrogation); he is a burnt-out case, to whom the mission offers two alternatives: either he will die – the logical result of his nihilism – or he will return and win back Jane, in which case he might be reborn, in the sense of rejoining the human race and rediscovering, through love, a purpose in life.

Since separating from Jane in 1939, Leith has, by his own admission, 'never cared about anything much', and it is ironic that he left her without warning because he was 'afraid' (of becoming too closely involved with another person), whereas Jane admits that she married Brand 'because he didn't run away'. The implication, therefore, is plain; in his own way, Leith can be cowardly, since he fears life itself, as is made evident when he tells Jane about the risks involved in the expedition, and resorts to sarcasm and irony rather than admit his true feelings for her:

JANE: What if he [Brand] doesn't come back?

LEITH: Then he and I and you become a part of history, of its futility.

JANE : Don't talk to me in riddles, Jimmy.

LEITH : It's a long time since I was in Libya. The Romans built wonderful cities in Libya: dead bones sticking out of the sand. War rolled over them. It'll be good to see them again.

JANE : You always seemed to prefer stones to people.

LEITH : I've learned things from stones.

JANE : What?

LEITH : All that people have forgotten in the centuries.

JANE : I seem to remember I was less than a stone to you. I loved you, Jimmy.

LEITH : We'd better go in. There isn't much time.

JANE : What can I say to him?

LEITH : Tell him all the things that women have always said to the men before they go
to the wars. Tell him he's a hero. Tell him he's a good man. Tell him you'll be waiting for him when he comes back. Tell him he'll be making history.

Until the attack on Benghazi, Brand's cowardice is shown only in his bullying interrogation of Jane about her former relationship with Leith, in which he gives vent to his
irrational jealously, twisting her replies to suit his purpose. In the raid, however – a night
sequence beautifully shot and constructed, with Ray making superb use of crumbling
white buildings and dark shadows, and with very little dialogue – Brand's true nature
reveals itself, as he finds himself unable to kill a sentry whose death is necessary if the
documents are to be stolen. Leith, by contrast, can and does kill the man, his groan suggesting both pain and pleasure as he plunges the knife into the German's back, as if the
death were his own. When Brand and Leith discuss the incident afterwards in the desert,
the former denies that he was afraid, and asks Leith if he will tell headquarters that he
failed; characteristically, Leith washes his hands of the affair, claiming that it is 'between
you … and you'. It is here that the *real* difference between the men (both cowards and,
finally, killers) is first revealed, thus setting in motion their deadly conflict: whereas Leith
realises that his struggle is within himself, Brand refuses to face up to his inner torments
and repeatedly tries to displace his failings on to others. As Leith later explains, he is like
Brand's mirror-image, which is why Brand wants to kill him.

Brand's first attempt to rid himself of this witness to his cowardice comes when he
leaves Leith behind to tend the wounded. Leith is accompanied only by two soldiers who
reflect his torn conscience: Dunnigan offers the injured men compassion, while Wilkins
– a criminal before the war – offers to kill them, so that the able men can move on and
not fall prey to German patrols. Unable to make a decision, Leith sends the men away,
but the choice must still be made; he kills a dying German, but when he comes to fire
at one of his own men, who begs him to get it over with quickly, his gun is empty, and
notwithstanding the wounded man's accusations that he is a coward, he begins to carry
him across the sand. The man soon dies, however, prompting Leith to acknowledge the
impossible absurdity of his role in the war: 'I kill the living, and I save the dead.' When
Mokrane, who has stayed behind, points out that, 'It's certain for everyone to die; it
makes no difference', Leith replies, 'Except for that little matter of when, and for what.'

Clearly, for Leith, there is little meaning in death, since there is no longer any purpose
in his life. That he sees himself as somehow separate from the rest of humanity is evident
when he and Mokrane catch up with Brand and the platoon at a ruined Berber city which
Leigh says is 'too modern for me'; a Welshman who regards himself as 'of the desert', he
is literally out of place and out of time, trying to live in a dead past that cannot really touch
him. But this detachment, expressed through sardonic irony, is itself ironic, not only in that
he is inevitably forced to live in the present (the source of his problems: he simultaneously
wants and does not want to be integrated into the world), but also in that it gives him an
unusually lucid perspective on those around him, most notably, of course, on Brand.

'I kill the living and save the dead': Leith (Richard Burton) confesses his contradictory ethos to Mokrane (Raymond Pellegrin).

What Leith discovers in Brand's cowardice is, in fact, an alienated condition that is merely the obverse of his own. During a long discussion in which Leith accuses his superior of leaving him to die in the desert, Brand says that after thirteen years in the army he still cannot kill a man in cold blood, to which Leith replies that the only difference between war and murder – between killing a man by means of a sharpshooter or arranging for him to die away from oneself, and killing him at close quarters – is distance; while Leith is able to stab a man but reluctant to become closely involved with the living, Brand, conversely, is able to live with Jane but fears having to confront his own capacity for killing at close range. Brand is not especially afraid of dying (in fact, he drinks water from a well that may have been poisoned by the Germans, in order to prove to his men that he is no coward); but he *is* afraid of losing the respect of the living – of Jane, his commanding officers, and his men – and, therefore, of being alone. Ironically, it is this obsession with being *seen* to be a good man that drives him both to kill Leith and to distort the truth about himself, acts which in turn alienate those whose respect he needs and desires; whereas Leith – whose interest in speaking the truth, however grim, derives from his sense of not caring for anyone – inspires the affection and esteem of those whom Brand courts.

As often in Ray's work a resolution to the problems set out by the narrative can only be achieved through sacrifice: Leith's death, after Brand fails to bring his attention to the scorpion climbing up his leg as he sleeps, paves the way for a kind of bleak redemption for Brand. Leith, poisoned by the sting, rejects Brand's offer of water and instead offers him a knife to cut into his leg to remove the venom; secretly desiring Leith's death and unable to face pain at such proximity, Brand inevitably refuses, so that Leith must plunge the knife into his own body. When, however, Mokrane, who has observed Brand's silence during the scorpion attach, attempts to kill him, Brand is forced to defend himself, and after shooting the Arab point-blank asks, 'Is it that easy to kill?'

That lesson learnt, he decides the following morning to leave the crippled Leith in the desert, again, despite the objections of the platoon, twisting the rules to suit his own murderous purposes (he had earlier told Leith that duty demanded he stay behind with the wounded). Leith, strangely happy that death is near, tells him, 'We're all murderers now, aren't we? Join the club', and points out that Brand is not the kind of man to kill for his woman, but would commit murder to prevent her finding out that he is a coward: 'You're not a man, Brand, you're an empty uniform, starched by authority so it can stand up by itself', to which Brand replies, with some justification, 'But I'm standing.' Then, having told Brand to tell Jane that she was right (in wanting to marry him, presumably) and to ask her forgiveness, Leith taunts him ('If you haven't got the courage to kill me, don't try to save me') before pulling him down to the ground to protect him from a sandstorm that has suddenly arisen, crying, 'I contradict myself, I always contradict myself.'

Leith's final decision to save his own killer is indeed an act of self-contradiction, but not in any sense a piece of dramatic contrivance on the part of Ray and his writers: with his suicidal tendencies, Leith has long seen death as at least providing a *potential* meaning to his own life, and in choosing to save Brand, he is merely remaining true to his sense of his own contradictory nature and performing an act of love for Jane, the one person who hitherto had made him feel a part of the world. Through his self-sacrifice, he is again killing the living (himself) and saving the dead (Brand, whom he regards as somewhat less than a complete, feeling human being), and acknowledging the absurdity of war in particular and of human existence in general.

Just as the captured German's near-success in destroying the documents reveals to Brand the waste of human life caused by the mission, so Leith's final words and act of self-sacrifice reveal to him the destructive futility of his (self-)deceptions. Back at headquarters, where Jane is visibly upset by the news of Leith's death, he at last attempts to give her an inkling of the truth, by saying that although the platoon members think he killed Leith, he wanted to save him, but it was too late. Then, still more bravely, he tells one last lie (ironically in an attempt to win Jane's love more honestly than before), saying that Leith's last words were, '"Tell Jane …" and then the wind drowned him out. I suppose he would have said, "Tell Jane I love her." Those would have been my last words, too.' His new-found courage has come too late, however, to preserve her love. As Patterson – the most pompous, gullible and dishonest character in the film, who boasts of his pride in the men 'under my command', and makes vacuous promises that, in writing to the dead men's families, he will say 'exactly what happened' – awards Brand the Distinguished Service Order, the men look on in contemptuous silence, and Jane simply walks away in despair and disgust. Left alone, Brand, who has always judged his own worth by the opinions of others, cannot but realise the absurdity of Patterson's words, and feel a bitter remorse for his own despicable, cowardly behaviour towards Leith. As if recalling Leith's words before dying (he described Brand as 'a stuffed dummy

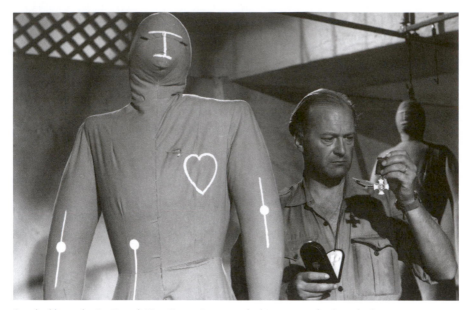

Starched by authority: Brand (Curt Jurgens) savours the bitter taste of military kudos.

with medals on his chest'), he pins the DSO on to the outline of a heart painted on a bayonet-practice dummy and achieves, through self-knowledge, a kind of redemption.

Ray's final image is of the dummy itself, after Brand has walked off-screen: Brand's belated enlightenment offers no happy ending, since all that he has come to recognise is the hollow futility of his own attempts to impress others. The film is, in fact, one of the director's most bleakly pessimistic works, akin even to Greek tragedy. Its lethal conflict is played out under a corrosively scorching sun in the starkest of environments. The vividly characterised platoon members serve as a chorus, observing and commenting on Brand's vengeful private war against Leith, while the frequently ironic dialogue provides a discursive argument as abstract as Ray's austerely poetic images.

Shot in CinemaScope and harsh black and white, the film is both palpably realist, in its successful evocation of the effects of sand, sun and wind upon the platoon members, and almost geometric, with its precise narrative and visual symmetries and oppositions. In every respect, indeed, it must, despite the problems encountered during production, be considered an artistic triumph: the performances – most notably Burton's Leith, which is quite probably the finest of his film career – are for the most part superb, while Maurice Le Roux's magnificent score (Ray originally wanted Shostakovich, but the Soviet authorities denied him the composer's services) perfectly complements the mesmeric tendency towards abstraction of Michel Kelber's camerawork. Perhaps most fascinatingly, the film (more meditative than action-packed, even allowing for Ray's virtuoso staging of the raid on Benghazi) wholly transcends the hackneyed conventions of the war-movie genre; besides being a characteristic Ray film, it also touches, in its observations on courage, fear, hypocrisy, ambition and self-knowledge, on emotions and issues that are timeless and universal.

Wind Across the Everglades (1958)

SYNOPSIS: Walt Murdoch arrives in turn-of-the-century Miami to teach natural history, and is arrested for removing a plume from a woman's hat. He loses his job and accepts work as a game warden for the Audubon Society, whose prime intent is to prevent a gang of poachers, led by the anarchic Cottonmouth, from killing birds in the Everglades swamps in order to meet the fashionable demand for hat plumage. A first inconclusive encounter with Cottonmouth persuades Murdoch of both the risks and the necessity of his task, even before the poacher sends one of his gang – Seminole Indian Billy One-Arm – to trick Murdoch into visiting the swamps, where he will be abandoned. But after Murdoch expresses sympathy for the Indians' plight, Billy decides not to leave him, with the result that Billy is caught by Cottonmouth's gang and killed by being bound to a poisonous tree. Murdoch, meanwhile, is rescued by Billy's wife and returns to Miami, where he presently exposes a businessman's illegal traffic in bird plumes. The judge, however, will only issue a warrant for Cottonmouth's arrest on the condition that Murdock serve it personally, in the Everglades. Murdoch, therefore, makes the long trip to the gang's camp, where he becomes embroiled in a drinking contest with their leader. Cottonmouth agrees the next morning to accept his punishment in Miami if Murdoch can manage to ferry him there and survive his attempts to kill him. When Murdoch, lost and feverishly fatigued, shoots at a branch he mistakenly believes is a snake, Cottonmouth hits him with an oar. After realising Murdoch's error, however, the poacher pulls him out of the water, deciding to take him back to Miami. But before they can set off, Cottonmouth is bitten by a venomous snake, and after insisting that Murdoch leave him alone, he dies, belatedly recognising the birds' beauty and inviting the vultures to feast on his body.

After the difficulties of making *Bitter Victory*, it must have seem a good idea to Ray to work with Budd Schulberg on *Wind Across the Everglades*. He had met Schulberg through his friend Elia Kazan, whose *On the Waterfront* and *A Face in the Crowd* Schulberg had written. Sadly, however, the making of the film (produced by the writer's brother, Stuart) was, by all accounts, as fraught with tension and ill-feeling as Ray's previous assignment. Again, the locations, in and around the swamps of southern Florida, were none too conducive to a good atmosphere on set; both Ray and his lead actors fell sick. More crucially, Schulberg reputedly expected the director to film his script to the letter, and proved so resistant to any suggestions for changes that Ray, in later interviews, would often claim that the writer wanted to direct the film himself. Those involved in the film's making have also spoken of the excessive drinking habits of both director and writer. At the same time, Warner Bros., financing the Schulberg brothers' first production, were apparently concerned by the high shooting-ratio and by the lack of a strong, straightforward story in the rushes sent to the studio. At any rate, Ray himself, for whatever reason, did not shoot the film's final sequence (which, according to Burl Ives, was filmed by virtually anyone who happened to be around), nor was he given any say in the final cut, which reduced the running time from an initially impractical three hours to a little more than half that length.

The result, as Ray recognised, is a movie whose narrative continuity is often creaky. None the less, though in later years both director and writer tended to dismiss their collaboration as almost wholly disastrous, the film remains a remarkable achievement, years ahead of its time and, notwithstanding all the various problems in making it, a key work in the stylistic and thematic development of Ray's *oeuvre*.

For one thing, it brings into the foreground his interest in ethnography and folk-culture (and consequently in ecological and conservation issues), which had already manifested itself to a lesser degree in earlier works such as *The Lusty Men, Run for Cover, Hot Blood* and *The True Story of Jesse* James, and which would reach its apogee in *The Savage Innocents*. For another, it also foreshadows *The Savage Innocents, We Can't Go Home Again* and *Lightning Over Water* in the sense that, into an essentially narrative format, Ray introduces sequences that are resonant less of fiction than of documentary. Indeed, the film is perhaps Ray's most bizarre hybrid; where several of his earlier movies function partly as generic concoctions (the thriller mixed with the love story, *film noir* with the social-conscience drama, and so on), *Wind Across the Everglades* not only mixes traditional Western motifs with costume melodrama and ecological pleading, but contrives to bring together poetry, metaphysics and violent action in a stylistic format that is partly mainstream Hollywood storytelling, partly art-movie and partly semi-documentary historical reconstruction. At the same time, for all that Ray and Schulberg failed to see eye to eye, the film is characteristically 'Ray' in terms of its protagonists and their rivalry, and in the way they are related to the environment in which they live. In fact, while its setting is in extreme contrast to the desert of *Bitter Victory*, the basic situation it depicts is remarkably similar to that in the previous film, and indeed, much of Ray's earlier work.

Since the film's narrative structure is very like that of a traditional Western – a stranger enters a town on the brink of becoming 'civilised', and takes on, almost alone, a murderous band of poachers (rustlers in Westerns) living out in the wilderness – it is easy at first to regard Murdoch as the hero and Cottonmouth as the villain. As the film proceeds, however, Ray blurs the lines that mark their characters so that, as with Leith and Brand, both their differences and their similarities are stressed. Both are outsiders and rebels. Cottonmouth, literally, inhabits a world that is only tenuously connected, through his trafficking in bird plumage, to the 'civilised' community of Miami, and lords it over an unruly, lawless band of equally disreputable outcasts (escaped convicts, a failed jockey, a cynical former 'professor' and an Indian thrown out of his tribe for lying); while Murdoch, a newcomer to the town who is immediately branded as a 'trouble-maker' after he plucks a feather from a woman's hat (asking her, 'How would you like it if this bird wore you for a decoration?'), is also, due to his heavy drinking and to his sense of alienation from modern America ('Progress and I never got along very well'), something of a loner. (His love affair with Naomi, his landlord's daughter, is somewhat perfunctorily handled by Ray, although she, too, may be seen as an outsider, since she refuses to wear feather hats and is of foreign extraction.)

It is no accident, then, that Cottonmouth and Murdoch come to treat each other with a wary respect, as if half-fascinated and half-disturbed by their similarities: when the warden finally visits Cottonmouth's camp, the latter forbids his gang to harm his guest, challenging him to a drinking contest, the outcome of which is, not insignificantly, a draw. The contest also provides an easy-talking opportunity for the pair to discover their common interest in 'protest', to the point where Murdoch claims his evening with the gang has been the best evening he has ever known, and Cottonmouth believes that Murdoch might join the gang. Both, after all, are men who prefer to live uninhibited by the repressive constraints of bourgeois society, and to some extent, for all their enmity, Murdoch comes to regard the hedonistic Cottonmouth (who regularly speaks of his love for 'the sweet-tastin' joys of life') as a father-figure and teacher; as a living, breathing symbol of anarchic freedom.

Nevertheless, poacher and warden are differentiated by their diametrically opposed attitudes to the natural world, which each prefers to bourgeois 'civilisation'. Murdoch is initially an outsider to nature, who sees it from the point of view of a servant (he wants to save the flora and fauna of the Everglades from the ravages of human land development and profiteering) and of a poet; after his first journey into the swamps, he says they are 'sort of the way the world must have looked on the first day, when it was all water, and then the first land … beginning to rise out of the sea. You feel the life force in there in its purest, earliest form. Then Cain, and the bothers of Cain, raise their twelve-gauge shotguns, and fire into the face of God.'

His, then, is a romantic, nostalgic, almost mystical reverence for the power of nature at its most positive (his fundamental innocence is shown by the way the gang call him 'bird boy', and repeatedly refer to the tale of the spider and the fly: Cottonmouth, of course, being the spider and Murdoch the fly). Cottonmouth, on the other hand, who is named after a deadly snake, an example of which ('my best friend') he carries in his pocket, is *of* the natural world. He first appears in the swamps before Murdoch as the latter looks through his camera (in a remarkable subjective shot showing Cottonmouth upside down, thus both prefiguring the way he will overturn the warden's view of nature, and suggesting that he is, in a sense, his mirror-image) and, when Murdoch asks where he lives, replies: 'I gotta thousand places round here: every piece of high ground between here and Cape Sable. I was born here; when I'm three score and ten I'll die here, with the seeds of the swamp cabbage in my gut so a tree'll grow out and stand on top of me.'

Though part of nature, Cottonmouth mistakenly sees himself as somehow its god-like master, and where Murdoch values the swamps for their 'life force', Cottonmouth is overly preoccupied with killing. As Murdoch explains during their drinking contest – when Cottonmouth, toasting protest, says that he is 'agin everything' and that 'eat or be ate is the law of the glades' – Cottonmouth's slaughtering of the harmless birds is no longer anything to do with the balance of nature, but entirely motivated by greed. In forging his uneasy business alliance with the merchants of Miami – who, after all, are profiting from a useless, silly fashion – Cottonmouth has himself been corrupted, has

A question of class: Sawdust (Pat Henning) pretends he's unworthy of joining Murdoch (Christopher Plummer), Mrs Bradford (Gypsy Rose Lee) and the corrupt politicians and businessmen in the brothel's best bar.

broken the dog-eat-dog laws of nature, and has become almost as alienated from the cyclical inter-relationship between life and death as Murdoch. In order, then, for the true balance of nature to be restored, the men must somehow become one, their contradictory, complementary attitudes united and resolved through conflict.

Just as Cottonmouth is a grotesque mirror-image of Murdoch, so his gang is an obscene parody of the Miami bourgeoisie, who have built, pioneer-style, the remotest outpost of 'progress' (the town is explicitly shown as being at the end of a railroad). Almost to a man (with the exception of Murdoch, the landlord and his daughter, and the former warden of the Audubon Society), the townsfolk are portrayed as hypocritical, profit-motivated and self-protective, with the judge and sheriff repeatedly turning a blind eye to the illegal trafficking in plumes, and the pompous burghers lying to their wives about their regular visits to the whore-house which seems to be the social centre of the town. (Although Murdoch drinks in the brothel's saloon, he refuses the madame's offer of a girl's favours.)

By juxtaposing scenes of the town's social gatherings with the drunken antics of Cottonmouth's gang, Ray draws an explicit parallel between the two communities, at the same time as he shows the almost ritualistic, tribal nature of the gang's behaviour (the men dance with each other – just as the Miami businessmen dance with the prostitutes – and fight almost to the death merely to gain or retain possession of their bunks). Both communities, then, however superficially different, stand in stark contrast, in their greed and dishonesty (Cottonmouth's gang resort to deception to trick Murdoch), to the natural world of the Everglades, which for Ray is a place where beauty and cruelty are inextricably intertwined: neither dominates the other unless man changes the balance that exists between life and death.

Murdoch's first venture into the swamps begins with lyrical shots of birds, deer and other creatures, but Ray, never a director to indulge in picture-postcard glamorisation, swiftly acknowledges the harsh realities that are the inevitable concomitant of this profusion of beauty, with shots of a heron swallowing a fish, an alligator killing a duck and wide-mouthed fledgling egrets screaming in aggressive close-up directly at the camera. Death exists, for sure. On the other hand, the killing is carried out without trickery or greed. Besides Murdoch – initially too blinded by the birds' colours to recognise the deadly pragmatism of animal life – the one human in the film who comes completely to reject killing for reasons of money is Billy One-Arm, the Seminole Indian rejected by his tribe because, like (or from?) the white man, he had learned the advantages to be gained by telling lies. For Ray, then, progress and civilisation, as introduced by the Europeans, are malignant forces; only the animals and the few surviving Native Americans – who, Murdoch points out, have been as shoddily and brutally exploited as the birds themselves – remain morally and spiritually pure, in touch with the forgotten, ancient laws of a primitive Eden that is in very real danger of being destroyed by human ambition.

In this respect, at least, *Wind Across the Everglades* is, alongside *Bigger than Life*, Ray's most disenchanted account of American culture in particular and of modern Western civilisation in general; there seems no hope of recovering this paradise lost. There is, however, a small glimmer of hope for Cottonmouth and Murdoch; each man's real, if very different, love of nature offers the potential of redemption, but first, in order to achieve a more balanced understanding of the world, they must first try to understand one another. Intrigued, therefore, by Murdoch's determination and courage, Cottonmouth decides not to kill him outright but to make a bet with him, the stakes, characteristically, being their own lives: he agrees to let the warden try to ferry him back to town to be punished, but will try to kill him en route, and will given him no directions on how to get out of the labyrinthine swamp. Equally characteristically, since he now recognises his affinity with the poacher, Murdoch accepts, and the conflict, hitherto an affair involving gang and town, is transformed into a one-to-one battle of wits.

Inevitably, Cottonmouth, on his home turf, is at a distinct advantage, and Murdoch, having had to spend a night without sleep lest his rival kill him, soon becomes fatigued and feverish. Imagining that a branch is a snake (appropriately, in that he has mistaken the fundamentally decent Cottonmouth for a 'snake' – that is, someone treacherous and dangerous), he fires his gun, and Cottonmouth, who thinks that Murdoch is trying to kill him, clubs him with his oar. Having apologised ('I kept hopin' I wouldn't have to hurt yer; I ain't never done nothin' I been sorry for, but I'm bone sorry for this') and helped Murdoch out of the water to a dry hummock, the poacher commits his last act of *hubris* by boasting that the glades are all his (as opposed to God's).

As if in retribution, he no sooner agrees to take Murdoch back to Miami ('You feel

Duel to the death: Murdoch and Cottonmouth (Burl Ives) discover they have mortality in common.

gut deep about livin', don't yer, like me?') than the glades refute his claims to god-like power: picking up the hat he has dropped, he is bitten by a snake, and so comes to realise that 'the glades is stronger than anything'. Then, having rejected Murdoch's futile offer of help and sent him on his way to Miami, Cottonmouth looks up at the screaming birds, and admits, 'Maybe you was right … [about their beauty]. Guess I never had a good look at 'em before', before calling on the vultures circling above to come and feast on his flesh. The death of Cottonmouth therefore becomes meaningful, not only in that his body, as he predicted at his first meeting with Murdoch, will be 'reborn' by giving sustenance to the birds, but also because, in belatedly realising their beauty immediately before yielding to their appetite for food, he comes to a full understanding of the cruel wonder of the natural world. As Murdoch departs, he weeps, saddened by the death not only of a fellow rebel but of someone who has finally proved to be far more generous and closer to nature than himself; for Murdoch, Cottonmouth's demise offers tragic but enlightening proof of man's worth and limitations.

From this brief descriptive analysis of the film, it should, I hope, be evident that *Wind Across the Evergaldes* was no mere chore for Ray, but a project that touched upon many of his own preoccupations and gave him the opportunity to develop a number of themes already broached in his earlier work. Parallels abound with other films: the sardonic view of 'respectable' society, the sympathetic identification with outcast loners, the need for a family (Cottonmouth's half-wit son, due to the producer's final cut, is hardly seen in the finished movie, but his gang recalls similar surrogate families in various Ray films), the description of human characters with reference to animals, redemption through sacrificial death, the references to myth (in this case the book of Genesis), the nostalgia for a vanished era, and so on.

Ray's use of colour – particularly of burnished golds, browns and greens – is highly evocative, while many of the compositions are imbued with a sense of visual delirium that verges on surrealism; the world of the Everglades is depicted as primeval and chaotic, but also as fecund, wondrous and vibrant with life even as it is threatened by mankind. As in Howard Hawks's later *Hatari!*, much of Ray's wildlife footage has an immediacy and authenticity that occasionally shifts the film into the realm of near-documentary, thus rooting its more metaphorical moments in a palpable, material reality. Indeed, with the exception of a few lines of Schulberg's script (notably, those concerning Murdoch and Naomi's courtship) which are altogether too florid to be naturalistic, Ray manages, superbly, to balance lyricism and realism, fiction and seemingly irrelevant historical reconstruction, to create a surprisingly coherent narrative; every detail, however superfluous to the film's dramatic thrust it might initially seem, has meaning, despite the occasional continuity lapses to which Ray objected.

On screen, there is scant evidence of the problems he and Schulberg suffered; the movie remains for the most part admirably consistent in tone, thanks partly to the excellence of Burl Ives's and Christopher Plummer's acting (the latter, whose first film it was, giving what is arguably the best performance of his impressive if underrated career). If the film was not a commercial success, that is no reflection on its quality – it is consummately professional, to say the very least – but on Warner Bros.' inability to understand how to market an unusually ambitious film, with no simplistic heroes and villains, which dealt partly with the then unfashionable question of ecology.But then it was not the first time Ray's tendency to make films that were hard to categorise had brought failure at the box office, nor was it the last (the equally eccentric *The Savage Innocents* would also suffer widespread neglect). Sadly, even now, he was still very much the stranger in a strange land.

Party Girl (1958)

SYNOPSIS: In Chicago in the early 1930s, at a party given by gangster Rico Angelo, Tommy Farrell – a brilliant but cynical lawyer who works for the mob – meets nightclub dancer and 'party girl' Vicki Gaye. Though their first impressions of each other are not favourable, the suicide of Vicki's flatmate throws them together; after Vicki points out that Farrell, like her, has sold his pride for money, they begin a love affair which is mutually healing. When Farrell, after undergoing a successful operation on his crippled leg, decides to begin his career anew elsewhere, Rico threatens to harm Vicki unless Farrell defends Cookie La Motte, Rico's new partner-in-crime, who is to be prosecuted by State's Attorney Stewart for murder. Reluctantly, Farrell agrees, but after Rico's attempt to bribe the jury is exposed, and after his gang murders the young psychopath Cookie (to prevent him killing Stewart), mob war breaks out; Farrell is arrested and held as material witness to Rico's criminal activities. At first, the lawyer is worried that Rico will hurt Vicki, and refuses to co-operate with Stewart, who finally decides to release him, rightly guessing that Rico will believe that Farrell betrayed him. Farrell, who has now turned state's witness in return for police protection for Vicki, wanders the bars of Chicago knowing that Rico will find him. When he is finally taken to see the mobster, who threatens to disfigure Vicki's face with acid (his men had abducted her as she was travelling to the coast), Farrell plays for time by flattering Rico's vanity with a trick he often used in court. The police arrive, alerted by a message from Farrell, and a gun battle ensues in which Rico accidentally pours the acid over himself and falls to his death from a window. Now free to begin their lives afresh, the lovers walk away into the night.

Considering the various problems Ray encountered while working for independent producers on *Bitter Victory* and *Wind Across the Everglades*, it is perhaps not surprising that he chose to make his next film under the studio system, for MGM. The script, adapted by George Wells from a story by Leo Katcher, was already written by the time Ray became involved in the project, and he was unable to make any significant alterations to it; for MGM, the film was at least partly a means simply of justifying the salaries of its two stars, Robert Taylor and Cyd Charisse, whose contracts with the studio were about to expire. Nonetheless, Ray's interest was engaged by the story's setting – he had spent time in Chicago during the 1930s – and what might have been little more than a conventional contribution to the then fashionable cycle of nostalgic gangster movies became a characteristically personal account of embittered outcasts threatened, as so often in Ray movies, by a hostile world and redeemed by love. Indeed, though the film, with its psychotic hoodlums and its ambivalent fascination with the gaudy opulence and explosive violence of a bygone age, may be grouped alongside movies such as Don Siegel's *Baby Face Nelson* (1957), Roger Corman's *Machine Gun Kelly* (1958), Richard Wilson's *Al Capone* (1959), Budd

Boetticher's *The Rise and Fall of Legs Diamond* (1960) and Billy Wilder's comic *Some Like It Hot* (1959), both thematically and stylistically it remains first and foremost a Ray film.

In their characterisation Farrell and Vicki (like Dix and Laurel in *In a Lonely Place* and Johnny and Vienna in *Johnny Guitar*) may be seen simply as older, if warier and more cynical, versions of Bowie and Keechie in *They Live by Night*. Physically crippled after an accident in childhood, Farrell has also become a moral and spiritual cripple: emotionally remote ever since his wife turned him out of her bed in disgust at his game leg, he has allowed his brilliant legal mind to become 'a mouthpiece for the mob, guardian angel for punks and gunmen, and great believer in the quickest way', as a means to earn a respect denied him in many areas because of his disability. His success in court is, in fact, due partly to his exploitation of his limp to gain a jury's pity; at the same time, however, he hates both his disability and the moral weakness it has produced in him. Like Vicki, he has sold his pride, prostituted himself in return for money and the high regard of others, his actual reward being self-loathing and loneliness; and it is because Vicki recognises his self-pity – as opposed to the legal genius others see in him – that she is able to bring about his regeneration.

Vicki, suspicious of men since 'being crowded into a corner' in her adolescence ('in a dark and dirty little bar back home in Oklahoma. I was 15. [It was] Very romantic'), has also been alienated from the world, and despite her ambitions to be a dancer, has settled for girlie-magazine modelling, prostitution (due to Hollywood censorship, this is conveyed by her accepting money to attend mobsters' parties) and exhibiting herself, semi-naked, in a nightclub 'meat parade': in the audience, Rico's men describe the showgirls as 'expensive merchandise'. Nevertheless, despite her despairing cynicism, Vicki has the moral fortitude and self-knowledge to drag herself out of the gutter, and thus to show Farrell the folly of his ways; forewarned of her potential self-destruction by her flatmate's suicide (the flatmate, also a showgirl, had been made pregnant and abandoned by her married lover), and recognising her own self-loathing after watching Farrell's tricks in court, she gains the courage and determination both to return the money she stole from lecherous gangster Louis Canetto, and to point out to Farrell, in no uncertain terms, his own pathetically whorish existence.

Following her example, Farrell too decides to go straight; then, after making their confessions to each other, they join forces against a corrupt and dangerous world in a mutually curative love affair. Vicki's abilities as a dancer (displayed after Farrell persuades Rico to give her a better job in the floor show at his Golden Rooster nightclub) are a physical manifestation of her greater inner strength, and it is only after she persuades him to see a doctor and undergo an operation on his crippled leg (an index of his sense of inadequacy) that Farrell rediscovers the ability to walk on his own two feet and to tell Rico that he intends to leave Chicago to set up a new, legitimate practice on the Coast.

Rico, however, plans otherwise. In terms of plot, his reason for wanting to retain Farell's services is one of self-defence: Farrell is not only the *best* lawyer he can afford, to protect both his young, upstart protégé Cookie La Motte and himself from the law; Farrell has also shown himself sufficiently cynical regarding the ethics of his profession to turn a blind eye to the guilt of his clients and to manipulate a court through deceit.

Even more crucially, Rico regards Tommy as a son, and interprets his decision to go straight as an act of personal betrayal. Indeed, there is a vivid Oedipal aspect to the triangular relationship between Rico, Farrell and Vicki: in order to consummate fully his romance with Vicki (her redemptive function makes Vicki something of a mother-figure for Farrell who, though older than she, repeatedly refers back to his childhood), Farrell must deny and eventually 'kill' his surrogate father; while Rico's decision to punish his errant 'son' by torturing Vicki with acid (by violating her virginal beauty – he says she has the 'face of an angel') carries strong undertones of metaphorical rape.

That the threat Rico poses to the lovers is associated with sexual violence is clear from the way their first kiss is immediately interrupted by a phone call from one of his mob. This drags Farrell away to a testimonial dinner at which Rico manically clubs a river gangster with a (phallic) silver billiard cue (this attack, incidentally, was inspired by a real-life beating meted out by Al Capone). Furthermore, Rico's perverse blend of macho sexuality and psychotic jealousy is plain when he is first introduced to the audience, drunkenly shooting at a photo of Jean Harlow (whom he has never met) simply because he feels betrayed by her recent marriage. But Rico is not merely a jealous, Freudian father-figure: he is also the embodiment both of Farrell's morally compromised past (both Tommy and Vicki are striving to unlearn the bitter lessons of their early years), and of a corrupt, callous, destructively dog-eat-dog world.

That Rico is only the most menacing of many threats to the love between Vicki and Farrell is apparent from the way the film's characters are related to one another through a complex web of bonds, to suggest an all-embracing social malaise. Had Vicki not decided to abandon her life of prostitution, she might have become a suicide like her flatmate, a downtrodden gangster's moll like Rico's 'secretary', a grasping, greedy opportunist like Farrell's estranged wife, or simply have remained a mercenary member of the 'meat parade' like her less fortunate colleagues at the Follies.

Likewise, Farrell's options are indicated not only by the other, less favoured members of Rico's 'family' – the wayward (and therefore expendable) La Motte, the unavailingly rebellious Louis Canetto, the servile Lou Forbes (successor to Tommy as Rico's crooked legal advisor) – but also by State's Attorney Stewart, who, in many ways, serves as a reverse mirror-image of Farrell. Where Farrell's actions are (at least initially) guided by his past, Stewart's political ambition – he hopes to become State Governor – looks firmly to the future; where Farrell defends the guilty, Stewart, in prosecuting Farrell to get at Rico, attacks the legally innocent; and where Farrell is the mouthpiece for the mob, Stewart represents 'respectable' society. Furthermore, in the same way that Stewart is as prepared as Farrell to employ trickery to achieve his purpose (he engineers a situation whereby Rico will believe, wrongly, that Farrell has betrayed him), so Chicago's seemingly law-abiding citizenry has much in common with the members of the underworld: at Rico's party, politicians and judges are entertained by gangsters and prostitutes, and when two policemen arrive at Farrell's apartment to arrest him, their garb and their boorish, threatening demeanour lead Vicki to think they are hoodlums sent by Rico. Crime, Ray seems to be suggesting, is so infectious and seductive a disease that it has become almost universal.

Were *Party Girl* simply a matter of vivid characterisation, it would remain no more

than a pleasing blend of love story and crime-thriller, a film with an uncommonly complex and sophisticated structure. Thanks to Ray's muscular direction, however, story and
characters are overlaid with a wealth of telling details that embellish and enrich the film's
every frame. As ever, décor and environment are of great significance in establishing personality and mood, with the apartments of Rico, Tommy and Vicki defined, respectively,
by gaudy, self-assertive opulence, tastefulness stressing bourgeois respectability and
homely, down-to-earth simplicity; similarly, the locating of scenes in rooms that are either
downstairs (the showgirls' dressing room) or upstairs (Rico's secret hideaway in the
Southside Club, the lovers' secret trysting-place in a hotel room when Stewart allows
Farrell a brief respite from jail) evoke, on the one hand, despair, and on the other, private escape. (A handful of exterior shots with shoddy back-projection, depicting Farrell's
and Vicki's brief European idyll after his successful operation, may be attributed either
to Ray's lack of enthusiasm for what is a clichéd montage-scene or – just as likely – to
the work of an assistant or second-unit director.)

Camera movement, too, is used expressively (when Vicki discovers her flatmate naked
and dead in her bath, the camera, rising from behind her to an overhead view of the
corpse, effectively conveys both curiosity and nausea), as are the elegant 'Scope compositions: the symmetry of the opening credits sequence, showing the girls in the 'meat
parade', has an abstraction that stresses their status as objects in a spectacle, while
Tommy's positions in the frame in relation to Rico (either towering over him, or sitting
below him) continually reflect the shifting positions of power and control the two men
occupy. Even Vicki's two dance scenes – presumably included because Charisse was better known for her dancing than for her acting abilities, although it must be remembered
that Ray had long wanted to make a musical – are fully integrated into the plot and mirror her predicament. In each, she is positioned between (and virtually fought over by)
two male dancers – who, it might be argued, stand in for Tommy and Rico – while in the
first she performs a striptease-style routine suggestive both of her past and of her desire
to attract Farrell, and in the second, dressed in a leopard-skin outfit, she acts out a dance
suggestive of nothing so much as a trapped, hunted animal.

But it is in his complex use of colour and symbolism that Ray reveals himself at his
most inspired, perhaps most notably in the way he achieves meaning and emotional
effect through the hues of Vicki's clothes. When she first meets Farrell at the party Rico
pays her to attend, she wears a scarlet dress so evocative of her way of life that the lawyer
immediately feels justified in commenting on her venality. At the end of the evening,
however, this apparently hackneyed visual shorthand is given further depth by a dissolve
that follows the red of her flatmate's blood in the bath with the same red dress, worn by
a severely shaken Vicki at the hospital: red has now come to signify not only sexuality,
but danger and death. Accordingly, when Farrell takes her back to his apartment to
recover from the shock, and she sinks into a sofa that exactly matches her gown, it is
clear not only that she will be at home there, but that their relationship will bring trouble.

As their love blooms and Vicki abandons prostitution for monogamy, so she takes to
wearing quieter browns, tans and fawns that fit in with most of Tommy's furniture and
decor, and only returns to wearing red when, in an attempt to seduce him into turning

A cue for violence: Rico (Lee J. Cobb) rewards Frankie Gasto (Aaron Saxon) for disloyalty.

state's witness, she visits him in the hotel room booked by Stewart. As a direct result of the tryst, she is abducted by Rico, who in order to persuade Farrell to retract his testimony against him, takes a bottle of acid from a white bag and pours it on to a red paper Christmas decoration, before bringing Vicki into the room, still in the red gown, with her face wrapped in white bandages. Without actually showing any violence against Vicki, Ray reveals – by associating her appearance with that of the paper bell, and through our memory of her flatmate's death – the vicious nature of the violence that threatens her. At the same time, her predicament is linked, through sound and place, with that of Frankie Gasto, the hoodlum Rico battered with the billiard cue; Gasto – like Vicki, who has taken Rico's 'son' Tommy away from him – challenged the mobster's authority. Not only is she threatened in the same room where Rico beat Gasto but, just as then (and just as before Bowie's death in *They Live by Night*), trains rumble deafeningly past outside the windows, as if they were omens of death.

Ironically, however, it is not Vicki's death but Rico's that the train noises foreshadow: when Canetto phoned Farrell to tell him he must be taken to meet Rico at an unknown place, the sound of the trains over the phone line forewarned the lawyer of his destination, and he was able to leave a written message for the police to follow him. Nevertheless, before help arrives, Farrell must delay Rico's decision to disfigure Vicki, and does so, with further irony, by using the very trick he had often used in court to defend the gangster. Taking from his pocket a watch he falsely claims was given him by his father, he plays for time by using time itself, by concocting a story in which, as a lowly street-urchin, he had his watch – stolen by a bully – returned to him by the gang-leader Rico, who subsequently became known as the 'king of the kids'.

By appealing to the gangster's pride, vanity, and sentimental memory of his past, paternal friendship with him, Farrell manipulates the situation with the result that he and Vicki are saved and Rico is killed. His tale is interrupted by gunfire from the police now gathered outside, and Rico realises that his 'son' has deceived him, but too late; approaching the lovers with the acid, he tells his betrayer half-sarcastically, half-admiringly, 'You got class, Tommy; that's why I like you,' before raising his hand and pouring, accidentally, the bottle over his own face. Blinded, he plunges through the window to the street below, finally toppled from his throne of seemingly unassailable power; Ray cuts, fittingly, to the red blood that oozes from his crushed, scorched head on to the sidewalk. At last Tommy and Vicki are free to embark on a new life, and before they walk off, alone together, into the night, Tommy furnishes proof that he is no longer in thrall to the past and that he now looks only to his future with Vicki; he gives Stewart the watch – symbol of memories, crime and compromise – as a souvenir.

The ending of *Party Girl* was arguably Ray's most positive and affirmative to date, even though Vicki's salvation is set in motion by her flatmate's suicide and though both Rico and Canetto need to die before Tommy can fully escape his past. Nevertheless, what sticks in the mind, beyond the generic scenes of violence handled by Ray with such breathtaking physical immediacy (mob war becomes a kind of abstract montage of crashing glass, shattered billiard balls and splintered doors), is the painful hesitancy of the lovers' relationship as they slowly progress from mutual recrimination, born of self-contempt, to mutual respect rooted in their recognition of each other's vulnerability: Ray's luxuriant, sumptuous imagery stands in ironic counterpoint to the stark and desperate emotions of his characters.

If, however, his account of betrayal, prostitution, jealousy and loneliness remains, finally, atypically affirmative in its emotional thrust, that speaks not only for the fact that he has made us care about Vicki and Tommy, but also for the sheer, enjoyable vigour and inventiveness of his direction, which as ever made use of every tool at his disposal. Most memorable of all, perhaps, besides the visual excellence, is the surprisingly high quality of the performances: Taylor (Ray initially felt unenthusiastic about him, but soon changed his mind once shooting began) contributed perhaps the finest work of his career, while Lee J. Cobb, perfectly cast as Rico, offered a study of unbridled and irrational villainy as complex as it was powerful, producing scenes that range across the scale from violent, megalomaniac outbursts to quieter moments of maudlin foolishness. The minor characters, too, are vividly drawn (with Corey Allen – Buzz in *Rebel Without a Cause* – especially effective and understated as the volatile, dandyish Cookie La Motte), while Charisse, never a particularly expressive actress, more than pulls her weight.

Finally, however, it is the way in which Ray moves effortlessly from action-packed scenes of violence to more meditative and touching sequences that helps the film to surpass its generic origins. Marked throughout both by his great professionalism and by his feelings of sympathy for his ill-starred lovers, the movie transcends the conventions of the nostalgic gangster picture to become a passionate, involving tale of moral and emotional rebirth.

The Savage Innocents (1960)

SYNOPSIS: Deep in the Arctic, the Eskimo hunter Inuk decides to take a wife; at first he is torn between Asiak and her sister Imina, but he finally chooses the former, and for a while they live happily together, accompanied in their travels by Asiak's mother Powtee. One day, however, while hunting a polar bear, they meet an Eskimo who kills with a rifle, bought from white men at a southern trading post in return for fox-skins. Inuk, who has hitherto hunted with a bow and arrow, is fascinated by the gun, and after killing a hundred foxes, goes to trade the pelts for a rifle of his own. But Asiak is afraid of the white man's madness, and believing it to be infectious she persuades Inuk to leave the post; soon, however, they are visited by a missionary, who admonishes them for 'living in sin'. When the priest rejects Inuk's offer of traditional hospitality (a dish of old meat with maggots and Asiak's sexual favours), he is accidentally killed by the offended Eskimo, who then returns to the northern wilderness. A year or so later, after Powtee has died and Asiak has given birth to a child, he is tracked down and arrested for murder by two Canadian troopers. One dies after falling into the icy sea, but the other's life is saved by Inuk, who takes him to his igloo to convalesce. Fully recovered, the trooper escorts Inuk to the trading post to stand trial, but he comes to realise and respect the difference between his own culture and the Eskimo's, and upon arrival he tells Inuk he is a free man. Bewildered, Inuk refuses to leave, and the trooper realises the only way to save him is to insult and punch him. Upset, Inuk leaves with Asiak, who concludes that the white man is even more unfathomable than the bear.

After the relatively conventional *Party Girl*, Ray embarked on one of his most ambitious and unusual films to date. Having read and liked Hans Ruesch's novel *Top of the World*, the film rights to which were held by Italian producer Maleno Malenotti, he threw himself into researching Eskimo life with great enthusiasm, even living with an Eskimo tribe for several weeks. Nevertheless, while the script was for the most part Ray's own, the making of the film – a US–Italian co-production shot partly in the Arctic, partly in London's Pinewood Studios, and also known as *Ombre Bianchi* and *Les Dents du Diable* – was beset by difficulties: besides the inevitable hardships associated with filming in extremely low temperatures, there were also the problems of dealing with a lead actor (Anthony Quinn) imposed on Ray by Malenotti, of using a multilingual cast and crew, and of matching the location footage with the scenes shot in the studio. This last difficulty was exacerbated when a plane carrying important exterior footage crashed, destroying the film stock and so ensuring much greater use of special-effects photography than was originally planned; worse still, Ray, by his own admission, was misguided in using for his matte-shots the 'blue backing' process, which was unfortunately to result in blue haloes surrounding the figures of the actors. Nonetheless, despite these problems and flaws, the film, finally shown in two very slightly different versions (one English, one Italian), remains an engaging, intelligent oddity, whose central ecological/anthropological theme – like that of *Wind Across the Everglades* – was years ahead of its time. (Interestingly, Bob Dylan's song 'The Mighty Quinn', written some years later, seems to have been inspired by Ray's film.)

Although the first half, whose narrative deals only with the comparatively uninteresting matter of Inuk's indecision over which of two sisters to marry, is documentary-like in its account of Eskimo customs and beliefs, the movie as a whole is very much a fiction with both characters and situations reminiscent of those in many of Ray's earlier films. Inuk, at the beginning, is a loner, unwed (unlike his friends) and more than a little innocent in his approach to courtship and hunting; indeed, within the context of his culture, he might even be regarded as a romantic, pointing out as he does to a colleague, who recommends that he adopt a more pragmatic attitude towards marriage, that a woman 'is not a seal or a walrus'. And like many of Ray's heroes, he is pushed into 'crime' (the accidental killing of the missionary, who attempts to introduce into Inuk's life the concept of sin) by a hostile world, and achieves happiness and insight with the help of a wiser, more mature woman: not only is Asiak's nurturing nature shown by the way she protects him from the cold by warming his feet with her breasts, but it is she who first recognises the risks involved in dealing with the white men at the trading post. Unlike earlier Ray protagonists, however, Inuk is at peace with himself; until confronted by 'civilisation', he is one with nature, acting in accordance with the environment he lives in, free to do as he pleases, and killing only what he needs to eat.

Inuk is, in fact, all too symbolically representative of his culture, seen by Ray as a kind of harsh Utopia where survival is difficult, and cruelty and corruption conspicuously absent: in an opening narration, we are told that the Eskimos – who proudly but simply call themselves 'the men' – share everything, and are 'so crude they do not know how to lie'. An entire race of outsiders (like the gypsies in *Hot Blood*), they have based their laws and taboos on a holistic view of nature, of which man is only one small part: when Powtee, too old to fend for herself, becomes a burden to Inuk and Asiak, she demands, according to tradition, to be left alone in the icy wastes as prey to the bears, who in turn will provide sustenance for her descendants (crucially, the birth of Asiak's child follows soon after Powtee's death, stressing the cyclic continuum of life and death). The Eskimos' customs revolve around a positive *acceptance* of mortality and the vicissitudes of existence: animals are to be hunted for food and respected; blood is a symbol not of violent death but of the life-force (after the Canadian trooper has begun to suffer from frostbite, Inuk kills a husky and plunges the trooper's frozen hands into its warm gut, the dog's death thus saving a man's life); and the long, dark winter night – lasting a third of the year – is seen as an opportunity for making love (or, as the Eskimos call it, 'laughing').

In 'the age of the atom bomb', however, this untainted, icy Eden is invaded by pioneers from Western 'civilisation', bringing with them capitalism, Christianity and needless destruction. When Inuk first encounters the Eskimo with the gun, the men take turns in firing it haphazardly; its potentially lethal effect on Eskimo culture is made clear when Asiak, peering curiously down the barrel, nearly has her head blown away. We have

Paradise on the brink ... Inuk (Anthony Quinn) saves the life of a trooper (Peter O'Toole) sent from the land of capitalism, Christianity and corruption.

already seen Inuk hunting seals by imitating them (in order to kill them at close quarters); the gun, in contrast, offers a more impersonal (and so, arguably, a less responsible/respectful) method of killing, which goes hand in hand with the white man's paying for the slaughter of animals simply in order to meet a fashionable, unnecessary demand for fox-fur. (In this respect, as in the film's portrayal of a threatened Eden, *The Savage Innocents* resembles *Wind Across the Everglades*.) Naïve innocents, Inuk and his friend are too amazed by the gun's magic to realise its lethal power; but Asiak, noting the white man's desire for 'so many useless skins' and wary of the drinking and gambling she finds at the trading post (whose owner, she sees to her bewilderment, nevertheless forbids people to 'laugh' on his premises), decides that the invaders' craziness is catching, and deliberately leaves the weapon behind when they leave.

What she understands and Inuk, at least initially, does not, is that the white man, when visiting strange lands, 'should bring your wives and not your laws' – this is what she tells the convalescent trooper who says he must arrest Inuk even though Inuk has saved his life. In allowing Eskimos into the trading post, the owner expects them to conduct themselves like white men, and turns off the jukebox as soon as Inuk (made drunk by his alcohol) looks as if he might be going to 'misbehave'; in lecturing Inuk and Asiak on the glory of the Christian God and the evil of living together unwed, the missionary too is in effect striving to corrupt them; and in arresting Inuk for murder when he himself rightly insists that 'my father's laws have not been broken' (the priest's death was accidental, and the result of *his* having broken *Eskimo* laws by refusing Inuk's hospitality), the troopers are attempting to impose an alien, destructive law (Inuk faces the death penalty) on a land in which they, and not the Eskimos, are the outsiders. To Ray, the white men are the aggressors, their harsh, unbending 'Christian' morality and profit-motivated commerce leading them to offend and exploit not only man but nature itself; taking their own social conventions as moral absolutes, they try to control the world by re-creating it in their own image and, in so doing, bring unnecessary killing and anguish into a community hitherto defined by its honesty, placidity, friendliness and generosity.

Finally, chastened by Asiak's words, by Inuk's generosity, and by the ludicrous, terrible intrusion into an otherwise silent, white wilderness of the thunderous sound of loud rock-'n'-roll echoing from the trading post's jukebox, the surviving trooper realises that the white man's laws have become 'stronger than the people who made them', and that prosecuting Inuk would achieve nothing: the authorities would never be able to accept or understand his innocence, nor his justification for attacking the missionary. He is at least partly enlightened, therefore, and sets Inuk free. But though Inuk is allowed to return home with Asiak to the serenity of life in the North, Ray's ending is hardly optimistic. While trooper and Eskimo have, by saving each other's lives, come to respect and like one another, they still do not understand each other; their cultural differences, ultimately, are such that they can never really communicate properly. Worse still, at the end of the film, the trading post continues to blare out its noisy music across the frozen wastes: the destructive onslaught of Christian, capitalist 'civilisation' into the Arctic cannot be stopped. The fragile balance of nature, so long supported by the Eskimo culture, is not merely threatened but doomed, and like the Everglades, the ancient hunting grounds of 'the men' will become a paradise lost.

As if reflecting the moral innocence of Inuk and Asiak, Ray's story and direction are unusually simple and straightforward; the film has almost the feel of a fable. Visually, the CinemaScope compositions stress the massive purity of the Arctic wastes, and the smallness of the humans struggling to live in them. At the same time, the Eskimos' grey and white parkas blend with the landscape for more harmoniously then the reds, browns and blacks worn by the invaders yet to realise that 'ice and snow can be friends'.

Without architecture at hand, Ray's use of décor is inevitably limited, but, instead, he reveals the Eskimos' sense of unity with their environment through a robust physicality of gesture (perhaps most notable in the scenes showing eating, dancing and laughing), and through long, elegantly fluid takes whose unbroken rhythms stand in contrast to the febrile, nervy tempos of most of his earlier, more anguished work.

Many of the performances, too, contribute to a sense of natural spontaneity; Ray used mostly unknown actors (usually Chinese or Japanese) to play the Eskimos, though Quinn, playing Inuk rather as if he were Zorba the Eskimo, seems too broadly and deliberately expansive in his gestures and delivery of lines to convince entirely. Otherwise, the casting is somewhat haphazard, a common flaw in international co-productions: Peter O'Toole (uncredited and, perhaps, dubbed) is plausible enough as the Canadian trooper whom Inuk saves, but Lee Montague, for example, simply does not look like an Eskimo.

It is perhaps in Ray's dialogue that the film is at its clumsiest: in attempting to duplicate the Eskimos' idioms by having them speak in the third- rather than first-person (they refer to themselves as 'someone' or 'a man' instead of 'I'), he often achieves, instead of the poetry he intended, a stilted pidgin English all too reminiscent of the lines commonly put into the mouths of Indians in Hollywood Westerns. Sadly, the effect is often jarring, all the more so because otherwise, in Ray's detailed, almost documentary-like account of Eskimo customs, he handles the ethnographic elements of his film unusually well.

The Savage Innocents, then, is neither bad nor formulaic; rather, it is half-successful, a fascinating but flawed attempt to examine cultural conflict not through war but through a poetic comparison of two very different ways of life. Those who have rather fatuously dismissed the film by comparing it to Robert Flaherty's classic documentary *Nanook of the North* have not only mistaken Ray's purpose – clearly, for all his romanticism, he does not see the Eskimo simply as a 'noble savage', as did Flaherty – but have forgotten that the earlier film, too, was something of a fiction, with the director manipulating his real-life subjects according to his own purposes; such comparison is largely irrelevant. Far more pertinent to any assessment of Ray's achievement is his use of Inuk as cultural cipher: while the Eskimo does share several basic characteristics with earlier Ray heroes, he is never wholly convincing as an individual, so burdened is he by Ray's decision to make him represent an entire society. As a result, the film lacks the dramatic complexity of Ray's finest work, and although the consequently simplified narrative has enormous charm as a fable, not to mention considerable power as an indictment of Western society's determination to colonise, economically, morally and spiritually, even the most arid wastes of our planet, it none the less occasionally suffers from a well-meaning naïvety which is altogether absent from Ray's best films.

King of Kings (1961)

SYNOPSIS: When, some sixty years after the Roman invasion of Judaea, Herod – a Bedouin
appointed King of the Jews by Rome – orders that all new-born sons be slain, Joseph and
Mary flee to Egypt with their child Jesus. Twelve years later, they return to a country where
rebel uprisings against the occupying forces are so troublesome that, finally, Pontius Pilate is
sent as governor. Aided by Herod Antipas, son of the late Herod, Pontius Pilate attempts to
destroy the subversive influence both of Barabbas – leader of an underground resistance
movement – and of prophets like John the Baptist, who is first to recognise the now adult
Jesus as the Messiah. Having survived Satan's temptation in the desert, Jesus gathers
apostles (including Judas, a former follower of Barabbas) to help to preach the Word of
God. They soon encounter opposition; after John the Baptist is beheaded by Herod Antipas
as a favour to his stepdaughter Salome, Jesus' message of peace, heard by thousands at the
Sermon on the Mount, and his ability to perform miracles convince Pilate that he is a threat
to Roman power. Barabbas is caught after disastrously rousing to rebellion a crowd
assembled to hear Jesus, while Jesus himself realises that he will be betrayed by Judas, who
believes that the Messiah, once arrested, will use his miraculous powers to defeat the
Romans. After taking a last supper with his disciples, Jesus is arrested in the garden of
Gethsemane and, having been tried by Pilate and Herod Antipas, is sentenced to
crucifixion. According to tradition, a criminal is pardoned at the Passover; Barabbas, rather
than Jesus, is chosen. After seeing Jesus die on the cross, Barabbas finds the body of Judas,
who has hanged himself. The morning after the Messiah's entombment, Mary Magdalen, a
reformed harlot, discovers that Jesus' body has disappeared from the sepulchre, and meets
him, seemingly alive once more; he promises to appear to the disciples on the shore of Lake
Galilee before he ascends to heaven. This he does, and the apostles, their faith restored, go
out into the world to spread the Word of God.

In Rome after completing *The Savage Innocents*, Ray decided not to return to America,
and spoke of making low-budget movies about simple, everyday life. It is perhaps ironic,
then, that his next film should have been for the independent producer Samuel
Bronston, who had recently set up his own alternative to Hollywood just outside Madrid,
and who would specialise in making expensive, spectacular historical epics like *El Cid*
and *The Fall of the Roman Empire* (both directed by Anthony Mann).

Bronston's first major production was a life of Christ which, under titles such as *Son of
Man*, *The Sword and the Cross* and *The Man from Nazareth*, had originally been planned as
a film for John Farrow or John Ford to direct; in the end, however, Ray was assigned to
the project. He hired Philip Yordan, the writer of *Johnny Guitar*, to work on the script, and
Yordan in turn suggested the title *King of Kings*. Since Ray himself had for some time been

considering making a film on Christ, his initial dealings with Bronston were amiable and fruitful; but Bronston's financing and production methods were so disorganised that Ray once again found himself involved in a chaotic shoot over which he had little artistic control. Various stars – including James Mason, Richard Burton and John Gielgud – dropped out of the cast; Ray's chosen cameraman, Franz Planer, fell ill, to be replaced by Milton Krasner; and when Bronston, in need of money to set up *El Cid*, sold shares in the film to MGM, Ray was once again deprived of his right to the final cut. Scenes were changed or removed; an explanatory narration, written by Ray Bradbury and read by Orson Welles, was added; and the film's running time reduced by three-quarters of an hour. But despite this interference, Ray's basic conception remains intact: Jesus is a moral and spiritual 'rebel' preaching the value of peace and love in a violent world, while Ray's decision not merely to create a series of *tableaux* inspired by Christian paintings ensures that the story looks as if it were 'taking place for the first and only time, that it was of *that* moment, not of a Renaissance moment, not of a Flemish moment, not of a Byzantine moment'.

Of course, any life of Christ not intended to blaspheme (and Bronston, fully aware of the benefits of publicity gained during production, obtained script approval from Pope John XXIII) will involve certain constraints on individual artistic expression; story and characters must conform with what is written in the Gospels. But, within those limitations, emphasis and context may provide a more personalised approach to Christ's life and teachings, and Ray's account reveals once again his own special interest in the lone innocent living in a hostile environment. Where Cecil B. DeMille's *The King of Kings* (1927) and George Stevens's *The Greatest Story Ever Told* (1965) opt for a far more conventional, reverential piety towards Christ as an individual, and where *The Last Temptation of Christ* (1988), as directed by Martin Scorsese and scripted by Paul Schrader from Nikos Kazantsakis's book, is primarily concerned with Christ as a man tormented by his divine calling, Ray's film anticipates Pier Paolo Pasolini's *The Gospel According to Matthew* (1964) in situating Christ within a clearly defined social and political context: primarily, it is Christ's ideology that sets him apart from the world around him and makes him of interest.

Unlike Pasolini, however, whose stark treatment of the story led him to downplay Christ's emotions and to use him as a barely characterised ideological mouthpiece, Ray manages to merge the political and the personal, with the result that his is arguably the richest of all films portraying the life of Christ. (It is a great pity that Carl Theodor Dreyer died before he could make his long-planned film on Jesus which, judging from his other work, would probably have stood head and shoulders above all such films, at least in its depiction of Christ's spirituality.)

Despite the contemporary nickname for *King of Kings* – *I Was a Teenage Jesus* – Ray's Messiah is unusually convincing both as a human and as the Son of God. Like Salome, played by teenager Brigid Bazlen, Christ is represented by an actor of the right age (Jeffrey Hunter – Frank James in *The True Story of Jesse James* – was in his early thirties). And like so many Ray protagonists, he is an innocent outsider whose isolation from society leads him to adopt a surrogate family – the disciples – and drives him along a thorny path of betrayal and self-doubt towards a violent death: here, crucifixion, a form of hanging which loosely connects with Ray's interest in lynch-mob mentality. Mostly, despite Jesus' short-lived fear of dying and his (characteristically for Ray) unsettled relationship with his father ('My God, my God, why hast thou forsaken me?'), Jesus, like Inuk, lives in harmony with himself and the natural world; here, the conflict is against, on the one hand, Roman oppression, and on the other, the spirit of violent resistance personified by Barabbas; neither can see, as Christ does, that salvation comes through peace and love.

That the Romans' control of Judaea is rooted in violence is made evident in the remarkable first sequence of the film, which, employing images and Bradbury's narration as opposed to dialogue, deftly and economically introduces the war-torn world into which Jesus is born and against which he will have to fight:

> Thus, for more that fifty years after Pompey's invasion, the history of Judaea could be read by the light of burning towns. If gold was not the harvest, there was a richness of people to be gathered; the battalions of Caesar Augustus brought in the crop. Like sheep from their own green fields, the Jews went to the slaughter; they went from the stone quarries to build Rome's triumphal arches. But Caesar could find no Jew to press Rome's laws on this fallen land, so Caesar named one Herod the Great, an Arab of the Bedouin tribe, as the new, false and maleficent King of the Jews. But from the dust at Herod's feet, rebellions of Jews rose up, and Herod, in reply, planted evil seeds from which forests of Roman crosses grew high on Jerusalem's hills. And Herod, passing pleased, bade the forest multiply.

The ironic use of agricultural metaphors implies that Roman aggression is an offence against not only the people of Judaea, but the very land, that is, against nature, and thus against God, its creator. Just as Bradbury's poetic writing draws on the elemental world of nature, so Ray's initial images of a turbulent, ravaged Judaea stress reds and browns, equating fire and spilt blood with the scarlet cloaks of the Roman militia. Indeed, clashing colours and metaphorical use of the natural elements recur throughout, as in *Johnny Guitar*, to dramatise conflict and symbolise character and ideology. While the Romans – whose harsh oppression of Judaea in the face of organised underground resistance evokes the Nazis' occupation of Europe – are predominantly clad in scarlet, the corruption of the court of Herod Antipas – of the collaborators, to continue the analogy – is signified by its opulent purples and golds. The natural moral purity of Christ, on the other hand, may be read from his clear blue eyes (seen in massive close-up across the 70mm frame when John the Baptist first recognises him as the Messiah), and from his clothes of white or pastel. Barabbas is for the most part clad in brown, reflecting his murky ethical dilemma of struggling to achieve peace through violence.

Christ and Barabbas, however, are – as the latter acknowledges – both fighting for the same cause (although the nature of the freedom they desire differs, as pointed out by Lucius, a Roman centurion who functions as a kind of chorus figure, commenting objectively – he does not initially believe in God – on Christ the man); if Barabbas is fire, then Christ is water, and Ray repeatedly shows the latter in scenes featuring water – in the river with John the Baptist, by the Sea of Galilee – while Barabbas' 'pollution' of Christ's pacifist ideals is embodied in the way the subterranean foundry where he forges his weapons turns a stream red with rust. (This twinning of Christ and Barabbas, of course, is reminiscent of Ray's treatment of Leith and Brand in *Bitter Victory* and of Murdoch and Cottonmouth in *Wind Across the Everglades*.)

Interestingly, like Scorsese and Schrader, who portray Judas as a *reluctant* betrayer of Christ, as a predestined instrument of his earthly death, Ray and Yordan offer a fresh and very credible interpretation of the character to emphasise the similarities and dif- ferences between Christ and Barabbas. Initially a follower of Barabbas, Ray's Judas is converted to Christ's pacifist cause partly because he feels that, if the two men fought against Rome together, there would be a greater chance of Judaea regaining its inde- pendence. Later, after Barabbas' arrest and the deaths of countless Jews, which come as a direct result of Judas' telling Barabbas that Christ is planning to preach in Jerusalem, the disciple is tormented by guilt; in his confusion, he imagines that, once Christ 'feels the Roman sword at His throat, He will strike them [the Romans] down with a wave of one arm'. Misguided, then, rather than mercenary, Judas becomes a somewhat more plausible disciple of Jesus than the figure described in the Gospels, and his suicidal guilt after the crucifixion is all the more tragically moving. (Equally interesting as characters whose feelings about Christ – and, therefore, about Rome's subjugation of Judaea – shift and develop as the film progresses are Lucius and Pilate's wife Claudia who, while not immediately converted by their encounters with the Messiah, at least come to question the Roman assumption that might is necessarily right.)

Indeed, all the characters – major and minor – are vividly, if economically, portrayed;

Symbol of peace: Christ (Jeffrey Hunter) seats the disciples at a strangely shaped table for one final supper together.

even Herod Antipas transcends mere villainy through his wary regard for John the Baptist and Christ. What is perhaps most surprising about *King of Kings* is the way Ray manages to insert so many significant details into a spectacular epic evidently intended by its producer to impress merely through sheer scale. Some of Ray's small details carry a resonance that extends beyond the Gospels (most notably, perhaps, a surprising over- head shot of the table used at the Last Supper, which instead of the long, straight tres- tle usually shown, is a three-spoked arrangement bearing a strange resemblance to the modern CND symbol!); other details, like Yordan's poetic but never clumsily archaic dialogue, lend immediacy and plausibility to a story that has all too often been turned, through excessively sentimental reverence, into little more than a fairy tale.

In dramaturgical terms, Ray sensibly opts for understatement rather than lurid spec- tacle. The miracles, for instance, are seldom actually shown being performed by Jesus; more subtly, his presence is conveyed by his shadow (as indeed it is in the final scene of the Ascension when it falls diagonally over the apostles' fishing nets to form a giant cross on the sand), or the miracles are merely mentioned in reports to Pilate. Similarly, the Sermon on the Mount is staged not as one unbroken monologue by a stationary Christ but, more plausibly, as a question-and-answer session in which he wanders freely among the multitude. The crucial effect of such sequences is to make Christ and his actions more comprehensible, in relation to everyday human experience, than they usually are in films of his life; at the same time, the simplicity of the story, the unpretentious nature of Jeffrey Hunter's performance and the very straightforwardness of Ray's direction cre- ate in the film a mythic clarity that encourages us to believe in Jesus' divinity.

All too often, *King of Kings* has been dismissed as just another Hollywood-style epic that vulgarises its subject-matter; such an assessment completely ignores the uncommon integrity and intelligence Ray brought to bear on the problem of transforming a poten- tially fantastic fable into an engrossing, believable story. The opening scenes of Pompey's invasion of Judaea (a lone horseman in red seen riding into a crowd of Jews who are garbed in gleaming white, and later violating Jerusalem's Holy Temple by running his sword through a scarlet silken gauze); the hubristic Herod's death and rejection by his son, shown by a lofty overhead camera; Salome's dance for her lustful stepfather, not the usual extravagant striptease with seven veils but a clumsy, none too enthusiastic attempt at erotic provocation performed by a petulant adolescent; Christ's painful pro- gression towards Calvary, his cross catching on street cobbles as he is surveyed not by thousands of adoring followers but by a handful of passers-by and acquaintances; the raising of the cross shown with a camera placed above Christ's head (interestingly, this dramatic point of view was also adopted years later in Scorsese's *The Last Temptation of Christ*): in every scene, Ray's ability to communicate mood and meaning through a pre- cise visual style transcends the clichés one usually associates with biblical epics and points up the story's contemporary relevance. Like most of his other films, it is about betrayal, solitude, the fruits of violence, and the value of love and being at peace with oneself. It is not necessary, therefore, to be a member of the Christian faith in order to become involved in the emotions on view. Ray's Christ, Barabbas, Judas and Lucius have their counterparts in the modern world; their hopes and fears are universal and timeless.

55 Days at Peking (1963)

SYNOPSIS: In China, in the summer of 1890, the killing of foreign residents by Boxer rebels is partly supported by an Imperial court keen to liberate itself from the influence of the Western powers, and the inhabitants of Peking's foreign compound are concerned that their lives may be at risk. After Major Matt Lewis of the US Marines is involved in an incident with the Boxers, the British Ambassador Sir Arthur Robertson advocates careful negotiations with the Chinese. But at a banquet to celebrate Queen Victoria's birthday, Lewis is so incensed by Prince Tuan's provocative display of Boxer martial arts that he insults the Prince. The next day, Tuan (who, unlike General Jung Lu, advises the Empress to opt for overt aggression against the Western powers) orders the Boxers to kill the German minister. When Lewis and Sir Arthur tell the Empress of Tuan's part in the murder, she warns them that it would be wise for foreigners to leave China at once. At a meeting of the allied powers, however, Sir Arthur – who expects military support to arrive within a few days – persuades his colleagues to remain in Peking; soon the Boxers lay siege to the compound. The foreigners' ammunition is severely depleted, and so many soldiers wounded that the Russian Baroness Natalie Ivanoff – with whom Lewis has begun a troubled love affair – abandons all hopes of leaving and takes to nursing. At court, meanwhile, Tuan's advocacy of aggression is supported by the Empress, and Imperial troops are dispatched to repulse the Western auxiliary forces. In desperation, Sir Arthur and Lewis plan a daring raid on the Peking arsenal; their success undermines Tuan's influence on the Empress, but fails to prevent a renewed Boxer attack. Lewis's attempt to reach the auxiliary forces in Tientsin ends in failure, and Natalie is killed during a mission to obtain opiates for the wounded, but just as all seems lost for the besieged, the auxiliaries arrive to repel the Boxer attack. The Empress escapes Peking disguised as a peasant, and Lewis departs accompanied by a dead colleague's daughter, whom he has agreed to take to America.

Ray's last commercial film was made, like *King of Kings*, for Samuel Bronston. It got off the ground after various other projects had come to nothing – including a circus story scripted with Philip Yordan (later directed by Henry Hathaway as *Circus World*) and versions of novels by William P. McGivern (*The Road to the Snail*), Henry Treece (about the children's crusade) and Nicholas Monserrat (*The Tribe That Lost Its Head*).

55 Days at Peking has been widely dismissed as, at worst, a mess, and at best, a thoroughly anonymous if craftsmanlike piece of hack-work. Such evaluations, however, seem to derive less from a considered assessment of the finished film, than from an awareness of the troublesome circumstances of its making. Understandably, given the effect that the production had on his health and his career, Ray himself seemed to prefer not to discuss it, other than to say that, besides an early interest in a theme of different nations trying to survive together in a strange, foreign land, his chief reason for accepting the project was that he saw it as a means to an end, as a way of obtaining sufficient finance (and, perhaps, status) to allow him to make more personal projects of his own choosing. Ray *aficionados*, too, have tended to regard it as a work with few redeeming features, largely, one suspects, because of certain events in the film's making. Ray collapsed from exhaustion on set (he had been the victim of regular interference from Bronston's executives, of antagonism among the members of his cast and of massive extravagance by others that sapped part of the budget while causing it to soar overall), and the producer's team of medical 'experts' virtually forbade his return to the set. As a result, the film was completed by Ray's second-unit director Andrew Marton (with the exception of a scene directed by Guy Green).

But though Marton (who, for most of the scenes he shot, followed Ray's and Philip Yordan's script) did in some cases change sequences by conflation and condensation, and though Ray was allowed no say in the editing, it is clear from a close analysis of the movie that, at least in theme and character, it may still be seen as Ray's creation. There are, quite simply, too many details which echo moments in his earlier work for the film to be taken merely as the product of artistic compromise. Moreover, it must be said that, despite a number of loose ends in the narrative – a result, one presumes of Marton having sometimes combined several scenes into one – the film remains an unusually ambitious and intelligent example of the epic genre.

Like Ray's previous movie, *55 Days at Peking* impresses by its careful balancing of the intimate and the epic, the personal – the story of Charlton Heston's Matt Lewis, an emotionally cold, alienated man of action redeemed by love – and the political. As so often with Ray, the film is fundamentally about conflict. Unlike *King of Kings*, which was primarily concerned with the occupied, *55 Days at Peking* focuses for the most part on the occupying forces, the leaders of the foreign compound. It is notable, however, that, like the US minister played by Ray himself in the film (he replaced an actor who withdrew from the cast at short notice), Ray the director never takes a partisan view of events by showing the Chinese as villains and the non-Chinese as heroes. Instead, he elects to abstain on the question of imperialism, giving equal weight to the arguments of the Chinese and the allies.

The film commences with a series of virtuoso crane- and tracking-shots of the twelve embassies in the foreign compound all raising flags and playing, to cacophonous effect, their national anthems, before cutting to two Chinese men, one blocking his ears, the other pointing out that the noise is from 'different nations saying the same thing at the same time: We want China'; the pointlessness of the violence that fuels much of the narrative is implied by the film's cyclic structure, which ends with that same terrible musical cacophony.

More crucially, both sides in the conflict are balanced against each other by means of the various characters advocating different strategies (and, therefore, ideologies). Sir Arthur, as played by David Niven, the epitome of decent polite behaviour and cool-headed rationality, is not merely a diplomat but an avowed man of peace who is reluctant to allow the situation in Peking to escalate to the point where full-scale international war is the outcome; and just as Sir Arthur would prefer to risk humiliation and the wrath of his government rather than forego his principles, so the Imperial General Jung Lu incurs the disapproval of the Empress by proposing not military aggression but prudence and patience. (Not insignificantly, each man is shown as being both willing and able to communicate and, to some extent, empathise with the 'enemy': in his negotiations with the Empress, Sir Arthur is fluent in the poetic, highly metaphorical language she uses, while Jung Lu, it transpires, has had an adulterous affair with Baroness Ivanoff, whose escape from war-torn Peking he attempts to faciliate.)

In contrast to these men of peace stand Lewis and Prince Tuan, whose blunt, pragmatic assessments of the tense situation – Tuan is no mere scheming villain but a passionate patriot who, like Barabbas in *King of Kings*, wishes to rid his country of its oppressors – are accompanied by a belief in attack as opposed to defence, war as opposed to negotiation. And while Ray clearly accepts that, in certain circumstances, the use of violence is not only inevitable but necessary, it is equally evident that his sympathies are with Sir Arthur and Jung Lu rather than Lewis and Tuan, whose proud, hot-headed tempers drive them to acts that only serve to increase tension between the warring factions. Like *King of Kings* (and to some extent *The Savage Innocents*), then the film deals with a lack of communication and understanding between cultures, and with the comparative value of peace and violence in striving to cope with that gulf.

At the same time, and on a more personal level, the film is once again about one man's redemption through a woman's love. All the female characters are, in some respects, wiser than their male counterparts: the Empress questions the justice of Western imperialism ('Prudence and patience? ... For what?'), and realises that what threatens China more than anything else is its lack of unity, as personified by Tuan and Jung Lu; Sir Arthur's wife Sarah likewise questions the very purpose of war, asking, after her young son is shot, whose ambitions he is serving, and who could profit by his death; and Natalie – rejected by the Russians, the lover of a Chinese and an American – challenges, by her behaviour, the very notion of racial and national purity. Finally, it is Natalie – in many respects an archetypal Ray outsider/outcast – whose words and deeds suggest a possible solution to the problems facing the warring nations, in that she alone recognises the harm caused by human beings' inability to communicate openly with each other. When she first meets Lewis, who in flirting with her warns that he can offer her very little time, she says, 'Keep drinking, Major; your tight uniform will hold you together'; almost at once she has noticed that his proud soldierly demeanour is only a mask for his inner insecurities and fears, and his immediate reaction to her comment is to confess that 'clever women' make him nervous and that, 'to a soldier, strangers make the best friends'.

Lewis, then, like so many Ray heroes, is afraid of being close to people (especially women), and so has chosen the lonely, nomadic life of a Marine rather than that of someone who has settled down in one place. His view of life, which he explains to his men as they enter Peking, is that everything has a price and can be bought; this is a cynical ethic that he acts upon when he tries to buy a Christian priest who is being tortured by the Boxers, and that is later echoed by his chauvinist evaluation of Natalie ('A soldier's pay buys a soldier's woman'). Lewis is alienated both from others and from his own feel-

Time to be brave: Lewis (Charlton Heston) faces his hardest battle ever when confronted by orphan Teresa (Lynne Sue Moon).

ings, and he has become an emotional cripple; it is hardly accidental that he first comes to question his cool attitude to others when he is told of Natalie's death by a crippled soldier she had been nursing. The soldier reproaches Lewis for his seeming lack of concern, and vehemently rejects Lewis's offer of help as he stumbles around on his crutches. It is therefore by being made to *confront* his own inadequacy regarding Natalie's death, to acknowledge his callous treatment of her when she was alive (though he knew she was wounded, he returned to the battle-line rather than visit her) that Lewis is granted, through her sacrifice, a chance of spiritual salvation.

But Natalie is now dead: redemption is now offered through his relationship with the orphan Teresa, the nine-year-old Chinese-American daughter of his dead colleague Andy Marshall. Early in the film, his dispassionate view of the girl's predicament (Andy complains that, because he is a Marine, he neglects her) is clear when he tells his friend that she could never be taken to America because she would be treated as a freak. Later, after Andy is killed, he tries to evade the responsibility of telling Teresa of her father's death. Even when he finally speaks to her, Ray's subtle direction – focused on *his* discomfort rather than, as one might expect in a potentially maudlin scene, on the girl – shows Lewis's inability to comfort her, so caught up is he in his own distaste at being forced to respond to another human's pain. Sitting at the far end of a bench from her, rarely looking into her eyes, Lewis lapses into long embarrassed silences, compelling her to fathom the sad truth for herself; clearly, he is concerned less with her feelings than with his fears of having to meet the emotional demands of a difficult (because intimate) encounter.

Thereafter, Lewis repeatedly neglects to fulfil his promise of discussing with the girl her desire that he should take her to America, as her father had vowed to do. (Interestingly, she calls America 'home' just as Sir Arthur's wife fears that her son, if he dies, will never go 'home' to the England he has never seen: the film, like many Ray movies, is partly about nostalgic desires for a resting place experienced by strangers in a strange land.) Only after Natalie's death and the crippled soldier's accusation that he feels no sadness at losing her does Lewis realise that he has buried his humanity – his ability to feel for and communicate with others – beneath a military uniform; action, for Lewis, has been less a matter of courage or staying true to one's principles (indeed, Sir Arthur tells him, 'It's easy [to be brave] when it's something you can see – a wall, a hill, a river; but how can you explain when it's for a principle?') than a means of avoiding close relationships and the responsibilities that accompany them. At the end of the siege, therefore, having realised his cowardly tendency to ignore the needs of others, Lewis confesses to Sir Arthur, who has asked him if he has a home to go to, that, 'I may have to make one yet.' Then, finally, as he mounts his horse and prepares to lead his troops out of Peking, he sees Teresa looking up at him from the crowd, and with unprecedented tenderness tells her, 'Here – take my hand', before lifting her up behind him and riding off towards a new life of emotional commitment – and even, perhaps, to a home.

The deeply moving close-up of Lewis's and Teresa's clasped hands recalls similarly affirmative celebrations of a redemptive coming together in both *On Dangerous Ground* and *Rebel Without a Cause*, just as the complex counterpointing of characters and communities (through contrast and likeness) echoes that in the majority of his films, most notably, perhaps, *The Lusty Men*, *Johnny Guitar*, *Wind Across the Everglades*, *Bitter Victory* and *King of Kings*. Indeed, the last two of these films are especially relevant if one wishes to examine *55 Days at Peking* within the context of Ray's *oeuvre*: the former, like *55 Days* a tough and challenging critique of notions of military courage, is frequently echoed by the later film, particularly in the tense night-raid on the Imperial arsenal and by a sequence in which Lewis completes a long and difficult journey with a wounded soldier on his back, only to discover that the soldier is dead; Ray's life of Christ, meanwhile, anticipates his next film in its discussions about the relative worth of peaceful and violent resistance as well as in its visual style.

Never merely opting for traditional epic spectacle – the use of lavish costumes and sets, and thousands of extras – Ray employed the resources he had been given to create meaning through colour, movement and composition. Filling the vast 70mm Technirama screen with a rich array of small but telling details (Sir Arthur kicks away a knee cushion, for instance, before addressing the Empress, revealing the determination and the sense of his own equality and dignity that underlie his politely deferential diplomacy), Ray enriches the skeleton of the written script with unexpected but entirely appropriate stylistic flourishes. As the humbled Empress (in a scene that prefigures a similar moment in Bertolucci's *The Last Emperor*) gazes one last time at her Imperial throne, Ray's overhead shot serves not only to conceal, initially, the identity of the woman (she is disguised as a peasant) but to evoke, perfectly, her sense of humiliation, oppression and despair; and as Sir Arthur and Lewis dive on to the arsenal floor in a last-minute effort to extinguish the dynamite fuses that could blow them to kingdom come, Ray's careful balancing of them within the frame and the characters' simultaneously timed leaps towards the camera reveal that at last, after arguing with one another for so long, they have been forced by desperate circumstances to work together and accept each other as members of a team.

Scene after scene, both intimate and action-packed, is constructed with an equally subtle eye for detail, just as Ray's use of colour and natural symbolism (red and fire for violence and menace; browns, blues, whites and water for contemplation and safety) adds still further dimensions to his assured control of mood. Indeed, though the sheer scale of the film, perhaps inevitably, means that Ray's more personal touches are less conspicuous than in his earlier, 'smaller' movies, *55 Days at Peking* is in no respect a failure. With strong, memorable performances, muscular but imaginative and lucid direction, and a narrative that moves effortlessly between exciting scenes of battle and quieter, more meditative moments to create a very real feeling of private lives caught up in the huge shifts of history, it remains one of the finest epic spectaculars ever made, and one can only regret that the painful experience of its production led its director to abandon – or be abandoned by – the world of mainstream movie-making.

We Can't Go Home Again (1973–76)

SYNOPSIS: At a time of great political unrest in America, former Hollywood film director Nick Ray (played, of course, by Ray himself) becomes a professor of film and decides to teach his students by helping them to make a film based on their own ideas and experiences. At first they view him with suspicion, but soon he becomes a kind of father-confessor to whom they come with their various anxieties about politics, sex and the widening generation gap. Ray becomes concerned that one student, Tom – who is unhappily in love, and confused by his feelings for his policeman father – may kill himself, and after he sees the youth enter a barn in which Ray has left a rope, the teacher follows to prevent his suicide. In the confusion that ensues, however, Ray accidentally hangs himself; his corpse counsels the students to love one another.

After the debacle of *55 Days at Peking*, Ray spent most of the 1960s in Europe, working on a number of projects that sadly never came to fruition: notably, adaptations of Ibsen's *The Lady from the Sea,* Dylan Thomas's screenplay *The Doctor and the Devils*, a Western scripted by novelist James Jones and a science-fiction project about youth rebellion called *Only Lovers Left Alive*, which was to have starred The Rolling Stones. That he was unable to see any of these films through was, admittedly, partly his own fault – alcoholism and drug-abuse, not to mention despair caused by his experiences with Bronston, had made him indecisive – but bad luck and the reluctance of producers to invest money in a supposedly troublesome director were also key factors.

Finally, however, after shooting footage for a never-to-be-completed film (*Wha-a-at?*) inspired partly by the events in Paris in May '68, he was tempted away from his home on the Baltic island of Sylt and back to America by a proposition that he direct a film about a court case involving a young drugs offender. Then, on his arrival in America, Ray became fascinated by a contemporary real-life courtroom drama – the Chicago Conspiracy Trial – and at once set about trying to make a movie about Judge Julius J. Hoffman and the 'Chicago Eight', the defendants whose involvement in various radical causes (student revolt, the anti-Vietnam War movement and the Black Panthers) had led to their being accused of conspiracy. After his cameras were denied access to the courtroom itself, Ray decided to reconstruct it in a studio and cast actors (including Dustin Hoffman as the defence lawyer and James Cagney or Groucho Marx as Judge Hoffman) to appear alongside the actual defendants; but once again his promised production finance fell through, so that the project had to be abandoned.

The experience was not, however, entirely fruitless: Ray's filming of events in Chicago was documented in Marcel Ophuls's TV documentary *Auf der Suche nach meinem Amerika* (1970), while the footage he had managed to shoot would finally appear, briefly, in *We Can't Go Home Again*, the film he made with his students at Harpur College, part of New York State University at Binghampton. Ray was appointed professor of film in 1971, and saw the experience of making a film as the best way to introduce his pupils to cinema in all its technical and artistic variety. The result was stylistically unlike anything he had made before. His interest, seen in *55 Days at Peking*, in filling the Technirama screen with a rich complexity of images had now developed into a fascination with multiple-screen work. In *We Can't Go Home Again* he incorporated up to four or five images – shot in various formats (35mm, 16mm, Super-8mm and video) – into any one frame. Scenes were fully improvised, often based on experiences and characters of Ray and his students, who – culled from the three classes he taught, and numbering about forty-five in all – both played themselves and worked, by rota, in various technical capacities. There was no formal plot, merely a series of sequences loosely linked by the themes of Ray's own premonitions of death and his relationship with his pupils. Indeed, the film was partly a self-reflective documentary on the circumstances of its own making.

It was, however, never fully finished. Although it was screened as a 'work in progress' at 1973's Cannes Film Festival, Ray continued to tinker with it until his death some six years later (his widow Susan, who worked with Ray on the basic 'script', told me in early 1991 that she was still hoping to produce a final definitive version, to première in 1992). The print described here, cut in 1973, is by all accounts rather different from and less polished, technically, than a 1976 version shown briefly in Ray's last film *Lightning Over Water*; it is therefore impossible to assess the film by any conventional critical method. Nevertheless, one can still discern Ray's basic intentions from his rough, fragmented mosaic of images – and often barely intelligible dialogue – that constitutes the version still currently circulating at retrospectives.

Described by the critic Jonathan Rosenbaum as 'cinema at the end of its tether', *We Can't Go Home Again* (which initially started out with the working title *The Gun Under My Pillow*, an explicit reference back to the confused Plato in *Rebel Without a Cause*) is indeed difficult to categorise, straddling as it does psychodrama, self-portraiture, documentary and avant-garde formal experimentalism. Jean-Luc Godard, whose later *Numéro Deux* and *Ici et Ailleurs* may well have been influenced by Ray's ambitious use of multiple images, once wrote that Ray alone seemed capable of 're-inventing' cinema; with his Harpur students, the American appeared to be attempting exactly that. The overriding impression one gains from seeing the film is of Ray striving valiantly, if finally in vain, to create a semblance of order from chaos, to find a new mode of expression in film that encompasses the personal and political.

Documentary footage – of the 1968 Chicago Democratic Convention, of campus riots and repressive police violence, of Richard Nixon and Hubert Humphrey, Jane Fonda and Tom Hayden – is clearly meant to place the main characters' private anxieties within the context of a nationwide *zeitgeist* of socio-political unrest and turbulence, of violence and despair; while the more conventionally 'narrative' scenes of the students' barely fictionalised interactions with Ray and each other are evidently intended to evoke the confusions of the era – the early 1970s – with a greater precision. But while the use of documentary footage (and, for that matter, of abstract sequences shot with Nam June

Father figure: Nicholas Ray makes a gift of his wisdom to his Binghampton students.

Paik's video-synthesizer) is of some formal interest, it ultimately contributes little to our greater understanding of modern America, other than to provide a rather vague sense of conflict and disintegration; as the film stands, these shots are too brief to do anything more than establish an overall mood.

Within what 'narrative' there is, however, many of Ray's abiding preoccupations may be discerned, and besides the film's function as an account of contemporary student *angst*, it also serves, to some extent, as a summation of the themes that had haunted his film career from its very beginning.

Ray's relationship in the movie with his fellow film-makers, explicitly that of a teacher to his pupils (a frequent motif in such earlier films as *Knock on Any Door*, *The Lusty Men*, *Run for Cover* and *Rebel Without a Cause*), is also that of a father to his children; but while Ray's very making of the film affirms his continuing sympathetic interest in the painful experiences of the young, the movie itself seems imbued with a cool bitterness, very different from the romanticism that distinguished his early films. As before, the young are essentially 'innocents', confused by their own sexuality, the various injustices of the world, the difficulty of genuine communication; here, however, they are also shown as self-obsessed, indulgent and harsh in their inability to accept or forgive the ways of an older generation. At the same time, Ray – as an observer, 'father' and mentor – not only proves helpless in his desire to ease their pain, but is someone who may betray any trust bestowed upon him. When Leslie, distraught after taking too many drugs, confides that she deliberately slept with a man who had syphilis, Ray suddenly orders the other students to pelt her with tomatoes; similarly when Tom, who like Ray is blind in one eye, approaches his teacher for advice on his unrequited love for Leslie, Ray tells him a parable about a man who visited the Sphinx in an attempt to discover some wisdom that would help humanity: 'and the Sphinx said, "Don't expect too much … don't expect too much from a teacher."'

While the students themselves are clearly far from models of human warmth and consideration (they argue constantly, wear tear-stained masks to hide their feelings from each other while making love and are openly hostile when Ray arrives to teach them), it is equally evident that Ray considered his own generation 'more guilty of betrayal than any other in history'. During the opening titles, he himself is seen wielding a whip; a girl complains that her parents are unhappy with her because they would like her to be a virgin all over again; and in a long, painful close-up, Tom (disenchanted after Nixon's unopposed presidential nomination at the Miami Convention of 1972) cuts off his beard (another 'mask', another self-destructive act), and confesses his enduring despair over his mixed feelings for his detective father, whom he loves but cannot communicate with because of political differences. Like cinema itself, Ray seems to be saying, America is coming apart at the seams, and needs to find new, more tolerant and understanding forms of communication to assuage the pain and loneliness that are the concomitants of trying to survive in a divided society.

Ray's solution, if such it be, to this problem is the unity of a real or surrogate family. Not only does the blues song heard over the opening and end titles ask God to

> Bless the family that stays together,
> bless the family that laughs and cries together,
> bless the family that loves.
> Bring them some happiness,
> shelter from loneliness,

but the film-making 'family' that Ray assembles is presented as *potentially* a mutually energising creative force. Not that the film-making process is in any way romanticised; in fact, film-making is explicitly shown, through the repetition of the scenes involving the tomato-throwing and Tom's admission that his father is a cop, and through Ray's baleful presence as chief tormentor and off-screen confessor (he tells Tom, 'Make me believe you'), to be exploitative of real-life emotions. But the *dialogue* that evolves when Ray and his students come together for a common purpose is at least a beginning in the struggle to achieve a new openness with one another and to overcome the generation gap. And it is in this context that Ray's posthumous sermon, after he dies accidentally ('I have been … interrupted') while attempting to save Tom's life, may be understood:

> Let him [Tom] sleep for a short time … not too long a time … just enough to get back his dream. The floodgates are opening, and the water is rushing like the people against the dams … and the goddams! But waken him in time. Take care of each other; it's your only chance of survival. All thus is vanity, and let the rest of us swing!

The view that this plea for mutual love and tolerance is to some extent a summation of Ray's lifelong message is supported, perhaps, by the various references within the film to his earlier works. For the most part, Ray is shown wearing a red jacket which recalls that worn by James Dean in *Rebel Without a Cause*; his students ask if he was the direc-tor of *The Savage Innocents*, *They Live by Night* and *Johnny Guitar*; when Ray 'dies' a first time, knocked over by a car while dressed in red Father Christmas garb, he is taken to his funeral in a large wooden box that Tom Farrell (the student who plays Tom) has described as 'a red wagon' (*They Live by Night*'s original title was *Your Red Wagon*); the scene in the barn recalls Jim Wilson's confrontation with Danny in *On Dangerous Ground*; a student's explanation that he grew his beard after seeing Charlton Heston play Moses pays indirect tribute to the lead actor in Ray's last commercial film. Moreover, the focus on father–son and teacher–pupil relationships, and the idea that Ray's death by hanging is a sacrifice from which his students may benefit, look back to motifs that recurred throughout his career. His dying words at the end of a rope, therefore, are something of an epitaph to his own past as a Hollywood director: he was indeed 'interrupted' when he still had a great deal to contribute. *We Can't Go Home Again*, then constitutes a cinematic resurrection which has enabled Ray to return from the 'dead' (for thus was he regarded by most Hollywood producers), in an attempt to forge a new kind of filmic language.

It would be difficult to argue from the evidence of currently available prints of *We Can't Go Home Again* that Ray was entirely successful in achieving his aims; all too often the multiplicity of images, instead of adding extra dimensions to the film's meaning, serves to confuse and obfuscate. Nonetheless, as a student exercise made under very difficult conditions (it was shot for the most part at night, so that the students could continue with their daytime courses, and the budget was so low that Ray had to finance it partly him-self), the film remains an impressive, if inevitably dated, achievement. Throughout, one senses Ray's passionate involvement with both his students and the production of the film itself; impressive too is the way he interweaves his concerns both with theirs and with the overall vision of an America on the rocks. The result may finally seem less a finished film than a rough blueprint for something that, more than likely, would have proved imposs-ible to achieve – but that fact merely speaks for his restless ambition, for his enduring commitment to a concept of cinema as a subject of exploration.

Lightning Over Water (1980–81)

SYNOPSIS: On 8 April 1979, Nick Ray – ravaged by cancer and visibly dying, despite three operations – is visited by his friend and admirer, the German film director Wim Wenders. They decide to make a movie together – the subject will be Ray himself – before Ray dies. Wenders' crew, itself filmed on video by Ray's former student Tom Farrell, shoots their discussions in the New York loft Ray shares with his wife Susan; a lecture given by Ray to students at Vassar after a screening of *The Lusty Men*; Ray working with his actor friend Gerry Bamman on a stage adaptation of Kafka's *Report to the Academy*; and, in hospital, a scene inspired by *King Lear*, performed by Ray and Wenders's wife Ronee Blakley. This last scene is then reworked in reverse as Wenders's nightmare: Ray visits him in hospital, saying that he is too sick to continue. Finally, on 16 June, Ray dies, and a wake is held by the film crew aboard a sailing ship on the East River which is carrying an urn of Ray's ashes.

In the years between the shooting of *We Can't Go Home Again* and his death on 16 June 1979, Ray kept himself remarkably busy, in spite of the ravages of alcoholism (he began attending Alcoholics Anonymous sessions in 1976) and the cancer which was diagnosed in November 1977. With a great deal of help from his wife Susan, he continued to work on clarifying the narrative and soundtrack of *We Can't Go Home Again*. After that film's Cannes screening, he contributed a short called *The Janitor to Wet Dreams*, a compendium of soft-core pornographic fantasy sequences assembled by the Dutch painter Max Fischer and directed by, among others, Dusan Makavejev (under the pseudonym of Sam Rotterdam), the writer Heathcote Williams and Fischer himself. In Ray's segment, he takes the two leading roles: a puritanical preacher whose hypocritical sermon provokes an orgy, in which he receives oral sex from, among others, a girl who may be his own daughter; and a cinema janitor – the preacher's *alter ego*? – who, repelled by the sight of his double's sexual antics projected on screen, fires a shotgun at the image. The segment, improvised overnight, is certainly no great shakes, but nor is it the salacious disaster of reputation; indeed, Ray's witty, tongue-in-cheek performance and his control of mood through sharp cutting make for an entirely watchable vignette.

Far more auspiciously, while three further projects came to nothing – *City Blues* (or *Murphy*), in which Rip Torn and Marilyn Chambers were to star, *The Sea Horse* and *The Truth*, a thriller co-written with British critic V. F. Perkins – Ray contributed a brief but resonant cameo role to Wim Wenders's *The American Friend*. The film, inspired by a Patricia Highsmith thriller about a placid picture framer who discovers his own capacity for violence, is something of a homage to Ray not only in its theme but in its casting of Dennis Hopper as Tom Ripley (Hopper had made his film-acting debut in *Rebel Without a Cause*) and in its Expressionist use of colour. Even more pertinently, the char-

acter Ray plays – Derwatt, an artist erroneously believed dead who survives by painting bogus posthumous pictures – clearly reflects, with sad irony, on his own predicament as an artist forgotten by the world at large; after leaving Harpur, Ray's chief source
of work had been as a teacher, first at the Lee Strasberg Institute, then at the New York
School of Arts.

But Ray's encounter with Wenders was to prove unusually fruitful: after another small
acting role as The General in Milos Forman's film of the musical *Hair*, Ray was finally
able to collaborate in the making of one last feature, when Wenders agreed to co-write
and direct *Nick's Film*, which later became known as *Lightning Over Water.*

Although the film's credits list both Wenders and Ray as its directors, and the initial
idea to make it came from Ray himself, it is without doubt a Wenders film first and foremost; while they arrived at the basic concept together, Ray was simply too ill to direct,
and obviously, due to the timing of the project, took no part in the editing. Nevertheless,
it is perhaps wrong to suggest that its overall structure – part fiction, part documentary,
part essay on the ethics of cinema and part home-movie – was entirely dictated by the
unusual circumstances of its production; although Ray's illness evidently did affect the
nature and quantity of the footage shot, the finished film, structurally, bears more than
a passing resemblance to *We Can't Go Home Again*. Again, as in the earlier work, the
line between 'reality' and performance is often obscured; again, references to Ray's previous films are frequent (he even first appears wearing a *red* T-shirt as his nightshirt);
and again, the film expands, through a labyrinth of connections, from a portrait of Ray
the individual to a consideration of wider concerns, including the nature of cinema,
father–son relationships and, inevitably, death. While Wenders directed and cut the
film, it is indelibly marked by Ray's personality and preoccupations.

To some extent, of course, the movie is a tribute from one film-maker to another, or
even, given Wenders's long-term love of Ray's films, from a pupil to his mentor, but even
on this level their collaboration is coloured by irony. Wenders, free to make the movie due
to a timely break in the filming of *Hammett*, his first American film, is a European 'art-
movie' director in exile, striving to come to terms with an America for which he has always
harboured mixed feelings of love and hate; Ray is also an exile, but from Hollywood –
many of his movies were deemed too idiosyncratically personal (or arty?) by the moguls,
so that eventually he had to leave for Europe in search of work. The contrast is emphasised when, to Wenders's confession that *Hammett* is budgeted at $10 million, Ray replies,
'For one per cent of that I could make … lightning over water.' While Wenders admires
Ray's Hollywood work and Ray thinks only of creating avant-garde films like *We Can't Go
Home Again*, the pair are nevertheless spiritual partners, with a shared interest in loners,
landscape, music, troubled father–son relationships, and odysseys in search of love and a
home. Finally, therefore, notwithstanding Wenders's acknowledgement of Ray's influence
on his own work, the film is no mere hagiography but an exploration, through the public
medium of film, of more private mysteries: of Wenders's feelings for Ray, and of how death
and the camera affect their friendship. And it is for this reason that the film's opening shot
– reminiscent of *The American Friend* as Wenders, like Tom Ripley before him, arrives outside Ray's home in New York – invokes the mood of *film noir*: in his quest for truth, the

Nicholas Ray takes a break from the screening of *The Lusty Men* at Vassar.

German is embarking on a voyage that will take him painfully close to human mortality, a journey, aesthetically speaking, undertaken by a son in search of his spiritual 'father'.

Ray, on the other hand, seems to interpret the experience of making the film as an opportunity not merely to make a few final comments on his life and the world around him, but to find a way to die calmly and fulfilled; to make sense of things. (To Ray, death seems not to be something to arouse fear but, as Tom Milne wrote, 'an untimely threat to his [Ray's] relentless self-examination'.) In a scene in which he discusses with Wenders the character he would like to play (or re-enacts his discussion – one can seldom in this film be entirely sure of what is real, what is performed and how far the performances match what actually took place before filming began), he envisions himself as a terminally ill Derwatt-like painter, who steals back his pictures and replaces them with his own forgeries, before leaving America on a junk slowly headed for China: the image is one of peace, belatedly rediscovered. And explaining the significance of *The Lusty Men* at Vassar, he says the film was about 'a man who wants to bring himself all together before he dies: a regaining of self-esteem for a once very highly successful man.' Given that Ray has already likened the unusually improvisational methods employed in making *The Lusty Men* to the experience of shooting the film with Wenders, one may only deduce that in referring to the earlier film's Jeff McCloud, Ray is also alluding to his own desire to die in a state of tranquillity and self-knowledge, however little of his career and reputation remain left to him. (In the clip shown here, to which Wenders himself had paid tribute in *Kings of the Road*, McCloud, crippled and at the end of his rodeo career, dives under his old home to retrieve a faded rodeo programme, a rusty gun and a tin containing two nickels: scant reward after a life of fame.)

The concerns of each man – one anxious to make a film that meets the demands of their friendship, the other keen to achieve a sense of achievement before dying – boil down, paradoxically, to the same thing: the problem of representation through cinema. Both men, finally, appear to want to create something honest and truthful through their collaboration, and in so doing repeatedly discuss their feelings: about the proximity of death, about their relationship, and about the nature and purpose of the film they have decided to make together. They want to make a fiction based on Ray's raddled self-image but, given the limitations imposed by his fragile body, are repeatedly forced to 'act out' realities that will not be too physically demanding: performance, normally considered a matter of artifice, here provides a pathway to the 'truth', as two directors, who normally elicit rather than give performances, reconstruct and distil their experiences together.

As a result, we are never completely certain of the spontaneity of what we are witnessing: the first scene – of Wenders's arrival at Ray's loft and their initial conversation about making a movie together – looks and sound 'real' enough, until our assumptions are undermined when Wenders cuts to show video footage shot by Farrell of this scene, with the addition of Ray (looking as frail and exhausted as he did in what we have just seen) asking if he looked like he was acting. Throughout the film, indeed, performance (whether Ray's lecture at Vassasr, Robert Mitchum's appearance in *The Lusty Men*, Ray's *King Lear* scene with Ronee Blakley, or his several encounters with Wenders) is shown to be a result both of the prerequisites of the film itself (to make a fiction movie you must have actors), and of the 'real' circumstances behind its making. Art and life are inextricably intertwined in a symbiotic relationship that mirrors that of Ray and Wenders, who not only depend upon one another's collaboration in order for the film to be made, but who, by their differences and similarities, illuminate both one another and their respective cinema careers.

At the same time, however, it is this blurring of the line between fiction and reality, between acting and being, that makes the film rather disturbing. Whatever Wenders's motives (there is no doubting the sincerity of his admiration for Ray), and however much Ray wanted to commit his last moments to celluloid, a problem remains in that the film is in certain respects tantamount to an intellectually respectable 'snuff movie'. Morally, it makes scant difference to Wenders's defence against charges of voyeurism that Ray – who in parts of the film appears to be somewhat befuddled – insisted on making the movie. Nor does it help that Wenders 'covers' himself by confessing to a certain queasiness about the project in hand (he even admits to Ray that he is worried he may be attracted to the older man's suffering, and rather fatuously expresses anxiety and shock at the way the camera mercilessly reveals how quickly time is running out for Ray). Voyeurism is, in the end, voyeurism, and had making the film merely been a matter of granting a sick man's request, then it might have been perfectly reasonable for Wenders to shoot the footage and never release it. Indeed, there is a scene which this writer at least finds more than a little grisly: when Ray 'visits' Wenders in the German's nightmare, he is barely able to speak, except to complain that Wenders makes him sick to his stomach and to say, 'I have to go now; I'm beginning to drool' – at which point Wenders's off-screen voice tells him he must say the word 'cut' himself. Facing the camera, Ray complies, but Wenders holds the shot and says, 'Don't cut'; only after Ray has repeated his request twice more does the filming come to an end.

This, situated before the wake on the 'junk', is the last we see of Ray, and Wenders's delay in cutting (reminiscent of a scene in his later *Tokyo-Ga*, when he fails to comply with a sobbing Japanese cameraman's request that he be left alone in his grief) suggests that his desire to catch human emotions honestly on film can be stronger than his respect for those emotions. Even in the case of someone like Ray, whose devotion to cinema was total, one may question Wenders's wisdom in putting the needs of a film above the explicitly stated needs of a fellow human being, and the scene as it stands, however 'honest' Wenders's inclusion of his own voice may appear, casts a dark, troubling shadow over the suffering and confusion that has been shown, admittedly without sensationalism, in earlier scenes.

That said, the film is finally rather more than a mere documentary about a dying man or a gratification of his last request, and many of the charges of voyeurism laid at Wenders's door seem to miss the point. Thanks to Ray's conspicuous courage, dignity, intelligence, wit and determination, *Lightning Over Water* serves as a celebratory tribute, not only to his past career as a great film-maker, but to his immensely strong will to survive; and despite the sad sight of a man grown ancient before his time, the effect of this cinematic epitaph is not depressing but uplifting. As a helicopter shot (fittingly, given the start of Ray's first feature) follows the boat bearing his ashes along the East River out towards the sea, with a Mitchel camera and a Moviola on deck and film stock fluttering wildly in the wind, we feel that Ray is going home, lonely and confused no more. Thanks partly to the help of his German friend, he had been able to find a kind of peace, by pushing one last time against the barriers erected by a cautious film establishment to safeguard emotional discretion.

In a diary, which Wenders reads during a break from filming, Ray had written, 'To experience death without dying seemed like a natural goal for me.' And in exposing to the camera his own struggles to remain true to himself even as death approached, Ray pursued his life-long passionate interest in the cinematic depiction of human pain, anxiety and solitude to its logical, characteristically extreme and profoundly moving conclusion.

Nicholas Ray in the Twenty-first Century

As time passes, films change – or, to be more precise, are changed. I am not referring to the 'director's cut', the work-in-progress or to the way celluloid discolours, disintegrates and is destroyed thanks to repeat screenings or rogue projectionists. Rather, I'm alluding here to the changes that can occur in terms of how a film is perceived – of what it *means* – due to changes that have taken place both in ourselves as individuals and in the world at large. One of the most striking aspects of Ray's work was his exploration of the charged relationship between his protagonists and the society in which they live; since he himself evidently found it necessary and useful to adopt a perspective that was at once personal and (in the broadest sense of the term) political, it would seem logical to take a similar tack in attempting to assess, for this updated edition of a book written some twelve years ago, the value of Ray's work in and for the twenty-first century.

In material terms, then, his films remain essentially what they always were. Prints have been struck, deteriorated and in some cases have been restored … and the advent of digital technology has certainly meant that, on the small screen at least, we are now able to appreciate some of the films in a condition probably closer to Ray's original aims and achievements than anything we've seen in decades: *Johnny Guitar*, for example, is now on DVD in a version that does far greater justice to its exquisite colour palette than the faded, scratchy prints that would sometimes turn up in art-houses. Notwithstanding a few welcome restorations, however – most notably, perhaps, of *In a Lonely Place* and *Bitter Victory* – there have been no amazing rediscoveries of lost, alternative or extra footage. Even in the case of *We Can't Go Home Again*, which Ray's widow Susan has long hoped to make available in a version that would conform to what might be described as his final wishes, we are still dependent on the version shown at the 1973 Cannes Film Festival; as I write, it seems sufficient funding is yet to be found for her project. What we can now actually see of Ray's work, then, remains the same as when I wrote this book at the start of the 1990s.

So how do the films stand up? When the book first appeared, Ray's earliest movies were already around forty years old, and even *Lightning Over Water* had been made a decade beforehand; now, Ray has been dead for almost a quarter of a century, and it is fifty-six years ago this month since he was shooting *They Live By Night*. That's a long time, and the film made with Wenders is more than twice as old now as it was when the book was first published. But watching the movies again and reading what I wrote, I find I hardly feel like retracting a word; I still stand by what I then felt, thought and said about Ray and his work. Now and then, while revisiting a film, I thought, 'I bet I didn't pick up on that detail! *That's* something to add!' – only to discover on rereading the relevant chapter that it already covered any such 'fresh' insights. That's why I haven't rewritten the book, which for better or worse I prefer to remain intact as a document of my thinking at that time about this woefully underrated director. (And despite the success of recent Ray retrospectives in Ontario, New York and elsewhere, he *remains* unjustly neglected, there still being no serious book-length study of his work in English other than this volume and what's written in Bernard Eisenschitz's definitive biography.) I'll simply try, then, to add here a few new comments in the hope that we may perhaps better grasp what Ray's films have to offer us so many years after they were made. In short, has his work any relevance today? Does Ray still matter?

To answer those questions, it's necessary to consider several others. How has the world changed? How has film culture changed? And, while we're on the subject, how have I changed since writing the book? Take an example: just weeks before I finally got married, I found that my heart was in a perilously poor condition. Those two unexpected developments changed how I live and how I feel about my life in many ways; they also inflect, as will be seen, my reading of *Bigger than Life*. Sadly, unlike Ed Avery, I haven't yet learned how to avoid working too much. I remain a film critic (roughly half my week is still spent working for *Time Out*), but now, as I used to before becoming a professional writer, I'm also trying to pass on my passion for movies by programming a cinema. With (to me) pleasing coincidence, for the last four years I've been head of programming at London's National Film Theatre, the very venue whose programmer in 1986, Sheila Whitaker, let me curate a Ray season, thereby encouraging and to some extent enabling me to write this book. (Almost 18 years later, needless to say, I'm about to bring Ray's work back to the NFT for a new generation of cinemagoers.)

But has my taste changed? That's relevant only in that it brings us to the second, more important issue of changes in film culture: changes which have inevitably affected how I respond to film in general and Ray's oeuvre in particular. In the preceding pages, I alluded repeatedly to Ray's maverick status in the studio system of the late 1940s and 1950s; on the first page of the Introduction, I wrote of his 'perennially troubled relationship with ...' and 'profoundly personal contributions to what was, and still is, something of a factory conveyor belt, specialising in the production of homogenised, undemanding mass entertainment'. If that were true of Hollywood when Ray was there, how much more so was it when I wrote those words! And isn't that even more dispiritingly the situation now, with studios run by committees of accountants for multinational conglomerates? American mainstream film-making – which for these global corporations is just a drop in the financial ocean – is more than ever undertaken as if there were a formula for success. The 'majors' and their imitators, absurdly faithful to tried-and-trusted clichés, churn out sequels, copies and gimmicky by-the-numbers blueprints (as opposed to properly crafted films with coherent, credible stories, rounded, consistent characters and themes that might appeal to intelligent adults curious about the world they live in). According to this lowest-common-denominator ethos, novelty is acceptable, even desirable as long as it can be marketed successfully, but anything truly original, eccentric, deeply felt or 'difficult' is mostly kept at arm's length. Ray found it hard enough to work as he wanted in 1950s Hollywood; it's almost impossible to imagine him surviving at all there now. Most contemporary American auteurs who insist on making movies their way – people like Jarmusch, Haynes, Lynch and Altman – have had to find funding from non-Hollywood

Tough Tinseltown truths: Dix Steele tells autograph-hunters he's just 'a nobody' in *In a Lonely Place*.

sources, often from abroad. Of those distinctive, independent-minded auteurs who do work with the majors, some (like Mann or Malick) find themselves making fewer films than they'd like; others (Soderbergh, say) have confessed to the need to come up at regular intervals with a comparatively calculated hit; some (like Spike Lee or Schrader) have had to settle for reduced budgets; others (Demme, Rudolph, Hill) have effectively been marginalised; and all too many have yielded to compromise. Even Scorsese's career has with *Cape Fear* and *Gangs of New York* shown signs of strain in recent years.

To some extent, then, I, like many others, have become increasingly disenchanted with the 'product' that Hollywood is forever trying to sell us. The Tinseltown way, as *In a Lonely Place* demonstrated, was always partly about making a quick buck, but is it too cynical to suggest that the old programme-filler ethos of 'never mind the quality, get the bums on seats' has spread from what used to be called B-movies to infect most American mainstream fare, including even the most prestigious, expensive blockbusters? How else can one explain a film like *Titanic* where – for all the cash, talent and energy lavished on eye-catching special effects – the standard of storytelling, characters, dialogue and acting rarely rises above that of the hoary old clichés one used to find in kids' serials? There's no point in arguing, 'But that's the point of this particular movie', if the same charge can be laid against most studio fare made these days. If in the past Ray's value as a filmmaker lay in his genuinely personal style and preoccupations and in a readiness to engage with the uncomfortable realities of the world in a way that was intellectually curious, emotionally passionate and artistically adventurous, surely those qualities now count for even more in a film culture where caution, conformism, philistinism and an apparently escapist apathy about the state of the world are prevalent.

Not that all American cinema should be tarred with the same brush, of course – I have name-checked just a few of the notable exceptions to the rule – nor can one equate the US mainstream and its imitators worldwide with film-making in its entirety. Not all film culture is primarily about money and mass consumption, and happily there now seems to be a growing interest in 'world cinema'. It used to be that 'art-house' exhibitors, distributors and audiences tended to favour a half-dozen or so film-producing nations – France, Italy, Japan, maybe Russia or Germany, along with vintage Hollywood, of course – but now the field has widened, and open-minded film fans are just as likely to sample fare from Iran, Argentina, South Korea, Portugal, Canada or Mauritania. This tendency may in part be a response both to the artistic impoverishment of today's Hollywood and to its stranglehold over most of our cinema screens; if you love movies but are repeatedly disappointed by what the American mainstream has to offer, you're likely to start looking elsewhere. And one suspects that Ray, interested in ethnography and experiment, would have been enthused by this development; surely the man who made *Hot Blood* would have been fascinated by the work of Romany director Tony Gatlif (*Lacho Drom*; *Gadjo Dilo*)? Wouldn't the man who played with fiction and reality in *We Can't Go Home Again* and *Lightning Over Water* have appreciated Kiarostami's *Close-Up*, *The Taste of Cherry* or *10*? Wouldn't the maker of *The Savage Innocents* have welcomed Zacharias Kunuk's *Atarnajuat: The Fast Runner*? With *10* and the Inuit film, it wouldn't only have been the insights into other cultures that might have fired his imagination, but digital technology. Ray was a restless talent, and the experimentation with multiple image and sound in *We Can't Go Home Again* – anticipating among other recent works Godard's *Histoire(s) du Cinéma* and Mike Figgis's *Timecode* – was just one aspect of his iconoclastic attitude to film convention. In the late 1970s, for example, while bemoaning Hollywood's constant futile search for a formula, he spoke of how he'd like 'to help create a new concept of film as a living, continuously breathing thing', and one can't but feel that he would have greeted the creative opportunities afforded by digital technology with open arms:

> I long for the day when I can be certain there's a film-maker in every family, when the form of communication is not limited to the word or page, when each kid can have a crack at giving a full expression to something of himself. How much richer the neighborhood would be, just one square block. We should be equipped and surrounded with the materials that creative activity calls for … (Nicholas Ray, *I Was Interrupted*, ed. Susan Ray, University of California Press, 1993)

* * *

Other aspects of our modern world, however, would probably have pleased Ray rather less. Since the first edition of this book, we've seen globalisation continue apace, with the multinationals increasing their power. Indigenous cultures are under threat from the total Westernisation (or, rather, Americanisation) of large parts of the world. Rainforests are being felled, species are vanishing at an unprecedented rate, the ice-caps are melting, the oceans rising and climate change is now regarded as a serious threat by almost every-one except those who have much to gain in the short term by pretending the threat does-n't exist. A blind faith in technology has probably created as many problems as it has solved, and the chasm between haves and have-nots seems to be getting deeper and wider all the time. There have, then, been enormous changes since Ray made his films. Nevertheless, it's possible, when considering certain aspects of our post-9/11 world, to discern distant but very distinct echoes of the world Ray depicted in films as diverse as *On Dangerous Ground, Johnny Guitar, Run for Cover, Wind Across the Everglades, Party Girl, The Savage Innocents* and *King of Kings*. In film after film, Ray showed characters who felt themselves above the law, driven by an arrogant belief in their own righteous-ness, prone to presume others guilty until they can prove themselves innocent; crowds turning into lynch mobs, with strangers at their mercy simply because they're strangers; political and civic corruption and the careless rape of the wilderness, fuelled by greed for money and power; one culture imposing its customs and laws on another, by force if needs be. So many Ray films show how fear, ignorance and a need to convince your-self of your moral superiority to those around you can lead to a belief that might is right; watching Ward Bond's Walter Brent (*On Dangerous Ground*), Mercedes McCambridge's Emma Small (*Johnny Guitar*) or Charlton Heston's Major Matt Lewis (*55 Days at Peking*) in an era when George W. Bush mutters dark warnings about an 'axis of evil' makes for fascinating if unsettling viewing. Just as Ray's films have become, with the passing years, ever more interesting and treasurable as rare examples of Hollywood movies made with a profound degree of personal investment, so, sadly, they seem horribly relevant in their critique of aggressive paranoia, eye-for-an-eye ethics and a shoot-first-ask-questions-later attitude. I may be wrong, but I suspect that the man who made *Bitter Victory* and intended to cast Groucho Marx as Judge Julius J. Hoffman in a film about the Chicago Conspiracy Trial would have had little sympathy not only for Osama bin Laden and Saddam Hussein, but also for the likes of Bush and Tony Blair.

*   *   *

Since Ray has long been one of my favourite film-makers, I have frequently revisited many of his movies purely for pleasure. But watching all the films again for the purposes of this new edition, in chronological order and within a period of about three weeks, I've been struck by a number of thoughts and observations, some doubtless of comparatively minor import. It's intriguing, for example, to see how he used certain actors more than once, and in some cases very often, in supporting or minor roles: Ian Wolfe, particularly fine as the seedy justice of the peace in *They Live by Night*; Jay C. Flippen, who among other things served as best man when Ray married Gloria Grahame in Las Vegas; Curt Conway, in numerous pleasing cameos from *They Live by Night* to *Wind Across the Everglades*; Ray's nephew Sumner Williams, turning up almost anywhere but especially notable as a hapless child-killer in *On Dangerous Ground*; Gus Schilling, Royal Dano, Corey Allen, John Ireland, Frank Ferguson, Denver Pyle, Will Wright, Rusty Lane, Jimmy Conlin, Robert A. Davis and others. There were, of course, many better-known performers he cast twice or more – not just stars like Bogart, Ryan and Grahame but familiar B- or C-list faces like Ward Bond, Ernest Borgnine, John Derek, Viveca Lindfors, Jeffrey Hunter and dear old John Carradine – but there's something strangely satisfying in encountering someone like the otherwise apparently unappreciated Gus Schilling in role after small role: it helps you find your bearings, along with all the other tell-tale details of *mise en scène* that make a film distinctively 'Ray'. It's indicative, perhaps, of Ray's very personal approach to the film-making process: keeping it as far as possible within an extended 'family' of friends, much as Ford, Hawks, Welles and Capra, not to mention a whole host of European auteurs – Bergman, Truffaut, Godard and Fellini, to name but a few – repeatedly turned to a repertory troupe of actors. Maybe, for better or worse, it's just another symptom of a film-maker having a distinctive artistic signature.

A crash course of viewings reveals not only Ray's abiding concern with violence and rough justice, but also what seems to have been a healthy wariness of judges and lawyers (*They Live by Night, Knock on Any Door, Wind Across the Everglades, Party Girl*), and of law-enforcement officers (*In a Lonely Place, On Dangerous Ground, Johnny Guitar, Run for Cover, The Savage Innocents*); far more than most Hollywood directors of his era, Ray tended to find their integrity open to question. One wonders whether this is merely a reflection of an overall anti-establishment sensibility on his part, or whether it speaks of a more specific lack of faith in the American system of crime and punishment. It could have been both, of course: certainly, the more one revisits Ray's work, the more its specificity in terms of period and place is apparent, whether in the Depression-era dustbowl setting of his début, the unusually unglamorous Hollywood of *In a Lonely Place*, or the turn-of-the-century Florida of *Wind Across the Everglades*, where judges and politicians sit in brothels, on boats and beaches alongside big businessmen, poachers and murderous criminals. (And people claim Carl Hiaasen was on to something new!) As often as not when one recalls a Ray film, what first springs to mind is not its story, stars or even genre, but its setting; in this respect, his work to some extent anticipates that of John Sayles (who made his own Florida film with *Sunshine State*) and the Coen Brothers – though the Texas, Minnesota and California in movies like *Blood Simple, Fargo, Barton Fink* and *The Big Lebowski* are primarily imaginative states of mind rather than rooted in meticulously researched socio-historical reality, as was much of Ray's oeuvre.

Another facet of Ray's films illuminated by watching them in quick succession is the way he so often found space for black characters. While one cannot make any great claims for radicalism in this matter – it is very minor roles we are talking about – African-Americans turn up rather more regularly in his work than in most studio films of the time. Moreover, the parts in question are seldom simply that of a mute or 'comical' servant, the options then most readily available to black actors. The aforementioned Robert A. Davis, for example, has a small but significant part as Nick Romano's friend in *Knock on Any Door* and as a florist's assistant in *In a Lonely Place*; in the former film we even see, in the opening montage, a black cop arresting a white suspect. In *Born to Be Bad* we merely glimpse two black servants, but in *Party Girl* Tommy Farrell is evidently used to seeking advice about domestic arrangements from his black butler. *They Live by Night, In a Lonely Place* and *Wind Across the Everglades*, meanwhile, all feature scenes centred on black singers and musicians, and in *Bigger than Life* we see a number of black hospital staff (one prompt-ing Richie's telling observation to his mom, 'Some people work *awful* late, don't they?'). Even one of the three magi in *King of Kings* is black, but perhaps most interestingly, and with pointed perversity, the very last close-up in *Rebel Without a Cause* is of Plato's gov-erness (Mariette Canty), weeping over the dead boy after Jim and his new girl Judy have walked away from the scene along with Jim's chastened and thus reconciled parents. It's an extremely intriguing cut-in, reminding us once more, before the film closes on a long shot of a mystified Nick Ray walking up to the steps of the Planetarium, that Jim and Judy's 'happy ending' was achieved at a terrible cost: the death of Plato, now abandoned in the arms of someone whose presence and feelings – she's 'only' a black female employee, after all – the middle-class white folks barely register. Ray, however, doesn't forget her, just as, in his own small way, he refused in those of his films which were set in modern America to abide by Hollywood convention and pretend that ordinary, dignified, decent, intelligent African-Americans just didn't exist.

This admittedly minor but far from trivial element in Ray's work may perhaps be traced back to his interest in music and the time he had spent researching American folk cul-ture with the Lomax brothers during the late 1930s, when he had met and befriended the likes of Huddie 'Leadbelly' Ledbetter, 'Blind Lemon' Jefferson and Billie Holiday. One other aspect of his personal life, however, which doesn't seem to have been reflected on screen, even though it brought Ray some posthumous publicity when Gavin Lambert's book *Mainly About Lindsay Anderson* was published in 2000, was his bisexuality. (Though Ray had been married several times, rumours had long circulated about his also having had sexual relationships with men, and Lambert's account of being seduced by the direc-tor gave such stories added credibility.) Frankly, one looks in vain for any real evidence that Ray's films were made by someone with bisexual or homosexual leanings. The only character of note one might categorise even as a closet gay man would be Mel Ferrer's Gobby in *Born to Be Bad*; a bitchy, faintly camp confidant to the scheming Christabel, the painter displays no interest in her (or for that matter in any other woman) other than as an amused observer of the chaos she creates and as someone who might profit finan-cially from having painted her portrait. There is also, of course, Plato, in *Rebel*, though his childlike innocence tends to counteract a fully gay reading of his possessive, hero-worshipping attitude towards Jim; one should also beware of confusing the sexuality of the character with that of the actor playing him. Elsewhere, certainly – even in *Johnny Guitar* and the various studies of intense male relationships marked by feelings of guilt, jealousy and betrayal (*Knock on Any Door*, *Run for Cover*, *Bitter Victory*, *Wind Across the Everglades*) – it would be difficult to make a convincing case that the dynamics between any characters of the same gender were in any significant sense sexual. (What is a little intriguing, however, is the slight facial resemblance of three of Ray's young actors – Farley Granger, John Derek, Sal Mineo – to the youthful Nick Ray; the curious should check out the photographs on pages 17, 37 and 55 of the English edition of Eisenschitz's biog-raphy and especially the portrait on page 65 of the French edition.)

*   *   *

As stated above, the comments that follow on individual films are not meant to be seen as retractions or reassessments of what I wrote previously, but as further thoughts about the films' longevity, proffered somewhat in the spirit of the notes a wine-taster makes after he has opened another bottle of a *grand cru* to savour the progress of a vintage he last tasted a year or so ago. Sometimes, you will see, I have little to add; elsewhere I've been more expansive. But before we proceed, there are two points I wish to make. The first is the one and only significant modification I should like to make to something that appeared in the first edition. In the Introduction (see page 2), when proposing possible reasons for Ray's neglect at the hands of British and American critics, I suggested that some might have dismissed his work because it rarely fulfilled expectations of polished perfection: classical notions of balance, restraint and tastefulness were neither Ray's forte nor, probably, his concern. I now feel that in arguing on behalf of Ray's 'imperfections' against what are widely upheld to be less conspicuously flawed works – in what often used to be characterised as the 'Ray or Ray?' debate (who's tops, Nick or Satyajit?) – I was missing the point. What does it mean to talk about films in terms of 'imperfections' when there is no such thing as 'perfection' in the movie world? I am not merely refuting the existence of some kind of Platonic form of 'perfection' in which certain films might partake; I am arguing that there is and can be no such thing as a perfect movie. One might conceivably argue that a film would be perfect if it achieved everything its maker wanted it to – but how are we to apply this argument to specific cases? What if the film-maker's ambitions were actually very meagre or, worse, as misguided as the glorification of, say, the Third Reich? Best, surely, to forget any such dreams of 'perfection', and then we can stop worrying over how to describe or defend all those films with 'imperfections'.

The other observation I offer is a slightly unusual but confessional one. Judging by my own experiences and by those of colleagues I've discussed this with, sometimes, when you're writing a study of an artist whose work you admire, you ask yourself if you might be 'talking things up' a little – a possible consequence of lavishing attention on a subject for months on end. As I was preparing for this new chapter, therefore, I wondered whether firing myself up to write this book had blinded me to Ray's weaknesses or led me to exaggerate his achievements. This time, I'd be more detached, more objective.

What did I find? First, that I'd been pretty sensible, first time out. When, after watching *A Woman's Secret*, I returned to the book expecting to find I hadn't been hard enough on the film, I was relieved to discover I hadn't been betrayed by my auteurist impulses. (It's a useful methodology, but I've always taken the view that it's also fallible: any great auteur can make a bad movie just as any hack has the potential to surprise us with a masterpiece.) Second, I found that despite my determination not to get fired up, it just isn't possible to remain detached about Ray's work. He made most of his films with great personal passion, and they retain a rare power to induce similarly strong feelings in the viewer. Once you adjust to his peculiar rhythms, compositions, camera movements, colours and those magic moments when a piece of acting of wholly plausible subtlety brings everything together in harmony: once you are caught up by all that, in any one of the dozen or so truly great movies he made – so long ago now – the excitement returns, gloriously undimmed.

They Live by Night

A case in point: while aware that this was an extraordinary début, each time I think about watching the film again, I feel I'm probably too familiar with it. But then I start, and once I'm past that strange little Brechtian prologue I'm hooked – mainly, these days, due to the authenticity of its depiction of the rude simplicity of rural life during the Depression; it feels far more 'real' than most of the *noir* thrillers and fugitive-lovers movies Hollywood has given us. That's because Ray worked *against* genre: he eschewed hard-boiled wise-guy dialogue, focused on everyday settings like a run-down garage or a bus-station diner, and – long before *Reservoir Dogs* – very intriguingly *didn't* show the bank robbery in which T-Dub dies; Chikamaw's death in a liquor-store hold-up is also something we hear about rather than see. It was brave not to show the demise of two of the four main characters, but then this is a film of beautiful but unlikely tiny details: the bitter-sweet deadpan comedy of the twenty-dollar wedding (no photos, no microphone, no organ, just a witness with a bad cold, and a whole lot of love); or the droll scene when Bowie and Keechie ask a motel manager for a secluded cabin, and the obliging but faintly pompous man tells his son, 'Learn that, Alvin; just married people like to be alone' – to which the seriously earnest Alvin responds, with a wisdom beyond his years, 'I should think so.' Humour wasn't mentioned much in the first edition, but it's there, even in this still chilling dissection of not-in-my-backyard ethics: no wonder Mattie won't sleep nights.

A Woman's Secret

Still without doubt Ray's least interesting movie, notable (just) for the way Grahame tries to inject some acid into the proceedings and for the unsympathetic portrait of bullish, bigoted GI Lee Crenshaw (Bill Williams) – a little surprising so soon after the war.

Knock on Any Door

Improbable as it may seem, the nature/nurture arguments centred on juvenile delinquent Nick Romano are still with us, in the movies and in real life, though the film does look a little old-fashioned. Some of Bogie's sermonising doesn't help, nor does angelic Emma; why didn't Nick stick with the blonde? But Ray's *mise en scène* is a treat: the opening montage is particularly pacy and stylish, and he milks the trial scenes for all they're worth. Indeed, the tacit suggestion that courts are as much about the theatrical expertise of the attorneys as they are about any proper commitment to the truth will ring terribly true for anyone who's ever sat on a jury – or, these days, seen a hearing on TV. An idea: Romano's 'Live fast, die young and have a good-looking corpse' has been much quoted, but could his 'Nobody knows how anybody feels' have inspired the Coen Brothers to have Gabriel Byrne's Tom repeatedly insist that 'Nobody knows anybody – not that well' in *Miller's Crossing*? (Another Chicago-set crime drama, incidentally, about betrayal and distrust rocking the friendship of a young man and his older mentor.)

Born to Be Bad

Thoroughly entertaining hokum about money, sex, class, love, gender roles, art and other unimportant things – but do people like Christabel get found out in real life? At least the coda has the good subversive sense to let her carry on unrepentant in her scheming. One wonders, by the way, whether it was an extremely subtle private joke on Ray's part to have the man who's utterly bemused by modern art at a gallery preview played by the same actor who in *Knock on Any Door* had played the sketch-artist at Romano's trial.

In a Lonely Place

In the first edition I drew attention to the importance of seeing – and, indeed, hearing – in this film, and it's fascinating, now that we live in a world where surveillance of some sort is an accepted fact of everyday life, to see how the paranoia shown in the movie about being watched and investigated by others – clearly pertinent to the HUAC era – is also very relevant to life post-9/11. We acknowledge that security measures are necessary to protect us – from crime or terrorism – but how far are we prepared to see civil liberties eroded? (Sadly, all too often we vehemently insist on our own rights while turning a blind eye to how others, especially foreigners, are treated.) Watching this film, even though we aren't *totally* certain that Dix didn't follow and kill Mildred after she left his apartment, we can't help feeling that Capt. Lochner is in the wrong, overstepping the mark in terms of the ethics of investigation and entrapment. Why *do* we dislike and disapprove of this cop so much – he's just doing his job, after all – even as we root for a man whose violent, even murderous, temper we've witnessed more than once? (Are writers so special they may be excused such behaviour? I think not!) A movie of many dark, unsettling ironies, that grows richer with the passing years.

On Dangerous Ground

We're used to police brutality now, but even post-Rodney King this retains the power to disturb, despite Wilson using only his bare hands. The questions about crime and retribution haven't gone away, and Walter Brent's desire to empty his shotgun into his daughter's killer will be frighteningly familiar to anyone unlucky enough to have heard paranoid hysteria voiced about paedophiles, sex-killers, asylum-seekers, ethnic and sexual minorities, or anyone merely perceived as different enough to constitute a threat. The tabloids and certain politicians thrive on fanning the flames of fear – Michael Moore's *Bowling for Columbine* is a wayward but entertaining thesis on this topic – and hearing Capt. Brawley tell Wilson a cop should not be 'a gangster with a badge' calls to mind those who believe it is their personal, God-given mission to police the world, regardless of what the rest of us think. The disregard for the due process of law shown first by Wilson and then by Brent is something we should all unreservedly condemn.

But enough of political or metaphorical readings – this is one great movie. Ray's cutting and camerawork, from sudden handheld action to lingering close-ups, from silent twilight walks to lovely highway dissolves, were never more elastic or expressive. The use of snow (think *Fargo*!) to contrast with soiled city nights is poetically fitting and beautiful. Bernard Herrmann's score is something even he seldom bettered. Dialogue, performances and direction have an unusually plausible naturalism – see Brawley order more peas while reading Wilson the riot act – that is never swamped when the plot tilts towards redemptive fable. And the moment when Brent finally realises Danny's 'just a kid' is heart-breaking.

Flying Leathernecks

Routine but efficient war heroics, reasonably restrained in terms of flag-waving despite the stuff about a country that will always fight against any aggression that threatens freedom; it was propaganda, after all. A very dry run for *Bitter Victory*, distinguished mainly by its genuinely delicate Technicolor hues, unusual in an actioner of this kind.

The Lusty Men

Arguably the most underrated of all Ray's films, partly because it's seldom been seen in its complete version outside of the USA, partly because it's a rodeo-movie – a small, hard-to-sell, somewhat obscure sub-genre. But this features some of the most unflashily *honest* film-making in Hollywood's history – small wonder Wenders, in *Lightning Over Water*, recycled the clip of McCloud leaving the windswept arena at sundown to return to his rundown family farmstead. (One is only bemused why he didn't continue through the superb scene with chatty old Jeremiah, and that he managed to forego some of the electric stuff – the pot-roast scene, say, including Louise's lovely, belated smile at Jeff's words of appreciation about her dress – with Mitchum and Hayward both on peak form.) Does the rodeo, with its rivalry, its addiction to money, myths and quick thrills, and its blind denial of danger and the outside world, stand for the States? Who can tell? Who cares, when it's one of the best studies of masculinity on film? That astonishingly moving roll away from the camera of McCloud's bare shoulders as he takes his final exit speaks volumes about love, loss, loneliness, and the need for pride, privacy and a sense of purpose in life.

Johnny Guitar

Is this film really getting less strange with the years, or is it just my personal familiarity with it that now makes it seem oddly logical, despite the non-sequiturs in the dialogue and some obscurely motivated moments in the action? (What precisely *is* the point of the Kid's dance with Emma, besides showing he lives up to his name?) Maybe those recent blockbusters where 'story' is little more than a series of spectacular set-pieces linked only by the constant presence of a handful of cardboard cut-out heroes and villains have helped to accustom us to things not having to be particularly explicable. And at least this Western is *about* something – something still, sadly, all too relevant. The way it treats the xenophobia, prejudice, hysteria, hypocrisy, cowardice and cruelty that can take over an inward-turned, ignorant, self-serving society tells us twice as much as Lars von Trier's *Dogville* (the recently premiered first instalment of what will apparently be a whole new trilogy) in half the time and with far less self-aggrandising ballyhoo.

Run for Cover

This, too, could be said to anticipate *Dogville*, perhaps even more closely, in fact, despite being far more conventionally classical in style than *Johnny Guitar*. Perhaps that's why it's not as well known as it could be, nor even as highly thought of as it should be among Ray fans. For it's actually a very fine Western, fascinating for its frank treatment of rough justice and for how it takes on a strangely abstract/metaphorical tone when Matt and Davey go off alone into the desert, ending up at that Aztec fortress. And the beautifully acted scenes Cagney shares with Viveca Lindfors and Jean Hersholt are deliciously tender, funny and touching.

High Green Wall

I've nothing new to say here except that, problems of ethnic representation aside – its age is very visible in that no-budget studio depiction of life in the jungle – this is far more ambitious and satisfying than most of the mindless fare served up by television today.

Rebel Without a Cause

Always a little tough to get to grips with – not so much because of the Dean cult, more because the film itself has become so *iconic*. (I hate that much-misused word, but it's the right one here.) Ironically, this can seem more dated than many of Ray's lesser-known films; that's probably because, being about teenagers, it's a film in which fashion – not only in clothes, but in speech, gestures and how the kids get their kicks (all that guff about *sincerity*!) – plays a more conspicuous role than elsewhere. But what does strike one as bold and modern is that the film begins with three kids – strangers to one another – at the police station, and then proceeds to fill in their separate stories before starting to weave them gradually together, tighter and tighter; it almost feels like a precursor to some of the narrative strategies Altman would be trying out about a decade and a half later. But there is also the way the best scenes feel as if they are developing organically before our eyes – the results, presumably, of the improvisational methods Ray was experimenting with, especially with the younger actors. At such points the more schematic aspects of the plot and the characterisations simply slip out of sight.

Hot Blood

The theme of cultural and ethnic traditions and identity being threatened with erosion or eradication by modern Western life is probably even more relevant now than when Ray made the movie; minorities are so easily ignored or outvoted, subsumed, seduced or just sidelined – or even, if nobody's looking, slaughtered. So one applauds Ray's aims here, though the outcome of his slightly bizarre strategy of making a semi-musical is more questionable. Was I a little too kind about the movie? Much of Les Baxter's music feels wrong now, especially since the increased availability of world music has meant that we are probably now more familiar with authentic gypsy fare; films, too, like those of Tony Gatlif and Emir Kusturica, have given a clearer view of contemporary Rom culture. That said, *Hot Blood* retains its vitality. Moreover, I may not originally have appreciated how important the title is: as with the range of reds used inventively throughout, the film explores 'blood' according to a variety of meanings, metaphors and associations, to do with life, love and sex, family and race, violence and death.

Bigger than Life

I watched this film again for this edition while my wife was visiting her father Sebastian in the Basque Country; he lay dying in hospital in Donostia (San Sebastian). Those sad circumstances enabled me to see what is still probably my very favourite Ray film from a fresh perspective; fresh for me, at least, even though I'd seen it several times since I'd been in hospital undergoing angioplasty. At last I realised that, besides the various levels of meaning I'd pondered over the years, there was one to which I'd never paid adequate attention: I'd been so caught up by the film's metaphorical aspects that the most visible and literal one had virtually passed over me. Besides the many nuances explored in my chapter on this film – nuances I still believe are important – there's an extraordinarily accurate, insightful portrait of what it's like to be told, suddenly and in early middle-age, that your health is such that you might die at any moment; that you need to be operated on at once, that you'll need to be monitored and have to take medication every day for the rest of your life – which, if you're careful and lucky, might just last as long as you'd always, until now, presumed.

Thanks in no small part to its origins in the fine Berton Roueché essay adapted by Ray and his colleagues, the film is extremely good on the consequences of such a trauma. Both essay and film are about the potential effects of cortisone; what the film also gets right is how the kind of (common) experience described above can affect your thinking, behaviour and entire existence, regardless of reactions to drugs. Of course some mood swings can be attributed to that daily regime of pills, but also of great importance is the

The benefit of wisdom that comes from recognition of one's own mortality: Ed Avery (James Mason) lays down the law in *Bigger than Life*.

increased awareness of your fragility and mortality. This new, deeper, constant sense of vulnerability can cause anxiety, depression, self-examination, contemplation of spiritual and philosophical questions, and reassessment of relationships; it can create a sense of urgency, solitude and dependency, and give rise to caution about your ability to perform certain basic acts you've always taken for granted. But there can also be an elation arising from the notion that you may have been given a second chance: that you've survived the really dangerous stuff and can start anew with a clean slate. You start taking better care of yourself, and so feel a little fitter, trimmer, younger even; you even wonder whether this fleeting glimpse of death's presence may have given you better insights into yourself, even into life itself. You ask yourself if you've spent your time wisely. Is it too late to change? Is it best to hang in there, take it carefully, hold on to what you've got, and think about the far-off future; or to pack in the job, sell the house, spend the savings and take off on some exotic holiday of your dreams because you may not last long anyway? You may feel sorry for yourself, or you may feel magnanimous, but one way or another your emotions often seem heightened, and you react to others accordingly.

Ed Avery does all this – or, rather, goes through all this. Because he misuses the cortisone, he ends up going much further than I did, but the film rings frighteningly true as an honest, sensitive, very precise account of the consequences of the sudden realisation that you *will* die, no question, and it may be sooner than you think ... tomorrow, or today. Notwithstanding all those disease-of-the-week telefilms, all the Hollywood weepies, and all the great art-movies about illness and dying – think Kurosawa's *Ikiru*, Bergman's *Cries and Whispers* or Todd Haynes's *[Safe]* – notwithstanding the long, rich history of cinema, Ray's film has no serious rivals in terms of getting this very widespread, very particular aspect of human experience exactly right. Quite literally, the movie improves with (my/our) ageing.

The True Story of Jesse James

Mercifully, there's less of me in this movie! Not a great deal to add, though isn't it heartening to see a film that tries to understand someone like Jesse James, rather than simply demonising and dismissing him as 'evil'? Oh, and isn't it nice to see a good, solid Western? We get so few now.

Bitter Victory

A wonderful and terribly underrated war movie; what is striking now (apart from how it anticipated, in various respects, both Lean's *Lawrence of Arabia* and Minghella's *The English Patient*) is the sheer, unflinching intensity of some of the scenes: Leith stabbing the Nazi guard, his mercy-killing of the wounded Nazi soldier, his being bitten by the scorpion, Mokrane's killing of the camel for ammonia. The dramatic heat is intensified still further by the way Ray focuses attention on stark, mythic elements (sun, sand, stone, wind, water, fire), and by our awareness that the loss of life involved in what almost turns out to be an entirely fruitless expedition counts for little indeed among the top brass, shown by Ray to be callously resigned to incurring high casualties in the furtherance of their plans. *Plus ça change* ... .

Wind Across the Everglades

I'm a bird-watcher, interested in ecological conservation issues; how could this film not look more relevant, prescient indeed, with each passing year? Politicians, business folk and, sadly, many other people don't appear to have got the message: plundering, ravaging, over-exploiting or simply not taking care of our dwindling natural resources, be they in Alaska, Antarctica, an Amazon rainforest or the *rias* of Galicia, is short-sighted, unsustainable, ultimately self-defeating and morally wrong. The film captures the ethos of machismo that inf(l)ects the culture of hunting, the lobby for which sadly remains all too powerful; it also suggests that politicians, entrepreneurs and downright criminals have long managed to get along quite comfortably in the Sunshine State.

Party Girl

More of Ray's lawyers of questionable integrity, but perhaps the most striking aspect of this film is that while the story now looks fairly conventional (albeit full of typical Ray touches, as I hope my original chapter made clear), the *mise en scène* is extraordinarily bold, so that it's almost possible to see the film as one of the most important progenitors of highly stylised crime sagas like *The Godfather, Miller's Crossing* and *Heat*. One thing I didn't for some reason notice first time around concerned the hero's name. What a coincidence that one of Ray's closest collaborators in his later years was a Tom Farrell, who worked on both *We Can't Go Home Again* and *Lightning Over Water*.

The Savage Innocents

I now think my original assessment of this film was not quite as positive as it should have been. Not that I didn't appreciate the importance of what it was saying; in its ecological, ethnographic and political concerns, it's arguably as significant and ahead of its time as *Wind Across the Everglades*. Rather, I feel I didn't quite get what Ray was up to in terms of performance: I'd always found Quinn, Yoko Tani and the other pretty conspicuously non-Eskimo actors (there can't have been too many Inuit thesps around whose services he could call on) a little too stilted, broad or one-dimensional. But now we've been able to see *Atarnajuat: The Fast Runner* and other films by Inuit film-maker Zacharias Kunuk, and it transpires Ray had it right all along. In getting his cast to laugh so often with the lack of self-consciousness one finds in children, in having them speak in a style we might sometimes consider repetitive or roundabout, he was simply getting them to behave like the Eskimos he'd encountered. Consequently, the film now feels far less clumsy than it did before digital technology enabled Kunuk to shoot in the kind of locations to which Ray, with his crew's less versatile or portable equipment, was very often denied access.

King of Kings

Watching this again in the light of the ongoing Israeli–Palestinian conflict, one is aware, of course, that it's no longer the Jews wielding slings to attack the occupying forces. When the film was made, the response of many to Zionism was probably rather different from the somewhat ambivalent view common now; the Holocaust was still all too recent, as may be divined from the opening prologue's shots of Jewish corpses being tipped into mass graves. That said, though time has changed the identities and roles of the peoples in conflict, Ray's concern with the question of the ethics and effectiveness of, respectively, peaceful and violent resistance is if anything even more relevant in a world preoccupied by a 'war against terrorism'. Yordan and Ray came up with some interesting advice for the Romans: for example, that it may be best to suffer leaders with a devout following, rather than punish them with death for their propaganda, thereby making them martyrs; and that it is unwise for an occupying power to try and impose its laws on a society which already has laws of its own. Because the film often seems more concerned with these still relevant issues than with trying to convince us, through spectacle, that Christ must surely have been the son of God because he had the power to perform some pretty nifty miracles, the film has aged considerably better than most biblical epics.

55 Days at Peking

As Major Matt Lewis confidently leads his Marines into Peking, he reacts to their leers at local women with the words: 'This is an ancient and highly cultured civilisation, so don't get the idea you're any better than these people just because they don't speak English!' Correct, except that he then proceeds to teach his men the Chinese words for 'yes' and 'no', reminding them that everything has a price – the respect he pays to other cultures is mere lip-service, given that he evidently believes that it's the laws of capitalism, rather than principles of honour, faith and tradition, that make the world go round. And while he's in some ways the (extremely flawed) hero, we soon sense that he's on the

Prince Tuan (Robert Helpmann) tests the limits of Western diplomacy in *55 Days at Peking*.

look-out for a fight now that he's come all this way to China; hence the anger and frustration he directs at Sir Arthur as soon as he's told his men are no longer needed. To Prince Tuan's provocation of bringing Boxer acrobats into the British embassy, Lewis responds with a display of strength and determination, totally disregarding Sir Arthur's warnings that his actions will increase rather than diminish the dangerous tensions between China and the Western nations that have been exploiting her. Later on, Lewis even suggests it might be a good idea to assassinate the Empress herself. Such hotheaded, nakedly militaristic aggression, Sir Arthur suggests, would be disastrous.

There are weaknesses in this film, the most obvious that of having Sir Arthur join Lewis and other top military officers in the risky raid upon the Chinese arsenal; even

Nicholas Ray and friend.

then stars had egos, and it seems Niven wanted a piece of the action, too, instead of just playing a wise diplomat anxious to avoid an international bloodbath. (If only some of today's politicians had Sir Arthur's patience and sense of fair play!) But again, for all the adherence to national stereotypes and epic conventions, there remains much of enduring interest in this tale of spiralling hostility between nations – or, more precisely, between their leaders and representatives, determined to save face, whatever the cost.

We Can't Go Home Again

Now more than in the late 1980s, the 1973 version of this experimental multi-screen collage looks like something from a bygone age; like *Rebel*, it's dated partly because it's about the young and is very explicitly about its time, which means it's the victim of changes in fashion. (All that hair!) But the complexity of the relationship between sound and image – which predates much work today – is also the reason it would be good to see a properly restored version approximating more closely to Ray's wishes in later years. Let's hope …

Lightning Over Water

Perhaps this film's bold blurring of 'documentary' and 'fiction' looks more significant now that there's virtually a subgenre of films which explore that fascinating, fertile no-man's-land: films like Erice's *The Quince Tree Sun*, Kiarostami's *Close-Up* and *10*, Moretti's *Dear Diary* and *Aprile*, Mohsen Makhmalbaf's *Moment of Innocence*, Breillat's *Sex Is Comedy*. I'm a little less sure, too, about my initial misgivings. Perhaps that's because Ray's been dead so much longer now. Perhaps it's because there've been so many films recently which are far less rigorous than this one with regard to the ethics of voyeurism, so that I've become a little inured to such problematic qualities. Perhaps I was a little unforgiving in the first place – at least Wenders was honest enough to include the moments where he's heard ignoring Ray's 'Cut!', so that are aware of his capacity to betray, briefly, a dying friend's wishes; he also left Ray's comments about 'stepping on my back' in the finished film. My worries haven't vanished entirely, but it's almost as if Wenders and Ray didn't want them to, anyway. What impresses me most now is seeing Ray continue his lengthy study of life in all its problematic, painful glory right up until those last few hours. As the final shot of his final film plays out – a shot, as it happens, of his funeral junk sailing peacefully past the Twin Towers – we are left with our memories not only of his courage but of the intense, passionate emotions poured so generously into his work. In that respect, his films really were bigger than life …

Filmography

Credit abbreviations: p – producer; exec p – executive producer; scr – script; ph – director of photography; art dir – art director; set – set designs; ed – editor; choreog – choreography; mus – music; lp – leading players. Release dates for US unless stated otherwise.

FILMS WITH RAY CREDITED AS DIRECTOR

THEY LIVE BY NIGHT (1948; RKO)

(also released as *The Twisted Road*; working title *Your Red Wagon*) p: John Houseman; exec p: Dore Schary; scr: Charles Schnee, from Ray's adaptation of Edward Anderson's novel *Thieves Like Us*; ph: George E. Diskant; art dir: Albert S. D'Agostino, Al Herman; set: Darrell Silvera, Maurice Yates; ed: Sherman Todd; mus: Leigh Harline; song 'Your Red Wagon' by Don Raye, Gene de Paul.

lp: Farley Granger (*Arthur 'Bowie' Bowers*), Cathy O'Donnell (*Catherine 'Keechie' Mobley*), Howard Da Silva (*Chicamaw*), Jay C. Flippen (*T-Dub*), Helen Craig (*Mattie*), Will Wright (*Mobley*), Ian Wolfe (*Hawkins)*, Harry Harvey (*Hagenheimer*), Marie Bryant (*Singer*), William Phipps, Regan Callais, Frank Marlowe, Jim Nolan, Charles Meredith, J. Louis Johnson, Myra Marsh, Tom Kennedy, Erskine Sanford.

Running time: 96 mins. Filming: June–August 1947. Released: GB June 1948; US 4 November 1949.

A WOMAN'S SECRET (1949; RKO)

p: Herman J. Mankiewicz; exec p: Dore Schary; scr: Herman J. Mankiewicz, from Vicki Baum's novel *Mortgage on Life*; ph: George E. Diskant; art dir: Albert S. D'Agostino, Carroll Clark; set: Darrell Silvera, Harley Miller; ed: Sherman Todd; mus: Frederick Hollander; songs: 'Estrellita' by Manuel Ponce, 'Paradise' by Nacio Herb Brown, Gordon Clifford.

lp: Maureen O'Hara (*Marian Washbourn*), Gloria Grahame (*Susan Caldwell*), Melvyn Douglas (*Luke Jordan*), Bill Williams (*Lee Crenshaw*), Victor Jory (*Brook Matthews*), May Phillips (*Mrs Fowler*), Jay C. Flippen (*Fowler*), Robert Warwick, (*Roberts*), Curt Conway (*Doctor*), Ann Shoemaker (*Mrs Matthews*), Virginia Farmer, Ellen Corby, Emory Parnell.

Running time: 85 mins. Filming: February–March 1948. Released: 5 March 1949.

KNOCK ON ANY DOOR (1949; Columbia)

p: Robert Lord, for Santana Pictures; scr: Daniel Taradash, John Monks Jr., from the novel by Willard Motley; ph: Burnett Guffey; art dir: Robert Peterson; set: William Kiernan; ed: Viola Lawrence; mus: George Antheil.

lp: Humphrey Bogart (*Andrew Morton*). John Derek (*Nick Romano*), George Macready (*District Attorney Kerman*), Allene Roberts (*Emma*), Susan Perry (*Adele Morton*), Mickey Knox (*Vito*), Barry Kelley (*Judge Drake*), Cara Williams (*Nelly*), Jimmy Conlin (*Kid Fingers Carnahan*), Sumner Williams (*Jimmy*), Sid Melton (*Squint*), Pepe Hern (*Juan*), Dewey Martin (*Butch*), Robert A. Davis (*Sunshine*), Houseley Stevenson, Dooley Wilson, Florence Auer, Pierre Watkin, Gordon Nelson, Argentina Brunelli, Curt Conway.

Running time: 100 mins. Filming: August–September 1948. Released: February 1949.

BORN TO BE BAD (1950; RKO)

p: Robert Sparks; exec p: Sid Rogell; scr: Edith Sommer, from Charles Schnee's adaptation of Ann Parrish's novel *All Kneeling*, with additional dialogue by Robert Soderberg, George Oppenheimer; ph: Nicholas Musuraca; art dir: Albert S. D'Agostino, Jack Okey; set: Harley Miller, Darrell Silvera; ed: Frederick Knudtson; mus: Frederick Hollander.

lp: Joan Fontaine (*Christabel Caine*), Robert Ryan (*Nick Bradley*), Zachary Scott (*Curtis Carey*), Joan Leslie (*Donna Fortes*), Mel Ferrer (*Gabriel'Gobby'Broom*), Harold Vermilyea (*John Caine*), Virginia Farmer (*Aunt Clara*), Kathleen Howard (*Mrs Bolton*), Dick Ryan (*Arthur*), Bess Flowers, Joy Hallward, Hazel Boyne, Irving Bacon.

Running time: 94 mins. Filming: June–July 1949. Released: 27 August 1950.

IN A LONELY PLACE (1950; Columbia)

p: Robert Lord, for Santana Pictures; scr: Andrew Solt, from Edmund H. North's adaptation of the novel by Dorothy B. Hughes; ph: Burnett Guffey; art dir: Robert Peterson; set dir: William Kiernan; ed: Viola Lawrence; mus: George Antheil.

lp: Humphrey Bogart (*Dixon Steele*), Gloria Grahame (*Laurel Gray*), Frank Lovejoy (*Brub Nicolai*), Carl Benton Reid (*Captain Lochner*), Art Smith (*Mel Lippmann*), Jeff Donnell (*Sylvia Nicolai*), Martha Stewart (*Mildred Atkinson*), Robert Warwick (*Charlie Waterman*), Morris Ankrum (*Lloyd Barnes*), William Ching (*Ted Barton*), Steven Geray (*Paul*), Hadda Brooks (*Singer*), Alice Talton, Jack Reynolds, Ruth Warren, Ruth Gillette.

Running time. 94 mins. Filming: October–November 1949. Released: 17 May 1950.

ON DANGEROUS GROUND (1951; RKO)

p: John Houseman; exec p: Sid Rogell; scr: A. I. Bezzerides, from Bezzerides's and Ray's adaptation of Gerald Butler's novel *Mad with Much Heart*; ph: George E. Diskant; art dir: Albert S. D'Agostino, Ralph Berger; set dir: Darrell Silvera, Harley Miller; ed: Roland Gross, mus: Bernard Herrmann.

lp: Robert Ryan (*Jim Wilson*), Ida Lupino (*Mary Walden*), Ward Bond (*Walter Brent*), Charles Kemper (*Bill 'Pop' Daly*), Anthony Ross (*Pete Santos*), Ed Begley (*Capt. Brawley*), Sumner Williams (*Danny Walden*), Frank Ferguson (*Willows*), Gus Schilling (*Lucky*), Cleo Moore (*Myrna*), Olive Carey (*Mrs Brent*), Richard Irving (*Bernie*), Pat Prest (*Julie*), Bill Hammond (*Fred*), Ian Wolfe (*Sheriff*), A. I. Bezzerides, Jimmy Conlin, Joe Devlin.

Running time: 82 mins. Filming: March–May 1950. Released: 28 November 1951.

FLYING LEATHERNECKS (1951; RKO)

p: Edmund Grainger; scr: James Edward Grant, from an original story by Kenneth Gamet; ph: William E. Snyder (Technicolor); art dir: Albert S. D'Agostino, James W. Sullivan; set: Darrell Silvera, John Sturtlevant; ed: Sherman Todd; mus: Roy Webb.

lp: John Wayne (*Maj. Dan Kirby*), Robert Ryan (*Capt. Carl 'Griff' Griffin*), Don Taylor (*Lieut. Vern 'Cowboy' Blythe*), Janis Carter (*Joan Kirby*), Jay C. Flippen (*Clancy*), William Harrigan (*Dr Curan*), James Bell (*Colonel*), Barry Kelley (*General*), Maurice Jara (*Shorty*), Adam Williams (*Lieut. Malotke*), James Dobson (*Pudge McCabe*), Carleton Young (*Capt. McAllister*), Steve Flagg (*Lieut. Jorgenson*), Brett King

(*Lieut. Ernie Stark*), Gordon Gebert (*Tommy Kirby*), Lynn Stalmaster, Brit Norton, Ralph Cook.

Running time. 102 mins. Filming: November 1950–January 1951. Released 28 August or 19 September 1951.

THE LUSTY MEN (1952; RKO)

p: Jerry Wald, Norman Krasna; scr: Horace McCoy, David Dontort, from a novel by Claude Stanush; ph: Lee Garmes; art dir: Albert S. D'Agostino, Alfred Herman; set: Darrell Silvera, Jack Mills; ed: Ralph Dawson; mus: Roy Webb.

lp: Robert Mitchum (*Jeff McCloud*), Susan Hayward (*Louise Merritt*), Arthur Kennedy (*Wes Merritt*), Arthur Hunnicutt (*Booker Davis*), Frank Faylen (*Al Dawson*), Walter Coy (*Buster Burgess*), Carol Nugent (*Rusty Davis*), Maria Hart (*Rosemary Maddox*), Lorna Thayer (*Grace Burgess*), Burt Mustin (*Jeremiah*), Karen King (*Ginny Logan*), Jimmy Dodd (*Red Logan*), Eleanor Todd (*Babs*), Riley Hill, Bob Bray, Sheb Wooley, Denver Pyle.

Running time: 113 mins. Filming: December 1951–February 1952. Released: 24 October 1952.

JOHNNY GUITAR (1954; Republic)

p: Herbert J. Yates; scr: Philip Yordan, from Ray Chanslor's novel; ph: Harry Stradling (Trucolor); art dir: James Sullivan; set: John McCarthy Jr., Edward G. Boyle; ed: Richard L. Van Enger; mus: Victor Young; song 'Johnny Guitar' sung by Peggy Lee, written by Young and Lee.

lp: Joan Crawford (*Vienna*), Sterling Hayden (*Johnny 'Guitar' Logan*), Mercedes McCambridge (*Emma Small*), Scott Brady (*Dancing Kid*), Ward Bond (*John McIvers*), Ernest Borgnine (*Bart Lonergan*), Ben Cooper (*Turkey*), John Carradine (*Tom*), Royal Dano (*Corey*), Frank Ferguson (*Sheriff*), Paul Fix (*Eddie*), Rhys Williams (*Andrews*), Ian MacDonald (*Pete*), Will Wright, Sumner Williams, Sheb Wooley, Denver Pyle.

Running time: 110 mins. Filming: October–December 1953. Released: 27 May 1954.

RUN FOR COVER (1954; Paramount)

p: William H. Pine, William C. Thomas; scr: Winston Miller, from a story by Harriet Frank Jr, Irving Ravetch; ph: Daniel L. Fapp (VistaVision, Technicolor); art dir: Hal Pereira, Henry Bumstead; set: Sam Comer, Frank McKelvy; ed: Howard Smith; mus: Howard Jackson; song 'Run for Cover' by Jackson and Jack Brooks.

lp: James Cagney (*Matt Dow*), John Derek (*Davey*

Bishop), Viveca Lindfors (*Helga Swenson*), Jean
Hersholt (*Swenson*), Grant Withers (*Gentry*), Jack
Lambert (*Larsen*), Ernest Borgnine (*Morgan*), Ray Teal
(*Sheriff*), Irving Bacon (*Scotty*), Trevor Bardette
(*Paulsen*), John Milhan (*Mayor Walsh*), Gus Schilling
(*Doc Ridgeway*), Denver Pyle (*Harvey*), Emerson
Treacy, Phil Chambers, Harold Kennedy, Joe Haworth.
Running time: 93 mins. Filming: May–June 1954.
Released: 29 April 1955.

REBEL WITHOUT A CAUSE (1955; Warner Bros.)
p: David Weisbart; scr: Stewart Stern, based on Irving
   Shulman's adaptation of a story by Ray (title from a
   book by Dr Robert M. Lindner); ph: Ernest Haller
   (CinemaScope, Warnercolor); art dir: Malcolm Bert;
   set: William Wallace; ed: William Ziegler; mus:
   Leonard Rosenman.
lp: James Dean (*Jim Stark*), Natalie Wood (*Judy*), Sal
   Mineo (*Plato*), Jim Backus (*Mr Stark*), Ann Doran
   (*Mrs Stark*), Corey Allen (*Buzz*), William Hopper
   (*Judy's father*), Rochelle Hudson (*Judy's mother*),
   Dennis Hopper (*Goon*), Ed Platt (*Ray*), Steffi Sidney
   (*Mil*), Mariette Canty (*Plato's governess*), Ian Wolfe
   (*Planetarium lecturer*), Frank Mazzola (*Crunch*), Nick
   Adams (*Moose*), Jack Grinnage, Clifford Morris, Gus
   Schilling, Nicholas Ray.
Running time: 111 mins. Filming: March–May 1955.
Released: 27 October 1955.

HOT BLOOD (1956; Columbia)
p: Howard Welsch, Harry Tatelman; scr: Jesse Lasky Jr.,
   from a story by Jean Evans; ph: Ray June (CinemaScope,
   Technicolor); art dir: Robert Peterson; set: Frank Tuttle;
   ed: Otto Ludwig; choreog: Matt Mattox, Silvia Lewis;
   mus: Les Baxter; songs: Ross Bagdasarian.
lp: Jane Russell (*Annie Caldash*), Cornel Wilde (*Stephano
   Torino*), Luther Adler (*Marco Torino*), Joseph Calleia
   (*Papa Theodore*), Jamie Russell (*Xano*), Nina Koshetz
   (*Nita Johnny*), Helen Westcott (*Velma*), Mikhail
   Rasumny (*Old Johnny*), Wally Russell (*Bimbo*), Nick
   Dennis, Richard Deacon, Robert Foulk, John Raven.
Running time: 85 mins. Filming: July–August 1955.
Released 23 March 1956.

BIGGER THAN LIFE (1956; 20th Century-Fox)
p: James Mason; scr: Cyril Hume, Richard Maibaum,
   from the *New Yorker* article 'Ten Feet Tall' by Berton
   Roueché; ph: Joe MacDonald (CinemaScope, De Luxe
   Color); art dir: Lyle R. Wheeler, Jack Martin Smith; set:
   Walter M. Scott, Stuart A. Reiss; ed: Louis Loeffler;
   mus: David Raksin.

lp: James Mason (*Ed Avery*), Barbara Rush (*Lou Avery*),
   Walter Matthau (*Wally*), Christopher Olsen (*Richie
   Avery*), Robert Simon (*Dr Norton*), Roland Winters (*Dr
   Ruric*), Rusty Lane (*La Porte*), Rachel Stephens (*Nurse*),
   Kipp Hamilton (*Pat Wade*), Betty Caulfield (*Mrs La
   Porte*), Gus Schilling (*Druggist*), Richard Collier
   (*Milkman*), Alex Frazer, Virginia Carroll, Renny McEvoy.
Running time: 95 mins. Filming: March–May 1956.
Released 2 August 1956.

THE TRUE STORY OF JESSE JAMES (GB title: THE JAMES
BROTHERS) (1957; 20th Century-Fox)
p: Herbert B. Swope Jr; scr: Walter Newman, from
   Nunnally Johnson's screenplay for Henry King's 1939
   film, *Jesse James*; ph: Joe McDonald (CinemaScope, De
   Luxe Color); art dir: Lyle R. Wheeler, Addison Hehr; set:
   Walter M. Scott, Stuart A. Reiss; ed: Robert Simpson;
   mus: Leigh Harline.
lp: Robert Wagner (*Jesse James*), Jeffrey Hunter (*Frank
   James*), Hope Lange (*Zee*), Agnes Moorhead (*Mrs
   Samuel*), Alan Hale (*Cole Younger*), Alan Baxter
   (*Remington*), John Carradine (*Rev. Bailey*), Rachel
   Stephens (*Anne*), Barney Phillips (*Dr Samuel*), Biff
   Elliott (*Jim Younger*), Frank Overton (*Maj. Rufus
   Cobb*), Marian Seldes (*Rowena Cobb*), Barry Atwater
   (*Walker*), Chubby Johnson (*Askew*), Frank Gorshin
   (*Charley Ford*), Carl Thayler (*Bob Ford*), Sumner
   Williams (*Bill Stiles*), Anthony Ray (*Bob Younger*), John
   Doucette, Robert Adler, Clancy Cooper.
Running time: 93 mins. Filming: September–November
   1956. Released: 22 March 1957.

BITTER VICTORY (AMÈRE VICTOIRE) (1957; Columbia)
p: Paul Graetz, for Transcontinental Films and Robert
   Laffont Productions; scr: René Hardy, Gavin
   Lambert, Nicholas Ray from Hardy's novel, additional
   dialogue by Paul Gallico; ph: Michel Kelber
   (CinemaScope); art dir: Jean d'Eaubonne; ed:
   Léonide Azar; mus: Maurice Le Roux.
lp: Richard Burton (*Capt. James Leith*), Curt Jurgens
   (*Maj. David Brand*), Ruth Roman (*Jane Brand*),
   Raymond Pellegrin (*Mokrane*), Sean Kelly (*Lieut.
   Barton*), Anthony Bushell (*Gen. Patterson*), Alfred
   Burke (*Maj. Callander*), Andrew Crawford (*Roberts*),
   Nigel Green (*Wilkins*), Sumner Williams (*Anderson*),
   Ronan O'Casey (*Dunnigan*), Christopher Lee
   (*Barney*), Fred Matter (*Lutze*), Raoul Delfosse, Harry
   Landis, Joe Davray.
Running time: 103 mins (France 97 mins; GB 90 mins;
   US 82 mins). Filming: February–May 1957.
   Premiered: Venice Festival, September 1957.

WIND ACROSS THE EVERGLADES (1958; Warner Bros.)

p: Stuart Schulberg, for Schulberg Productions; scr: Budd Schulberg; ph: Joseph Brun (Technicolor); art dir: Richard Sylbert; ed: George Klotz, Joseph Zigman.

lp: Burl Ives (*Cottonmouth*), Christopher Plummer (*Walt Murdoch*), Chana Eden (*Naomi*), Gypsy Rose Lee (*Mrs Bradford*), Tony Galento (*Beef*), Sammy Renick (*Loser*), Pat Henning (*Sawdust*), Peter Falk (*Writer*), Cory Osceola (*Billy One-Arm*), Emmett Kelly (*Bigamy Bob*), MacKinlay Kantor (*Judge Harris*), George Voskovec (*Aaron Nathanson*), Curt Conway (*Perfessor*), Sumner Williams (*Windy*), Howard I. Smith, Mary Pennington, Fred Grossinger, Mary Osceola.

Running time: 93 mins. Filming: November 1957–January 1958. Released: 20 August 1958.

PARTY GIRL (1958; MGM)

p: Joe Pasternak; scr: George Wells, from a story by Leo Katcher; ph: Robert Bronner (CinemaScope, Metrocolor); art dir: William A. Horning, Randall Duell; set: Henry Grove, Richard Pefferle; ed: John McSweeney Jr; choreog: Robert Sidney; mus: Jeff Alexander; song 'Party Girl' by Nicholas Brodszky, Sammy Cahn, sung by Tony Martin.

lp: Robert Taylor (*Tommy Farrell*), Cyd Charisse (*Vicki Gaye*), Lee J. Cobb (*Rico Angelo*), John Ireland (*Louis Canetto*), Kent Smith (*Jeffrey Stewart*), Corey Allen (*Cookie La Motte*), Claire Kelly (*Genevieve*), David Opatoshu (*Lou Forbes*), Lewis Charles, Ken Dibbs, Patrick McVey, Myrna Hansen, Erich von Stroheim Jr., Betty Utey.

Running time: 99 mins. Filming: March–May 1958. Released: 28 October 1958.

THE SAVAGE INNOCENTS (OMBRE BIANCHI/LES DENTS DU DIABLE) (1960; Paramount/Rank)

p: Maleno Malenotti, for Magic Films, Play-Art, Gray Films, Pathé and Appia Films; scr: Nicholas Ray, from an adaptation by Hans Ruesch and Franco Solinas of Ruesch's novel *Top of the World*; ph: Aldo Tonti, Peter Hennessy (Super Technirama 70, Technicolor); art dir: Don Aston, Dario Cecchi; set: Edward Clements; ed: Ralph Kemplen, Eraldo Da Roma; mus: Angelo Francesco Lavagnino; songs: 'Iceberg' by The Four Saints, 'Sexy Rock' by Lavagnino, Panzeri, sung by Colin Hicks. Narrator: Nicholas Stuart.

lp: Anthony Quinn (*Inuk*), Yoko Tani (*Asiak*), Peter O'Toole (*First Trooper*), Carlo Giustini (*Second Trooper*), Marie Yang (*Powtee*), Andy Ho (*Anarvik*), Kaida Horiuchi (*Imina*), Yvonne Shima (*Lulik*), Lee Montague (*Ittimangnerk*), Francis De Wolff (*Trading Post Proprietor*), Marco Guglielmi (*Missionary*), Anna May Wong, Anthony Chin, Michael Chow, Ed Devereau.

Running rime: 110 mins. Filming: June–September 1959. Released: Italy, March 1960; US, 24 May 1961.

KING OF KINGS (1961; MGM)

p: Samuel Bronston; scr: Philip Yordan; ph: Franz Planer, Milton Krasner, Manuel Berenguer (Super Technirama 70, Technicolor); art dir: Georges Wakhevitch; set: Enrique Alarcon; ed: Renée Lichtig, Harold Kress; choreog: Betty Utey; mus: Miklos Rozsa. Narrator (uncredited): Orson Welles.

lp: Jeffrey Hunter (*Jesus*), Robert Ryan (*John the Baptist*), Siobhan McKenna (*Mary*), Hurd Hatfield (*Pontius Pilate*), Ron Randell (*Lucius, a Centurion*), Harry Guardino (*Barabbas*), Rip Torn (*Judas*), Viveca Lindfors (*Claudia*), Rita Gam (*Herodias*), Brigid Bazlen (*Salome*), Frank Thring (*Herod Antipas*), Carmen Sevilla (*Mary Magdalen*), Guy Rolfe (*Caiphas*), Maurice Marsac (*Nicodemus*), Gregoire Aslan (*Herod*), Royal Dano (*Peter*), Edric Connor, George Colouris, Conrado San Martin, Gerard Tichy, José Antonio, Luis Prendes, David Davies, José Nieto, Michael Wager, Felix de Pomes.

Running time: US 168 mins; GB 160 mins. Filming: April–September 1960. Released: 30 October 1961.

55 DAYS AT PEKING (1963; Rank)

p: Samuel Bronston; scr: Philip Yordan, Bernard Gordon, with additional dialogue by Robert Hamer; ph: Jack Hildyard (Super Technirama 70, Technicolor); art dir: Veniero Colasanti, John Moore; ed: Robert Lawrence; mus: Dmitri Tiomkin.

lp: Charlton Heston (*Maj. Matt Lewis*), Ava Gardner (*Baroness Natalie Ivanoff*), David Niven (*Sir Arthur Robertson*), Flora Robson (*Dowager Empress Tsu-Hsi*), Leo Genn (*Gen. Jung-Lu*), Robert Helpmann (*Prince Tuan*), John Ireland (*Sgt. Harry*), Harry Andrews (*Father de Bearn*), Kurt Kasznar (*Baron Sergei Ivanoff*), Paul Lukas (*Dr Steinfeldt*), Elizabeth Sellars (*Lady Sarah Robertson*), Jerome Thor (*Lieut. Andy Marshall*), Lynne Sue Moon (*Teresa*), Ichizo [Juzo] Itami (*Col. Shima*), Jacques Sernas, Eric Pohlmann, Walter Gotell, Robert Urquhart, Alfred Lynch, Nicholas Ray.

Running time: 154 mins. Filming: July–November 1962. Released: GB, 6 May 1963; US, 29 May 1963.

WE CAN'T GO HOME AGAIN – A FILM BY US (1973–76
– uncompleted)

p, scr: Ray, in collaboration with Susan Schwartz and
students at Harpur College, Binghampton, New York
State University. Technical crew: Ray and Harpur
College students. Song 'Bless the Family' by Norman
and Suzy Zamchek.

lp: Ray, Tom Farrell, Leslie Levinson, Richie Bock,
Danny Fisher, Jane Heymann, Jim North, Steve
Maurer, Stanley Liu, Jill, Hallie, Phil Wiseman, Steve
Anker, et al.

Running time: approx 90 mins. First public screening:
Cannes Film Festival, May 1973; first public screening
of revised version: Rotterdam Film Festival, February
1980.

THE JANITOR, episode twelve of compilation film *Wet
Dreams* (1974; Film Group One (Amsterdam)/Cinereal
Film (West Berlin))

p: Dick Van Der Maarel, Peter Greulich; production co-
ordinators: Max Fischer, Jim Haynes; scr: Ray; ph
(16mm colour), ed: Fischer.

lp: Ray (*Preacher, Janitor*), Melvin Miracle, Anneke
Spierenburg, Dawn Cumming, Marvelle Williams,
Mary Moore, Kees Koedod, Falcon Stuart, Barbara,
Burnie Taylor.

Running time: 14 mins. Filming: May 1973. Released:
25 January 1974.

(Other episodes directed by Lee Kraft, Fischer, Jens
Joergen Thorsen, Hans Kanters, Heathcote Williams,
Sam Rotterdam [Dusan Makavejev], Oscar Gigard,
Falcon Stuart, Geert Koolman.)

MARCO (1978)

Made at the Lee Strasberg Institute of Dramatic Arts,
based on opening chapter of Curtis Bill Pepper's
Marco – A Novel of Love. ph: Robert La Cativa,
Danny Fisher; lp: Claudio Mazzatenta, Jim Ballagh,
Ned Motolo, Gerry Bamman, Connie, Charles W.
Joaquin.

Running time: 11 mins. Filming: December 1977.

LIGHTNING OVER WATER (NICK'S FILM) (1980–81;
Road Movies (Berlin)/Wim Wenders Produktion
(Berlin)/Viking Film (Stockholm))

Officially co-directed with Wim Wenders; p: Chris
Sievernich, Pierre Cottrell; scr: Ray, Wenders; ph: Ed
Lachman, Martin Schafer (Eastmancolor); video: Tom
Farrell; ed: (first version) Peter Przygodda, (final
version) Wenders, Sievernich; mus: Ronee Blakley;
song 'Nick One' written and sung by Blakley.

lp: Ray, Wenders, Gerry Bamman, Blakley, Cottrell,
Stephan Czapsky, Mitch Dubin, Farrell, Becky
Johnston, Tom Kaufman, Maryte Kavaliauskas, Pat
Kirck, Lachman, Martin Muller, Craig Nelson, Susan
Ray, Timothy Ray, Schafer, Sievernich.

Running time: 91 mins (first version 116 mins). Filming:
March–June 1979. First version premiered at Cannes
Film Festival, May 1980; final version premiered at
Venice Festival, September 1980.

DIRECTED FOR TELEVISION BY RAY

SORRY WRONG NUMBER for *Climax* series (1945; CBS)

p: John Houseman; scr: Houseman, Ray, from Lucille
Fletcher's radio play; lp: Mildred Natwick. Running
time: 30 mins.

HIGH GREEN WALL for *General Electric Theatre* series
(1954, CBS)

p: Leon Gordon; scr: Charles Jackson, from Evelyn
Waugh's story 'The Man Who Liked Dickens'; ph:
Franz Planer; lp: Joseph Cotton (Henty), Thomas
Gomez (McMaster), Maurice Marsac (Aubert),
Marshall Bradford, Ward Wood (search party).
Running time: 30 mins.

FILMS RAY IS BELIEVED TO HAVE CONTRIBUTED TO WITHOUT DIRECTORIAL CREDIT

1944 – as assistant on *A Tree Grows in Brooklyn* (dir:
Elia Kazan)

1945 – as dialogue director on *Caribbean Mystery* (dir:
Robert Webb) – as assistant on *Tuesday in November*
(dir: John Berry – short for Office of War Information
Overseas Branch)

1946 – as script collaborator on *Swing Parade of 1946*
(dir: Phil Karlson)

1949 – as co-director on *Roseanna McCoy* (dir: Irving
Reis)

1951 – as co-director on *The Racket* (dir: John
Cromwell)

1952 – as co-director on *Macao* (dir: Josef von
Sternberg)

1953 – as co-director on *Androcles and the Lion* (dir:
Chester Erskine)

1964 – as co-writer of original story on *Circus World*
(dir: Henry Hathaway)

1971 – as collaborator on original idea for *The Murder of
Fred Hampton* (dir: Mike Gray, Howard Alk)

FILMS IN WHICH RAY APPEARS

– *The James Dean Story*: documentary (dir: Robert
  Altman, George W. George, 1956, US)
– *America Revisited (Auf Der Suche Nach Meinem
  Amerika – Eine Reise Nach 20 Jahren)*: documentary
  (dir: Marcel Ophuls, 1970, W. Germany)
– *I'm a Stranger Here Myself*: documentary on Ray (dir:
  David Helpern Jr., James C. Gutman, 1974, US)
– *James Dean: The First American Teenager*: documentary
  (dir: Ray Connolly, 1975, GB)
– As Derwatt in *The American Friend (Der Amerikanische
  Freund)* (dir: Wim Wenders, 1977, W. Ger.) with
  Bruno Ganz, Dennis Hopper, Liza Kreuzer, Gerard
  Blain, Samuel Fuller, Peter Lilienthal, Daniel Schmid,
  Sandy Whitelaw, Jean Eustache
– *Garlic Is as Good as Ten Mothers*: documentary (dir:
  Les Blank, 1978, US)
– As the General in *Hair* (dir: Milos Forman, 1978, US)
  with John Savage, Treat Williams, Beverly D'Angelo,
  Annie Golden, Dorsey Wright, Don Dacus, Cheryl
  Barnes
– *The Dreamers* (dir: Bernado Bertolucci, 2003,
  Fr/It/GB)

UNREALISED PROJECTS (dates are inevitably approximatisations)

1956 – *Heroic Love*; *Passport*; *My Antonia*
1961 – *The Road to the Snail*; *The Tribe That Lost Its
  Head*
1963 – *The French Revolution*; *Circus World*; *Next Stop
  Paradise*
1965 – *The Doctor and the Devils*; *Only Lovers Left Alive*
1966 – *The Saga of Ghosta Berling*; *L'Evadé*; *Melody of
  Murder (In Between Time)*
1968 – *The Lady from the Sea*; *Wha-a-at?*
1970 – *Conspiracy: The Seditious Movie*
1975 – *Murphy – City Blues*
1977 – *The Sea Horse*
Other untitled projects include films about Cyrus and
  the Children's Crusade, a screenplay by Simone de
  Beauvoir and a life of Rimbaud.

SELECT BIBLIOGRAPHY

BOOKS ON RAY

Allan, Blaine, *Nicholas Ray – A Guide to References and Resources* (Boston: G. K. Hall, 1984).

Eisenschitz, Bernard, *Nicholas Ray: An American Journey*, trans. Tom Milne (London: Faber, 1993).

Erice, Victor and Oliver, Jos, *Nicholas Ray y su tiempo* (Madrid: Filmoteca Espanola, 1986).

Kriedl, John Francis, *Nicholas Ray* (Boston: Twayne, 1977).

Giuliani, Pierre, *Nicholas Ray* (Paris: Edilig, 1987).

Masi, Stefano, *Nicholas Ray* (Florence: La Nuova Italia, 1983).

Polan, Dana, *In a Lonely Place* (London: BFI, 1993).

Ray, Susan (ed.and Intro.), *I Was Interrupted: Nicholas Ray on Making Movies* (Berkeley: University of California Press, 1993).

Truchaud, François: *Nicholas Ray* (Paris: Editions Universitaires, 1965).

Wagner, Jean, *Nicholas Ray* (Paris: Rivages, 1987).

ARTICLES BY RAY

'Story into Script', *Sight and Sound*, Autumn 1956; reprinted in Richard Koszarski (ed.), *Hollywood Directors 1941–1976* (New York: Oxford University Press, 1977).

'Rebel: The Life Story of a Film', *Daily Variety*, 31 October 1956; reprinted in Allen Rivkin and Laura Kerr (eds), *Hello Hollywood* (New York: Doubleday, 1962).

'Always a Guest, Never a Host', *Hollywood Reporter*, 29 November 1962.

USEFUL MAGAZINE ARTICLES ON RAY IN ENGLISH

Biskind, Peter, 'Rebel Without a Cause: Nicholas Ray in the Fifties', *Film Quarterly*, Fall 1974.

Farrell, Tom, 'We Can't Go Home Again', *Sight and Sound*, Spring 1981.

Jost, Jon, 'Wrong Move', *Sight and Sound*, Spring 1981.

Leahy, James, 'Blood and Ice: Images of Nicholas Ray', *Pix*, no. 3, 2001, pp. 132–44.

Perkins, V. F., 'The Cinema of Nicholas Ray', *Movie*, no. 9 May 1963.

Rosenbaum, Jonathan, 'Circle of Pain: The Cinema of Nicholas Ray', *Sight and Sound*, 1973.

Thomson, David, 'In a Lonely Place', *Sight and Sound*, Autumn 1979.

Wilmington, Mike, 'Nicholas Ray – The Years at RKO, Parts 1 & 2', *The Velvet Light Trap*, nos 10 & 11, 1973–4.

Wollen, Peter, 'Never at Home', *Sight and Sound*, May 1994.

Wood, Robin, 'On *Bigger than Life*', *Film Comment*, September/October 1972.

USEFUL MAGAZINE INTERVIEWS WITH RAY IN ENGLISH

Cameron, Ian, Perkins, V. F., et al., 'Interview with Nicholas Ray', *Movie*, 9 May 1963.

Goodwin, Michael and Wise, Naomi, 'Nicholas Ray: Rebel', *Take One*, January 1977.

Houston, Penelope and Gillett, John, 'Conversations with Nicholas Ray and Joseph Losey', *Sight and Sound*, Autumn 1961; reprinted in Andrew Sarris, *Interviews with Film Directors* (New York: Avon, 1967).

Wilmington, Mike, 'Nicholas Ray on the Years at RKO', *The Velvet Light Trap*, 10, Autumn 1973.

OTHER FILM BOOKS IN ENGLISH WITH USEFUL MATERIAL ON RAY

Andrew, Geoff, *The Film Handbook* (London: Longman, 1989).

Durgnat, Raymond, *Films and Feelings* (London: Faber & Faber, 1967).

Finler, Joel W., *The Movie Directors Story* (London: Octopus, 1985).

Hillier, Jim (ed.), *Cahiers du Cinéma – Vol. 1: The 1950s* (London: Routledge & Kegan Paul, 1985).

Hillier, Jim (ed.), *Cahiers du Cinéma – Vol. 2: The 1960s* (London: Routledge & Kegan Paul, 1986).

Lambert, Gavin, *Mainly About Lindsay Anderson* (London: Faber, 2000).

McArthur, Colin, *Underworld USA* (London: Secker and Warburg, 1972).

McCarthy, Todd and Charles Flynn, *Kings of the Bs* (New York: Dutton, 1975).

Milne, Tom (ed.), *Godard on Godard* (London: Secker and Warburg, 1972).

Perkins, V. F., *Film as Film* (London: Penguin, 1972).

Roud, Richard (ed.), *Cinema – A Critical Dictionary* (London: Secker and Warburg, 1980).

Sarris, Andrew, *The American Cinema* (New York: Dutton, 1968).

Thomson, David, *A Biographical Dictionary of the Cinema* (London: Secker and Warburg, 1980).

Truffaut, François, *The Films in My Life* (London Allen Lane, 1980).

Wenders, Wim, Sievernich, Chris, and Eisenschitz, Bernard, *Nick's Film/Lightning Over Water* (Frankfurt: Zweitausendeins, 1981).

One should, perhaps, also mention the following autobiographies which both include interesting material on Ray:

Houseman, John: *Unfinished Business* (London: Chatto and Windus, 1986) – a condensed version of Houseman's three previous volumes, *Run-Through*, *Front and Center* and *Final Dress*

Kazan, Elia: *A Life* (London: André Deutsch, 1988).

Further writing on Ray and details of web resources can be found on the *Senses of Cinema* website: <www.sensesofcinema.com>

LIST OF ILLUSTRATIONS

Whilst considerable effort has been made to correctly identify copyright holders this has not been possible in all cases. We apologise for any apparent negligence and any omissions or corrections brought to our attention will be remedied in any future editions.

They Live by Night (1948), RKO Radio Pictures; *A Woman's Secret* (1949), RKO Radio Pictures; *Knock on Any Door* (1949), Columbia Pictures Corporation/Santana Productions; *Born to Be Bad* (1950), RKO Radio Pictures; *In a Lonely Place* (1950), Santana Pictures/Columbia Pictures Corporation; *On Dangerous Ground* (1951), RKO Radio Pictures; *Flying Leathernecks* (1951), RKO Radio Pictures; *The Lusty Men* (1952), Wald-Krasner Productions/RKO Radio Pictures; *Johnny Guitar* (1954), Republic Pictures Corporation; *Run for Cover* (1954), Paramount Pictures; *High Green Wall* (1954), Revue Productions/CBS; *Rebel Without a Cause* (1955), Warner Bros.; *Hot Blood* (1956), Columbia Pictures Corporation; *Bigger than Life* (1956), 20th Century-Fox; *The True Story of Jesse James* (1957), 20th Century-Fox; *Bitter Victory* (1957), Transcontinental/Robert Laffont Productions/Columbia Pictures Corporation; *Wind Across the Everglades* (1958), Schulberg Productions/Warner Bros.; *Party Girl* (1958), Euterpe Productions/ MGM/Loew's Incorporated; *The Savage Innocents* (1960), Magic Film/Play Art/Gray Film/Pathé/Joseph Janni; *King of Kings* (1961), Samuel Bronston/MGM; *55 Days at Peking* (1963), Samuel Bronston Productions; *Lightning Over Water* (1980–81), Road Movies/Wim Wenders Produktion/Viking Film

INDEX